The Sane Asylum

8.20.05
to Judy,
my Bible study companion
Louise Hogan Downer Davis

The Sane Asylum

✦

Memories of Spiritual Healing Through Extended-Family Living

Laurie Hogan Downes

iUniverse, Inc.
New York Lincoln Shanghai

The Sane Asylum

Memories of Spiritual Healing Through Extended-Family Living

iUniverse, Inc.

For information address:
iUniverse, Inc.
2021 Pine Lake Road, Suite 100
Lincoln, NE 68512
www.iuniverse.com

ISBN: 0-595-31171-7

Printed in the United States of America

Contents

Acknowledgments

I am eternally thankful for my daughter, Julie Streeter, who not only designed the book cover and shot the photo of me on the back cover, but helped me to edit the book and prepare it for submission to iUniverse. I was regularly encouraged during the writing process by the many friends and family members who supported me in prayer. I have to mention the weekly support and fellowship with my much-loved writers group, The Chuparosas of Sunland/Tujunga, CA. And I couldn't have finished this project without the generosity of the people who were able to financially support me: my sons, Jose' and Michael, my sister Carolyn Behr and her husband, Tom, my brother, Stephen Hogan and my mother, Margaret Hogan, my sister-in-law, Alice Adcock and my other sister-in-law, Eileen Rehg and her husband Virgil. Old friends since the beginning of my marriage, Joe and Joan O'Halloran and friends from the sixties, Ann and Walter Kron and our mutual friends, Gerri and Dick Shaver helped finance this venture. My dear friends, Maria Post and Sue Young, Sandy Darga and her husband, Ken, helped to keep me afloat and a niece and a nephew wanted to get on the bandwagon too, Nicole Smith and Kirk Baur. Last but not least I mention Don Williams, who started the whole thing.

Introduction

Far too many of us must go through our days unknown and unappreciated by our co-workers, friends and families. Experiencing only superficial relationships as we plow through our days our primary life is one of isolation. Our inner world suffers as most of us strive to meet the perceived expectations of the world we live in, instead of appreciating our own unique gifts enough to let them flow uncensored. And with the morning newspaper and the nightly television recap of the day's events pouring violence and chaos into our homes, we desperately need a place of sanity in the middle of it all.

In the early seventies, my husband and I and our eight children began putting into practice the wisdom we gleaned from the Bible. As our lives began to change, we, as a unit, became a surrogate home for people looking for a place of refuge. Ninety-five people came to live with us, some bringing their emotional baggage with them as well as their strengths. In our shared life, we discovered that the power in our love and encouragement of each other was a huge factor in the progress we each made toward our goal of becoming the person God had in mind when he created us.

With eyes of faith, God blessed me with this treasure of friends who are dear to me still, despite the years and miles between us now. The challenge and the joy which those individuals brought to my life changed me forever and gave me a deep respect for the resiliency of the human spirit. They showed me far more of God's grace and faithfulness than I could ever have shown to them.

Up until the mid-seventies, people obviously suffering from the inability to mentally cope with their surroundings used to be sent to insane asylums for treatment or custodial care. But then, new mental health statutes called for abandonment of the large state institutions and the placement of people in the least restrictive environment possible. This usually took the form of a system of small group homes staffed by social workers and medical personnel.

As a member of the Tri-County Community Mental Health Board for almost ten years in Lansing, Michigan, I was involved in the process of opening these small group homes. It was then that I became aware that our home was a *sane* asylum (double entendre intentional) and the thing that made the difference between our home and the others, was the presence of God in our midst. God was and is our source of sanity.

But the ministry described in *The Sane Asylum* was birthed in the loving environment of my childhood and the work that God was able to accomplish within me during the years predating the beginning of our extended-family. Looking back at the first half of my life, I saw that if God could make *me* into a usable vessel for him, then it was possible for him to work in anyone's life. When I decided to take God seriously I discovered an extraordinary life unfolding before me as that commitment blossomed into a closer relationship with him. Once I'd had a taste of his great love, I ardently desired to be in the center of his will for me. And as he comforted me, taught me, astounded me, hounded me and changed me, he drew me into a fierce love for him that is still my place of peace. With the help of my journals scribbled through the years, this writing reflects my search to understand my past and to sense his guidance in the present phase of my journey with him.

Bill and Marge

My only intimate experience with dogs occurred when I was bitten by a pit bull in Costa Rica. So a few years ago, when my sister, Nancy suggested that I live with her for a while, I wondered how I'd cope with the fact that her dog was part of the living arrangement. It was a relief to discover that our other roommate, Celise, was a calm delicate five-pound poodle. And, do you know what she did? She showed me something about myself.

Whenever I took Celise for a walk she had a wonderful time sniffing every square inch of ground we covered, her body quivering in excitement. But if we encountered a large menacing dog along the way, without skipping a beat she pointed her little face straight ahead and trotted as fast as her tiny feet would take her, looking neither to the left nor to the right until we were safely past the perceived danger. One day I recognized myself in her behavior. When emotions threatened to overcome me, I stuffed them down by intensely fixing my energy on a task in front of me. And I would tell myself, "Don't think, don't think, don't think!"

Sometime in my mid-thirties, after I had started taking my spiritual life seriously, I began to question my past behavior. Trying to find a reason to accept the person I was then, trying to slough off the deep self-loathing that frightened me from time to time, I cast my thoughts back to my formative years in Iowa to begin to unravel the puzzle that was me.

Cedar Rapids, Iowa, was a pleasant place to raise a family when I was born there in 1935 to Marge and Bill Hogan. My simple needs of housing, clothing, food and love were provided by parents who worked hard and didn't burden me with their worries. Leading protected lives far from the center of the evil that erupted into World War II, my siblings and I enjoyed a happy life within our family and neighborhood structures.

Daddy was the seventh of his nine brothers and sisters who were members of an Irish Catholic family that grew up on a large farm seven miles west of Cedar Rapids. Although they all worked hard from 4:30 in the morning until dusk, they played hard too. They still found time to dig a huge pond in the woods which friends and neighbors enjoyed for years. Swinging from rope swings knotted over tree branches to drop into the cool water on hot summer days, and ice-skating on the pond during the winter, were activities which broke the monotony of the labor needed to keep the family supplied with necessities. The farm was a gathering place for young people who used to come from the city to ride the horses or join the Hogan boys in dropping chickens from the top of the windmill to see if they could fly. The tales of mischief my father and his brothers got into on that farm have entertained me all of my life.

My father developed his love for flowers when working alongside his mother in the beauty she created outside of her house as well as within it. Although she died when I was only three, I was comforted by the love in his voice whenever he spoke of her. Many's the time I heard him say, "All mothers are saints." Her influence upon him, in turn gifted me with the same love of growing things of beauty, whether it be flowers or children.

The Hogan family lost their farm during the Great Depression when hog cholera decimated the herd of pigs they had planned to sell to make a mortgage payment. Daddy's anger toward the bank that turned them out of their home never abated nor did he ever emotionally cede his right to the land of his childhood. He continued to take his children and grandchildren with him to walk in the woods of that land until he grew too weak to do so, a year before he died, at the age of eighty-six. It had never mattered to Daddy whomever currently owned the property. There was no one who would challenge his right to walk where so much of his sweat was planted. And it was a great joy to us in later years, when friends, Bernard and Carol Witting, bought the farm and welcomed my father there whenever he came, now bringing his second generation of offspring.

Well I remember the rite of spring walks in Sisily Grove, as the woods were known locally. We would run through a plethora of young trillium and violets to see who would be the first to spot a jack-in-the-pulpit or a bleeding heart. Spring remains my most favorite time of the year because of those trips to the woods. The pungent sweet odor of lilies of the valley and lilacs always brings to me memories of the birthing of summer.

But after the farm foreclosure, since the family members had to find other ways to make a living, Daddy and his brother, Walt, approached the owner of a Mobil gas station and told him they'd give him all the money they had, if he would lease it to them. Never mind that they only had $3.54 between them, their gift of blarney won the owner over. Their hard work, servant hearts and Irish wit were the assets in what grew to be a very successful business. When someone pulled into their station for a quarter's worth of gas, the Hogan boys would swarm over the car, cleaning it inside and out. But success came after many years of working long hours with most of the money earned going back into the business.

My mother was the youngest of ten children growing up in Missouri. When she was eleven, her father suffered a severe head injury while at work for the railroad. Depressed and no longer able to provide for his family, he disappeared one day when Mother was 12, leaving my Granny and her two youngest children to fend for themselves, so they moved to Cedar Rapids to begin a new life near one of her older siblings who lived there. She continued attending school for a while but left when she was fourteen to work in a dime store in order to help support them.

She was twenty when she met my father at the CeMar Ballroom, a place where young people went to dance on Saturday nights. Since the ten cent admission price was within her budget she regularly went there with some of her friends from work. Although my father didn't know how to dance and claimed the only way he could carry a tune was in a bucket, he loved music and he had a car, so he regularly drove his friends to CeMar. He was leaning on the railing around the dance floor watching the fun the night that he spotted my mother and got someone to introduce them. When the dancing was over, he gave her and her friends a ride home and he continued taking her home as long as he lived. She never was willing to learn to drive a car herself.

Although Mother attended a number of Christian churches with childhood friends it wasn't until she went to the Catholic church with my father that she felt at home. She embraced the Catholic faith, studying our catechism books right along with us as we went through school. One of my earliest clear memories, is of her reading to us before bedtime from a simple illustrated book, *The Lord's Prayer.* I still have vivid brightly colored pictures from that book in my mind.

Childhood

I grew up hearing my mother tell the story of how she picked me up from my nap one day when I was two and noticed that my eyes were crossed. Knowing now what a perfectionist she is, I can imagine the distress she felt when she made that discovery. I remember her saying that there was no history of such a thing in *her* family background.

I knew she loved me, but perhaps I sensed her anxiety about my appearance during my formative years, because I've felt unattractive most of my life. My sister, Carolyn, born two years after me, has always been so beautiful that people comment on it still, so I grew up with the comparison of my appearance to hers and felt ugly.

Mother was devoted to us and used her considerable sewing skill to alter hand-me-down clothing in order to make pretty clothes for us. Having learned to be very frugal, she not only altered used clothing but she even made clothing from flour sacks which had floral patterns. She kept the house spotless enough that you could eat off her floors and did everything she possibly could to relieve Daddy of any work at home.

When we were little, every evening after supper she would bathe us and then read to us until Daddy came walking in the door after he'd closed the station at 7:00. He'd whistle two special notes as he called out to his "darling little daughters" and come to our bedroom to talk to us for a few minutes while my mother put the finishing touches on his dinner. Then she and Daddy had their private time with each other. Their love for each other was evident all through the sixty two years they were married, and they lavishly shared it with us.

One sunny summer day when I was five, I saw my father's car approaching the house as he came home for lunch and I ran excitedly down the sidewalk to meet him, calling, "Daddy! Daddy!" In my haste, I fell, skinned my face, hands and knees and broke my glasses. He carried me upstairs to the bathroom, where he stood me on the sink and comforted me as he gently washed my wounds. He always took care of me in times of trouble. My three sisters and I absolutely adored him and his unconditional love for me made it easy for me to identify with God the Father loving me.

I often saw my father on his knees by his bed saying his night prayers. He taught me to be thankful by expressing his own gratitude toward God. Many's the time I heard him say, shaking his head in bewilderment, "I don't know why God has been so good to me!"

He constantly went out of his way to serve people. It was not unusual for him to get out of bed in the middle of the night to go get an auto part someone needed. He had a profound respect for elderly people and would regularly do small services for them when he saw someone with a problem he could fix. He had no use however, for people who were lazy or dishonest and could eloquently use his sharp tongue to lambaste such behavior. I felt I would rather have died than do anything to make him ashamed of me.

Our extended family was a large one. Granny was always near us and we enjoyed close relationships with aunts, uncles and many cousins from both sides of the family. Poor we might have been in money matters but not in the riches of family and friends. And it was one of my father's friends who took us up in a small plane one night when I was only four. The magic of that night stayed with me and came back to claim me later in life.

In 1941, my sister, Nancy, was born and World War II encroached on us. Fortunately, Daddy had too many children to be called into service, sparing us from that anxiety, but gas-rationing resulted in business lagging at the service station. So he worked as a city fireman, on duty for 24 hours and then off for 24 hours, which allowed him to still work with Uncle Walt at the service station on his days off. Although there wasn't as much gas sold then, customers still came and appreciated more than ever those wise-cracking Hogan brothers.

Air raid sirens, black shades at the windows, and talk of my Uncle Bernard, who was on a ship in the Pacific, impinged on our lives. The Ryans down the street lost their only son in battle and nightly radio broadcasts were listened to very closely. We nurtured a "Victory Garden" a couple of blocks from our house in a big field turned over to the raising of food for the war effort. Mother and I went there to work in the hot summer sun, pulling weeds and picking beans. Afterwards, I would use one foot to encourage gentle movement of the front porch swing where Granny and I spent hours snapping beans and podding peas, while Mother plunged into the canning process in the hot steamy kitchen.

During the summer months before my eighth birthday, I made several trips with her on the inter-urban train which ran between Cedar Rapids and Iowa City. At the University of Iowa Medical School, I was seen by an ophthalmologist who performed two operations that straightened my eyes. When the surgeries were completed, we moved to the first house my parents ever owned, in time for me to enter the third grade at St. Patrick's School.

The school was under the firm command of the Sisters of Charity of the Blessed Virgin Mary. The majority of our social life revolved around St. Patrick's and the friends we made there. Although I was a good student, I quickly found out that some of the nuns were really tough to deal with.

One day that first year I was there, an important feast day occurred so we were herded into the church, class by class, where I knelt quietly with my peers and looked around. The altar was a blaze of candles. As I turned my head quickly to one side for a moment I noticed that the candles blurred into a lovely streak. I started experimenting, moving my head quickly back and forth and then up and down and back and forth again, entranced with the light.

Faster and faster I moved my head until, suddenly, I was brought back from my colorful heavenly vision by a nun who had noticed me making a spectacle of myself during the solemn liturgy. She roughly yanked me out of my pew and dragged me back to sit beside her in disgrace. Perhaps my tendency, even now, to feel like I am about to get into trouble comes from that experience and a number of similar ones. My childhood contact with school teachers was probably like all kids; some teachers were understanding and nice and others were not.

At home we always thanked God for our food at meals, we often prayed the Rosary together and we always went to Mass on Sundays and Holy Days. During the forty days of Lent, we attended the Stations of the Cross each Friday and followed the practice of giving up candy during Lent. Easter Sunday was near to Christmas in excitement because we always found candy strewn all over the dining room table when we came downstairs that morning!

There were lots of kids on our block. We played the usual games with each other and devised a few of our own as well in the lazy days of summer. Catching lightening bugs, building tree houses, pelting each other with green apples, having tea parties under the grape vines in the back yard, and digging at the melted tar in the cracks in the hot pavement were but a few of the ways we kept ourselves occupied. Tearing around the neighborhood on my second hand bike was the beginning of my lifelong love of cycling. We'd take a clothes pin and clip playing cards to the spokes of our bike wheels so the resulting sound made it easy to pretend we were riding motorcycles.

My sisters and I still talk about the dismay we felt when we almost always had to go inside to bed before the rest of the other kids in the neighborhood. Mother still settled us down for the night around 7:00 so she could have private time with Daddy. Ice skating, piano lessons, playing with our cousins, rides in the countryside to visit old great uncles and aunts; this was the fabric of my grade school years. The long hours that my father worked, and my mother's careful running of the household, created a good life for us.

Toward the end of my grade school years, the birth of my sister, Charlotte, and then my brother, Stephen, provided the hands-on experience with little ones that prepared me for babysitting jobs during my teens. I spent almost a year, though, curtailed by Osgood-Schatter's disease diagnosed when I was twelve. Hobbling around on crutches with one leg in a cast during the summer months and then having to be driven to and from school and forced to stay in the classroom through recess and lunch periods, caused me the discomfort of feeling different from the other kids. I read constantly, losing myself in the adventures contained in books, often using them to avoid the unpleasantness of my current reality.

High School Revisited

Just after my fourteenth birthday, while a friend and I were walking home from the swimming pool at Ellis Park, a car came up over the curb and struck me as we waited to cross Ellis Blvd. Thankfully, I was just bruised and scraped a bit except for a couple of teeth being knocked out where the door handle of the car had clipped me. But I began my high school days a little bit banged up and distracted as I tried to get used to having a temporary denture in my mouth. One day my teacher angrily ordered me to spit out my gum despite my protesting, "But I don't have any gum!" When one of my classmates shouted out, "It's her teeth!" I was mortified!

I always loved school, though, and putting crisp words on a clean sheet of notebook paper was a joy I still appreciate so I really looked forward to starting ninth grade. My class of thirty-six students would now ascend from the second floor of the school building to the third floor set aside for high school. There we would for the first time, change rooms and teachers for our classes.

My school day began with a Latin class taught by Sister Mary Leonella, my father's former teacher. Algebra seemed like another new language to figure out and participating in Glee Club was enjoyable because I really liked music. But it was my Religion class which graced me with a treasure that year. When I opened my ninth grade Religion book, I saw a prayer attributed to St. Augustine on the first page. I was so taken with it that I memorized it and the first seeds of a new understanding of my relationship to God were sown:

Oh God, I love thee for thyself, and not that I might heaven gain,
nor yet that they who love thee not must suffer hell's eternal pain.
Thou, O my Jesus, thou didst me upon the cross embrace.
For me didst bear the nails and spear and manifold disgrace,
and griefs and torments numberless and sweat of agony,
e'en death itself and all for one who was thine enemy.
Why then O Blessed Jesus Christ, should I not love thee well?
Not for the sake of winning heaven nor of escaping hell,

not with the hope of gaining aught, not seeking a reward,
but as thyself hast loved me, O ever-loving Lord.
E'en as I love thee I will love and in they praises sing,
solely because thou art my God and my Eternal King.

The prayer probably only remained with me for a few months, but twenty years later, during a time when I first experienced God in a deeply personal way all the words of the prayer came rushing back and have been vividly with me ever since. I began going to daily Mass before school, singing the Requiem Mass on a regular basis. But I was soon distracted from deep thoughts of piety when I fell in love with a new boy in our class, Owen Fields.

He usually met me at morning Mass and later walked me home from school. My perception of myself started improving from all the attention he gave me. We were both very inexperienced at romance and it was a year later before we exchanged our first chaste kiss, but by our junior year he had acquired a car and we began to experience the problem of what to do with raging hormones.

Coming home from a date with Owen, if we dallied in the car saying good-night, my mother would start flipping the front porch light on and off until he escorted me to my door. Incredible as it now seems, my mother was too reticent to say anything to me about sex. It's ironic that the only adult who even alluded to any information about sex was a nun telling us that we girls must keep even our ankles covered or we would be tempting the boys and go to hell. I was scared by the delicious feelings I had around Owen. So, worries of going to hell and/or disappointing my parents caused me to pull back from a relationship that was getting too intense.

We went to the Junior Prom together but things were beginning to unravel even then. And when Owen started dating a public school girl who had a dubious reputation, I was heartbroken. Although we were not a couple any more we still dated casually and I felt like I was on an emotional roller coaster much of the time. And although I dated other boys during my senior year I still had strong feelings for him.

Many of my classmates and I had been together since third grade but we were going our separate ways after graduation from high school. My parents could not afford for me to go on to college but in July I was able to began a two-month air-line communications course in Minneapolis, Minnesota, by working part-time while I focused on mastering the codes and acronyms needed to work in that field. Because I was already an excellent typist I had completed the course in one month and was on the verge of accepting a job placement in St. Louis, Missouri, when Owen drove up to see me on my birthday.

Homesickness had plagued me the whole time I was in Minneapolis so I welcomed the chance to ride back to Cedar Rapids with him. It was so good to be home that I decided to stay. My typing skills quickly got me a job that enabled me to pay my parents $10 per week for room and board so I settled back into my old environment, happily surrounded by family and friends. Then Owen joined the army and all but disappeared from my life.

In May of 1954 I drove to Ft. Riley, Kansas, to be Maid of Honor for my high school friend, Judy Kerns. We had missed each other but she was far enough away that she couldn't come home to assuage her homesickness and it was too far for me to drive down there on a weekend. But as I thought about our dilemma I realized that if I could learn to fly, it would be easy to scoot over to see her on a weekend. Also, I thought flying a plane would be fun and exciting! This proved to be true!

The guys at Wathan Flying Service had to put pillows under me and in back of me in order to help me reach the pedals of the Aeronca Champion they used for training but that didn't deter me. So a week before my 19th birthday, after eight hours of instruction, I soloed. Before long, I eagerly flew west to visit Judy over the weekend. The head-wind was stronger than I had expected, causing me to run out of gas before my first planned fueling station so I put the plane down in a farmer's field and was feeling pretty nervous as he came running toward me. It just happened that he was the Sheriff of Lucas County, Iowa, and also the head of the local flying club. He brought me some aviation fuel and bade me Godspeed as I resumed my journey.

At the army base, Judy and her husband introduced me to their friend, Harry, who consequently became one of my pen pals. And since we frequently had visitors in our home and I knew he had no family, I invited him to visit us for Christmas. But when he showed up with a diamond ring and asked me to marry him I was truly shocked! I was sorry to have to tell him that I did not think of him that way and I regretted the fact that he was not Mr. Right. I was very aware that I really did want to get on with the next phase of my life, that of marriage and children.

Several of my close friends had paired up with each other as early as the seventh grade and had gotten married right out of high school. Five of my six closest girlfriends from school were already married and the other one was engaged, so I began to earnestly pray that I would soon meet the man who would be my husband.

Courtship

Somewhere during my high school years at St. Patrick's, I had been told that if I prayed the *Hail Mary* one thousand times on March 25th I could ask Mary, the Mother of God, for anything I wanted and expect to receive it. This was not something taught by the Catholic Church but was one of those many beliefs more accurately described as superstitions prevalent among certain Catholics which varied depending on the cultural Catholicity you had inherited.

So in the spring of 1955 I decided that this was the time for me to pray that prayer one thousand times and request that I meet my future husband in a month. I got in the required amount of prayers on March 25th but the one-month deadline came and went without me meeting anyone new. Two weeks later, however, while I was attending a dance at a regional Newman Club event, Bill Downes stopped by the booth where I was sitting with my friends and asked me to dance.

Both of us were skinny, both of us wore glasses and we were both from the Midwest, but that was about all we had in common. I had first thought that Bill was only an undergraduate at Iowa State College in Ames, but he was actually twenty-eight and working on his Ph.D. in Entomology. I was nineteen years old and had never been to college. He had lived most of his life in St. Louis, Missouri, but had seen a bit of the world when he served in the army in Japan at the end of World War II. I was only ten when the war ended and had spent practically my entire life in Cedar Rapids. But mindful of my prayers for a husband, and because he was so different from the boys I had dated, I was interested in getting to know him better.

He invited me to come to Ames the next weekend for the annual spring festival there and followed the invitation up with a letter. I had been a licensed pilot for about a year then, so the following Saturday morning I rented a four-passenger Piper Tri-Pacer plane and flew three of my friends, Linda and Dave Schulte and Shirley Maloney, with me to Ames. Bill borrowed a car in order to meet us at the airfield and take us to enjoy the campus festivities. At the end of the day he squeezed into the plane and flew back to Cedar Rapids with us, beginning what evolved into a weekend courtship.

The following weekend, he came to Cedar Rapids and we went for long walks or just sat and talked. I don't think we ever went out on a real date. He was a brilliant man attending college under a National Science Foundation Fellowship and I was fascinated by the conversations we had, flattered that he was interested in me at all and that he seemed more interested in my mind than my body.

The third weekend, as we left the house of one of my friends, he said to me, "I think we should think about getting married on Labor Day weekend. That's probably the soonest we could do it." Stunned, I recovered enough to reply, "It's much too soon to be making any decision about that!"

But Bill wanted to move things along, so early in June we flew to St. Louis to meet his family. They were very sweet to me and I took to them at once. On the way back to Cedar Rapids on a hot sultry afternoon, we ran into severe weather which buffeted us so badly that I was forced to make an emergency landing in an alfalfa field. Bill seemed unperturbed by the incident and a hospitable farmer and his wife put us up overnight. As we took off at dawn the next day, I reflected that Bill seemed to have handled that crisis pretty well.

The following weekend he again suggested we get married in September but I told him, "It's too soon! I hardly know you! And even if we do decide to marry some day I would expect to have a long engagement." With that he became upset with me and shouted, "How am I supposed to get my thesis done if I have to keep running to Cedar Rapids every weekend!"

I was terribly naive. The only marriage I knew about was that of my parents' very loving and affectionate union. In spite of the fact that Bill hadn't shown any signs of affection toward me since he had talked about marriage, I assumed he must love me. And although I knew I was not in love with him, I thought I might learn to love him some day if I was meant to marry him. But the more I thought about it the more I worried about his behavior, and I finally decided to tell him by letter, that I did not believe we should marry at all. Since, to me, it seemed cruel to tell him that I didn't love him, the only barriers to our proposed marriage that I cited, were my lack of education, the differences in our ages and our lack of compatibility.

He quickly responded with more reasons why we *should* marry. And particularly, he told me that he had prayed a prayer of surrender shortly before he met me, telling God that he was going to give up trying to find someone to marry and resign himself to remaining a bachelor unless God brought someone into his life. So, dismissing my concerns, he still pressed for the September date. I kept leaving the issue hanging because I still couldn't bring myself to hurt his feelings by telling him I didn't love him.

The following weekend, I was visiting him in Ames when he made a phone call to his parents, and in the middle of his conversation with them he looked over his shoulder at me and said, "Shall I tell them we're getting married?" And for the life of me, I don't know why, I told him he could go ahead. It was just easier at that moment to acquiesce.

On July 1st, we went to morning Mass and he slipped a ring on my finger, making our engagement official. The next day I rented a Cessna 120 airplane and flew us to St. Louis, in order to spend the long Fourth of July weekend with his family. We landed at a small airport located fairly near the home of Bill's parents and I left the airfield employees with the usual instructions for my plane to be tied down, fueled, and ready for our departure on Monday. Unknown to me, this holiday weekend was also the weekend of the annual coast-to-coast race of women pilots known as the Powder-Puff Derby, a fact that would all too soon be brought home to us.

We spent an enjoyable weekend visiting with Bill's parents and siblings but an unusual thing happened to me when his sister, Eileen, asked me to take her for a ride in the plane. I began to feel uneasy and afraid. I was at a loss to understand my feelings. I had never been a fearful person and always enjoyed taking friends and relatives for rides. But now I was experiencing unreasonable unidentifiable fear at the thought of taking her up in the plane and I just couldn't do it. I don't remember what excuse I gave her or if I verbalized to anyone the dread I was feeling. And Monday morning, although I was very careful with my pre-flight check of the plane, when Bill and I started back to Iowa, we crashed.

We were only 400 feet in the air in the usual take-off pattern when the motor quit. Underneath our wings was a lush canopy of trees, the roofs of houses, and the Meramec River. I had received no instruction on forced landings on water but knew that plowing into the trees was not an option for us, so I headed for the river. I expected the wheels of the plane to flip us when we hit the water so I decided to keep the nose of the plane as high as I could. A rush of fear gripped me as I held the plane steady and prepared for the impact. A pilot on the river bank, who saw us smash into the water and nose over into it, talked to me later, saying, "You did a good job of setting the plane down but it was like hitting a brick wall at eighty miles an hour." Bill's distressed parents had seen our plane going down beyond the trees as they drove away from the airport and they turned around in panic.

We were both knocked unconscious but water rushing in through the broken windshield of the cockpit quickly revived us. Once the incoming water equalized the pressure we were able to force open the doors and swim free of the plane. We treaded water as people along the shore put boats into the water in an effort to come to our aid. The first boat to reach us had too many people in it to take on both of us. Once I was pulled out of the water there was no room for Bill! He kept treading water until a second boat rescued him and then a police officer rushed us to a nearby hospital. Bill noted, with some anxiety, that the car we were riding in was traveling over 100 mph, faster than we had been traveling in the plane!

Other than bruises and the need for a few stitches we were not seriously damaged, but the plane was another story. After being released from the hospital, we returned to the scene of the accident where the tail of the plane could be seen sticking up out of the water. We retrieved from it what personal belongings were still intact, and it was later dismantled and trucked back to Cedar Rapids for restoration.

An investigation into the cause of the crash revealed that the airport personnel had been extremely busy with the Powder-Puff Derby, and in the excitement generated by the unusual activity at their field they had failed to fuel my plane until just before I arrived to fly back to Iowa. The heat and humidity of the weekend had allowed water to condense in the gas lines, thus interrupting the flow of gas to the engine.

We returned to Cedar Rapids by train, and though our injuries were minor, news coverage of our accident was extensive. One result of the publicity was an anonymous letter I received, telling me, "God has saved your life for a purpose." The thought that God might have a purpose for my life, was foreign to me. At any rate, so much was happening that I had no time, then, to dwell on lofty things so I tossed the letter aside. And, although I've speculated about it from time to time, I never have figured out the source of the uneasiness I felt at the thought of taking Eileen up in the plane.

Meanwhile, to facilitate our weekend courtship, Bill bought an old Pontiac and left it with me so I could drive to Ames to visit him some weekends. On those occasions, I stayed in a room he rented for me just a few doors down the street from the apartment where he was living. In late July, anticipating our upcoming marriage, he rented a furnished apartment for us and moved into it. The first time I drove up to see the apartment I was in for a shock. As I got out of the car, I was stopped in my tracks as Bill came rushing out of the house, yelling angrily at me, "I don't want any kissing at our wedding!"

I couldn't believe it! He was acting crazy! Trembling with anxiety, I responded, "Well, *Auntie Betty* will want to kiss me!" He finally simmered down, saying, "I didn't mean *Auntie Betty*!" He then explained that he was upset because he had been at a wedding where everybody was grabbing the bride and kissing her. I was so shaken by this incident, that I cut short my visit and when I got back home I wrote him another letter telling him that I didn't believe we should marry. Again he insisted that we were supposed to be married and all would be well once we were.

My parents seemed to go along with the fact that I was marrying Bill. They are very private people and humble, not likely to offer any advice unless asked to, and they were awed by Bill's education. I never asked them what they thought about having Bill for a son-in-law. I didn't tell them of the conflict inside of me. Although I was frantic about the mess I had gotten myself into, I could not bring myself to cause the uproar I envisioned if I did call the wedding off, so I just kept earnestly praying for something to happen to stop the wedding. What a wimp I was! Nothing did happen.

Two days before the wedding, my high school sweetheart, Owen, called me. He was home on leave and wanted to see me. When I told him that I was getting married, he didn't believe me at first and reminded me of how we had talked of getting married someday. It's true that there was a time when we had daydreamed about marrying but I had left that dream behind a couple of years before. I'll probably always wonder why I had been able to tell Owen that it was too late for us even though I had been in love with him, and yet I couldn't seem to extricate myself from my relationship with Bill.

The night before the wedding, the house was brimming with relatives from as far away as California. Late that night, during a moment when I was alone with my father in the kitchen, he said to me, "Are you sure you want to go through with this?" Until that moment, not a single person had asked me that. And at that point, I didn't see how I could upset everybody by telling Daddy the truth so I told him it was okay. Mother told me later that he was heartsick about my marriage. He evidently sensed that all was not well but his natural reticence had kept him quiet too long.

Early Marriage

Since nothing had stopped the wedding, I prayed as I walked down the aisle for God to give me enough love to make the marriage work. The day passed in a blur of activity and festivity, as I luxuriated in loving attention from my family and friends. Afterward, when I looked at the pictures of our wedding I noticed that the only guests from Bill's side of the family were his parents, his brother, Jack, and his college friend, Joe O'Halloran with his wife, Joan. It seemed a little strange to me that none of his other friends were there, not even the ones from Ames, which was only 100 miles away.

Always concerned about having enough money, Bill combined our honeymoon with an insect collecting trip to Texas. We were supposed to drive south over into Missouri and stop at my Aunt Virginia and Uncle Fred's farm near Amoret, on our wedding night. But as we paused in Ames to unload presents from the car, Bill wanted to consummate the marriage immediately, so my initiation to wedded bliss took place on a messy unmade bed. I was disappointed that the encounter was a mere perfunctory mating. Both of us were very ignorant about sexual intercourse and we were too reticent to talk about what we would like from each other, so no words about the encounter were spoken.

The next morning, we drove to the farm in Missouri and then we continued south all the way to Padre Island, off the coast of Texas. Along the way, once we had found an inexpensive motel for the night Bill would take his net and go out to collect a few specimens of flies that he then put into a cyanide bottle. Back in our room, he pinned and labeled the flies and stuck them in neat rows inside a cigar box lined with Styrofoam. One night, as he flourished his net around the motel's outside lights he was stopped by a sheriff's deputy because someone had reported him as a prowler. This necessitated the delivery of a spontaneous entomology lecture for the deputy before he was allowed to return to our room that night.

As our honeymoon collecting trip progressed, I realized with a sinking heart that what I had thought was admirable restraint on Bill's part while we were courting was actually something between aversion to and disinterest in such things as kissing and cuddling. His embrace was always loose; the way he touched my body was very tenuous. The tenderness and intimacy I had seen between my parents was not there.

Another facet of his behavior that really bothered me was what I perceived as his attitude of suspicion around me. When I asked him questions about his life or his opinions about issues he would usually respond by asking me why I wanted to know. It frustrated me that he wouldn't just answer my questions.

My mother had brought us up in a fastidiously clean and tidy home, so it surprised and offended me that Bill felt it necessary to check the dishes and silverware I had washed, as if expecting to find them dirty. I would eventually learn that Bill was a brilliant scientist, but so absorbed in his thoughts that he had little awareness of the people around him, but I took his behavior toward me very personally and came to the conclusion that he didn't love me after all.

The three-week trip introduced me to more than marriage though. Life with Bill must have released a dormant desire for adventure within me because I certainly did enjoy the traveling and seeing different parts of the country. I can't say I was thrilled with sleeping on a blanket in a cornfield but camping on the beach at Padre Island was a joy. The waters of the Gulf of Mexico mesmerized me and I told myself this Iowa girl had finally seen something pretty amazing!

During the first nine years of our marriage, we lived in eight houses in five states and welcomed seven children into our family. When we had first talked of marriage we had agreed we'd like six children and I became pregnant on our honeymoon. I had transferred with Northwestern Bell Telephone Company to their Ames office but once I was five months pregnant I was forced to quit because of their company policy. Then many of my days were turned into nights when I accompanied Bill to a darkened lab where he was using a microscope to make drawings of the flies he was dissecting. While he worked until dawn I would read a book and eventually lay down on one of the lab tables to sleep.

Once it was established that I was pregnant, we qualified for married student housing and moved into Pammel Court, the Veterans Housing Project on campus. Our $25.00-per-month cracker-box-style duplex was furnished with twin beds, a kerosene stove and an icebox. With a card table, a couple of chairs, and a sofa bed in the living room, we didn't live like kings but the camaraderie with the other couples who were neighbors was great. Toward the end of each month when the money was really tight, we used to fill up on popcorn, the cheapest vegetable around.

I really hadn't had time to think about what it would be like to enter the academic community as the wife of a grad student. I met lots of educated people so I listened attentively and absorbed as much as I could. There had been no classical records in my home as I was growing up but Bill considered the classics the only music worth listening to. He liked working with the sounds of Beethoven, Bach and Brahms in the background so they eventually became familiar and soothing to me. I enjoyed our limited social life with other grad students and their families, and looked forward to the birth of our first child.

Joseph was born the last day of May 1956 after I was hospitalized with pre-eclampsia symptoms. This was in the dark ages when laboring mothers were knocked out with drugs and fathers were kept in a waiting room until given the news of the sex of their progeny. Only then, was the new father allowed to see his wife. Indeed, I had received virtually no instruction as to childbirth so I was intent on just getting through it all without causing anybody any trouble. It is only in retrospect that I realized how Mary Greeley Hospital epitomized the archaic birthing process of the time. Attempting to follow the orders of a Sargent-type head nurse five hours after Joey was born, I fainted as I got out of bed after she had commanded me to follow the other three women in my room down the hall to the communal shower.

Bill wanted me to nurse Joey instead of using formula, but I got off to a rough start until I met the wife of one the grad students who was nursing her baby and she gave me advice when I needed it. I was absolutely thrilled being Joey's mother! Because the love I felt for our blue-eyed blonde little son was so deep, I began to grasp for the first time, how much my parents must love me. Bill appeared to be as besotted with our firstborn as I was and we enjoyed a shared pride in him.

Bill's specialty in Entomology was with flies (Diptera), so when he had an opportunity to work in the Diptera collection of the Smithsonian Institute in Washington, D.C. he interrupted the work on his Ph.D. in order to identify flies there for a few months. We moved into an apartment that had been carved out of a stately building located across the street from the central fire station in Alexandria, Virginia, and across the Potamac from the National Airport.

There was an energy to the area that would have been invigorating to me, even without the noise of the fire engines and the planes. Since I had never been east of Ohio I eagerly explored my new neighborhood. Bill was at the museum most of the time so I would often drive across the Potomac and walk for hours pushing Joey's stroller up and down the mall, discovering the treasures housed in the capitol city of our nation. I still remember the excitement I felt being part of the crowd at the second inauguration of President Eisenhower.

When Washington's famed cherry trees were about to bloom we moved back to Ames, where Bill would finish his Ph.D. thesis and receive his doctorate. We lived in a Quonset hut in Pammel Court this time and a year after Joey's birth, I went back to the same hospital to deliver Tommy. I remember being struck by how exotic he looked, this second son of ours, with his dark hair and brown eyes.

Caring for the two little boys and typing my husband's 350-page doctoral thesis, I was always busy and short on sleep. Developing the creativity of a desperate mother, I put a plastic, cereal bowl of dry Cheerios in each of the boys' cribs when they first woke up in the morning. Therefore I could get a few extra minutes of sleep before they started clamoring for my attention.

Early in 1958 I began to think that motherhood was ruining my figure because my normally flat abdomen was sticking out a little, so I purchased a girdle. It wasn't long, though, before I realized that my abdomen was accommodating another pregnancy, and I knew right away that it was Michael John who was on the way. So I now had three little boys on my mind as we moved to New Haven, Connecticut, after Bill received his Ph.D. in March of 1958. There he did a stint at the Connecticut Agricultural Experiment Station and I did a repeat of my sojourn in Washington.

This time, we lived in the first floor flat of a three-story house surrounded by similar buildings teeming with people of Irish or Italian descent, people whose lifestyle was very different than what I'd experienced. Our first day there, I was shocked when I heard a woman screaming from her third floor porch to her child in the yard below, "Get up here right now or I'll break your arm off!" Once again. I was absorbing scenes filled with color and language that were new and intriguing to me.

Pushing the stroller for miles, it was wonderful being out among the people and my boys seemed to enjoy our long walks, too, as I admired the many specialty shops, with exotic looking produce and foods. As a family we spent many happy times on the weekends throughout the summer, exploring the beaches and beautiful state parks nearby. One Sunday Bill brought a huge king crab back with us and threw it in the bathtub to entertain the boys for a few hours.

Red-headed Michael was born the day after my twenty-third birthday, in August of 1958 back in Cedar Rapids. The boys and I had flown there in mid-July in order to take refuge with my parents while Bill was packing and moving our belongings to our next home in Urbana, Illinois. I had only three weeks left of my pregnancy when I arrived and met my new obstetrician, who tried in vain to train me to use hypnosis for a painless delivery. I had another 2½ hour labor and watched a priest who had asked permission to be present in the delivery room, pass out about the time Michael was born. Three weeks later, Bill arrived to collect us and we were off to his first, post-Ph.D. teaching appointment in the Entomology Department of the University of Illinois.

It had been wonderful being back with my family and friends, whose love and encouragement had brought home to me the lack of intimacy and affection which was now my lot. Just recently, I came across something I wrote dated October 1958: "By the end of the third year of our marriage, I now realize that married life is not going to be the bed of roses I had hoped it would be. I feel deep sorrow from the deteriorating relationship with my husband. That dream of every young woman, to live happily ever after, is not going to be a reality for me."

Although I don't remember writing it, I do remember the scripture I had also written on that piece of paper, because it has sustained me with its wisdom: *Do not give in to sadness, torment not yourself with brooding, gladness of heart is the very life of man, cheerfulness prolongs his days. (Sirach 30:21-22)*

This very good advice implied that gladness of heart was attainable, so I made a determined decision to enjoy my children and to keep focusing on what was beautiful around me. My sons were precious, and kept me so happily busy that I had much to be thankful for. I also had my father to thank for teaching me during my childhood to have an attitude of gratitude. It stood me well as I prepared to embrace another new living environment.

Homemaker in Illinois

In Urbana, we lived for the first few months in a university-owned rental house. It was a little Cape Cod with two bedrooms, all on one floor. Now that we were back in the Midwest we were only four hours from Bill's friend, Joe O'Halloran, and his wife, Joan, so they visited us from Chicago one weekend with their three little ones. We managed to find room enough for all of us to sleep and we enjoyed the antics of all of our children, theirs being the same ages as our three sons, but it was obvious we needed to find a home with more space.

In the spring of 1959 we saw a seven-room house in the nearby village of St. Joseph listed for sale for $6,000. We thought the price must be a mistake, but when we looked at it we discovered why it was so cheap: it was so old it had wooden pegs and square nails holding it together, no central heating, and nothing in the kitchen but a bare sink. But it had possibilities, we could afford it and we liked the idea of living in a little town, so we bought our first house.

Once we had a furnace installed and put plywood and tile down on the kitchen floor, we were able to move in, but it was definitely a bare bones environment that I was eager to embellish. Bill put up a couple of bare shelves in the kitchen but never was interested in what the house looked like and he didn't want to spend money just for aesthetics. But since there were pieces of wallpaper hanging off the wall in parts of the room we had designated as our family room, I couldn't stand it the way it was. My friend, Carol Prosser, came over one afternoon and helped me pull all the wallpaper down.

When Bill got home and saw what we had done, he was upset. He didn't think I knew what I was doing. However, the paint roller had been invented and I had a wonderful time applying gallons of paint and adding a few throw rugs to make our house feel like home. I paid only seventeen cents per yard for unbleached muslin and sewed drapes out of them for the living room. The plaster of the ceiling in our bedroom was so crumbly that we had a layer of fine sand on us when we woke up each morning. So I tore more of the cheap muslin into strips and pasted them up on the ceiling, and then I rolled a coat of paint on it. I was lucky the weight of the wet painted fabric didn't cause the whole thing to fall down on us!

I didn't say anything to Bill about painting the outside of the house, which was in dire straits, because I knew he wouldn't want to do it. But knowing what an absent-minded professor he was, and that he always pulled up on the south side of the house from the west when he came home, I started painting the north side of the house and then the east side of it. The neighbors were watching and chuckling, trying to guess how far I could get before he noticed. (I had two walls done and was working on the third, when he noticed it.) And yes, he was upset that I was painting the outside of the house. "Why can't you appreciate the fact that I'm industrious and am increasing the worth of our property?" I appealed to him. "Because if I gave you any encouragement you'd be bringing paint home by the truckload instead of by the bucketful!" he shot back.

Bill did get involved with the house eventually, though, and I found out that he had practical skills as well as cerebral ones. He did lots of electrical and plumbing rearranging in the house. He seemed to be able to do anything he put his mind to! He'd get a book about how to do something and then translate that into the actual task, even tearing down the wall in one room and putting up drywall with ease. But when he decided to plant his first garden ever, the many retired farmers of this little town were hooting and hollering about it over their morning coffee at Fannie Denhart's Diner.

The thing was, Bill decided to plant all sorts of things that I'd never eaten nor even heard of...things like kohlrabi, egg plant, Swiss chard, and okra. And his real triumph was squash. He hadn't realized what could happen if you planted two hills each, of seven varieties of squash and then had perfect growing weather for the aforementioned vegetable. They grew so fast and produced such abundance that Bill and I couldn't begin to keep up with it. In our attempts to stay ahead of it and not waste it, every household in St. Joe was offered our wonderful squash. I froze it, canned it, baked it, boiled it, chopped it, and mashed it until Bill was forced to start taking it to a local market every morning on his way to the university.

Located eight miles east of Urbana on I-74, St. Joseph was home to 1,200 souls, including some who thought all university professors were communists. The first night in St. Joseph that Bill went outside with his net to collect insects swarming around street lights, he was again reported as a prowler and had some explaining to do, when he was approached by the local sheriff. Once it was learned that he was another of those crazy professors, people were more understanding of his behavior and would sometimes even drop by to see what he was up to. Every time I go back to visit in St. Joseph, people start saying, "Remember the time..." and another story of his eccentric behavior would be told.

The best thing about St. Joseph, was that we were finally settled someplace where I would meet women friends who are still close to my heart. Some of us formed a group we called, The Crafties. We got together every other week in each others' homes to sew, knit or crochet. The women were wonderful fellowship for me as we shared our daily lives in that little town. They didn't hesitate to tell me, though, that they had a problem with me having so many children so close together.

I was having a problem in that regard, too, because I felt so used by Bill instead of cherished by him. My husband seemed to think that sexual intercourse was just part of the going-to-bed routine at night. The Catholic Church teaches that if we feel we need to space our children, for serious reasons such as health, finances or other true hardships, we had open to us only the use of abstinence, and Bill was not willing to practice abstinence.

When anyone in our Crafties group started complaining about her difficulties one of the other women would say, "at least you don't have it as bad as Laurie." But although Bill didn't help with physically caring for the children or spend much time with us as a family, I didn't think I had it bad because I was very good at managing the children's care and very happy with them. My mother had trained me so well that it was no problem keeping the house nice, and I certainly had a ball with the children, probably because I was an overgrown kid myself.

On March 23, 1960, Paul was born and endeared himself to me by coming three weeks early, thereby getting me out of last minute responsibilities for a spring style show I was co-chairing. The day I brought him home was as warm as any summer day, perfect for resting in the spring sunshine. However, Bill had just barely coped with our trio of little boys while I was in the hospital so the house was a mess. I couldn't stand a messy house so I was on my knees scrubbing floors when he was only four days old. I was foolishly determined to show everybody that I could keep my house clean and orderly and have the best dressed, best behaved kids in town. That determination came from my mother's teaching and was fueled by my own pride.

Paul was only six weeks old when he began having serious bouts of asthma. His bedroom had to be stripped of rugs and curtains and cleaned thoroughly every day, but in spite of my efforts he was hospitalized with pneumonia when he was only seven months old. Also, he had been born with one foot twisted inward, so I had bruises on my arms from handling him, because of a cast he had on one leg to straighten the foot. And, Michael, at that time, required a special diet for his food allergies, making it necessary for me to bake our own bread every day, the old fashioned way. Bread machines for the home weren't even dreamed of yet.

That was when I realized, if I wanted to stay healthy myself, I needed some help. When I appealed to Bill for help he suggested that I not iron his handkerchiefs since they just went in his pockets, nor the tails of his shirts since he tucked them in. When I asked him to pick up his clothes and put them in the clothes hamper, positing that he needed to set a good example for his boys, he just chuckled and said to tell them he was setting them an example of what not to do. So since Bill didn't have either the time or the inclination to physically pitch in I decided to hire a neighbor, Mrs. Asher, to come and babysit one afternoon a week so I could have some free time away from the house. It was one of the best decisions I ever made and it served me well.

One of my acquaintances in St. Joseph was an elderly woman, Marian Reese, who lived in a house that her husband had built for her when she was a bride. I fell in love with it the first time I visited there and once mentioned to her that I'd like to buy it if she ever got to the point where she was willing to part from it. When she decided to sell it to us in the fall of 1961, we sold our little house and made the move to the big house on Lincoln Street nine days after Julie's birth.

She was our first daughter, born in October of that year, and she was a beautiful brunette with blue eyes. I had been surprised and thrilled to have a girl after all this time, but my joy was tempered when I knew for certain before she was a week old, that she had the same eye muscle problem which I had shown when I was two. Because of that, I was really mad at God! "Why did you do this to me, God! How could you be so cruel as to give me a beautiful daughter and then afflict her with crossed eyes!"

Obviously, I was very immature in my understanding of God at the time. I remember looking down at that darling little one and fiercely vowing that I was not going to let her be hurt like I had been hurt. I don't know what I thought I could do to keep her from being hurt but I was determined! Thankfully, she never had to endure being taunted by other children at school as I had been, because surgeries she had when she was two years old corrected the problem.

Our new home had large gracious rooms, beautiful stained woodwork that didn't show fingerprints, and two pocket doors that I could smoothly roll to close off the dining room from the playroom or the living room. We had a six-car garage and a big yard with lots of room for a garden, too. Even though we had to heat the house with a coal furnace, and the kitchen was not modern, I was happy to be there. But while living in that house I was finally forced to recognize my resentment toward Bill that had been building for years, and the first outward sign of real disunity in our household occurred as a result of my parents giving us a television.

It was an old black and white set that they brought for us when they came to see their first granddaughter. I enjoyed watching a program or two when I was ironing in the evening, and the children got to watch the morning Captain Kangaroo program. But Bill became glued to the TV, often staying up into the wee hours of the morning, and after about six months of that he decided the TV would have to go. Since the children and I really liked the little bit that we watched, I objected to throwing it away. But throw it away he did, despite my indignation with the injustice of it all.

In exasperation he explained to me one night: "If I was an alcoholic you wouldn't insist on having wine in the house so you should just accept the fact that we need to do without a television set." In an attempt to get me to understand his decision he started ferreting out books and articles describing the dangers of television. While agreeing with him that our children needed to be busy doing things instead of sitting passively in front of a TV screen, I still resented having to get rid of it just because he couldn't handle it. And I recognized that I had begun to lose respect for him because I thought that his real reason for getting rid of it was his lack of self-discipline.

Bill and I could talk about surface things but when I touched on areas of our relationship or disagreed with him about something, he usually dealt with me by clamming up and giving me the silent treatment for days. One night though, when the children were all in bed, my attempt to have a serious talk with him about our relationship escalated to the point that some of the children remembered it from the loud voices below their bedrooms. We were in the kitchen when I turned to Bill and told him how lonely I was, how much I wished he would tell me that he loved me and would act like he was glad I was there.

"That's what you get from reading all those Hollywood novels!" he retorted angrily.

"No!" I protested. "You don't understand! I'm not expecting things to be perfect but this isn't at all the way things are supposed to be! Why is it too much to expect some personal attention and affection like my parents show each other?"

"I am not your father!" he roared back at me.

"I don't expect you to be like my father, but why can't you at least sometimes show me some appreciation for all that I do!" I cried desperately. "I can't keep living like this! I seem to exist in a void as far as you're concerned!" I felt like I was at the end of my rope.

Trembling with fury, he said, deliberately, "I am not going to change. If you don't like it, then get out!"

Then he picked up a piece of a two-by-four that was leaning against the pantry door frame and smashed it into pieces across the kitchen table! End of discussion.

Although I would try again and again through the years, to get him to talk about our relationship, to go to counseling, to do something to make our marriage more tolerable for me, he would angrily reply in the same way, "I am not your father and I am not going to change! You need to accept me as I am!" I didn't think that I expected him to be like my father, just more loving in our relationship, more caring. I didn't accept his statement that he couldn't change. I always thought that he just didn't care enough to want to change.

Kids and Critters

Although I kept praying for God to help me and guide me, sometimes during those years of so many babies and so much loneliness I would wonder if God ever heard my cries for help. Knowing that my children needed me, the joy I received from them, and the sheer workload every day, kept me so busy that I didn't have time for much introspection. But I often cried myself to sleep at night after Bill had rolled over and begun to snore. Sometimes I would get up and go downstairs and just walk through the rooms, thinking and praying.

Three weeks before David was born, one of my friends, Marilyn White, came over for the afternoon with her two little daughters, six-month-old Mara, and three-year-old Melissa. We took our children for a walk and afterwards sat at my dining room table, visiting over a cup of tea while our children played next to us in the playroom. The Whites had recently moved to St. Joseph from the Philippines, where her husband had been stationed with the U.S. Army. She had been concerned about his difficulty adjusting to civilian life, but that day, she said he had a new job and was in good spirits, so I rejoiced with her at the happy turn of events. The next morning I awakened to the horrible news that he had just shot and killed all of them, including himself.

Our mutual friend, Bev Connell, and I walked and talked all morning trying to comfort each other. After lunch when I went for a checkup with my obstetrician, Dr. Trupin, he discovered I was in labor but had been too agitated to notice. Since some of my past labors had been short he had me admitted to the hospital and dropped into my room frequently all night, not only to check on my condition, but to talk and to listen to each other, as we pondered this tragedy. My labor stopped by morning so I went home, giving little thought to my natal condition, so shaken by the events of the previous day which made my problems seemed negligible and still solvable.

When I came home after David's birth on April 2, 1963, I had to laugh when Bill asked me if I was in the habit of serving the children green oatmeal for breakfast. "I put green food-coloring in the oatmeal when you were in the hospital," he said, "and they didn't say a word about it. They acted like they had it that way every day!" I think it was such a rare thing for him to be in that domestic role that they probably were too shocked to question him.

Thankfully, as I plunged back into the business of keeping track of my busy brood, all of the children seemed to be thriving. Small town life in the summertime was filled with fun. It was easy to be out and about since I didn't have to bundle everybody up against the cold, and released from the regimen of school, we spent the lazy days visiting with my women friends and their children. Although I didn't enter much into open disagreement with Bill, we both knew my attitude toward him was not good. My resentment flared up again when I had to go to the homes of my neighbors to watch the coverage of President Kennedy's funeral, because I couldn't watch it in my own home.

Concurrent with the death the President, was my awareness that I was nurturing new life in my womb again, but instead of a smooth ride through this pregnancy I suffered two blood clot episodes. Dr. Trupin, had a fit about the first one, put me on some medication and told me to stay off my feet. Right! When the second clot formed he told us that he would no longer be willing to accept me as a patient if I became pregnant again. According to him I could very well die with another pregnancy, so Bill had to pay attention to him. With Anne-Marie's birth in July of 1964 we had already passed the number of children we had hoped to have so Bill agreed to begin using Natural Family Planning to avoid another pregnancy. That method, perfected by Dr. John and Sheila Kippley, and taught by the Couple to Couple League, worked fine for us.

As if having a passel of kids wasn't enough excitement, we had a houseful of animals too. I had never had a pet as a child, unless you could count the time I got a light blue, baby chick for Easter. I named it Powder and kept it in a cardboard box when I wasn't playing with it until it matured into a chicken and we ate it for dinner.

But at our first house in St. Joseph Bill had brought home a couple of hamsters one day and gently introduced me into a more intimate knowledge of animal life than I ever cared to have. He put them in a cage on the kitchen floor and I had to admit that we all had great fun watching the antics of the little rodents. After that success, the next thing Bill brought home was a guinea pig. Again, it was an animal in a cage but it was possible to take this one out and cuddle it a little. I got used to the hamsters and the guinea pig, eventually enjoying them as much as the kids did.

But once we bought our second house the animal population in the Downes house got a bit macabre. The day that Bill found a bat hanging in the basement of our house he didn't just dispose of it like most normal husbands would have done. No, he liked it! He started calling her The Old Lady and his curiosity about her led to a research project raising bats in captivity by developing an artificial diet for them.

When Bill started raising bats in our house, I couldn't help but remember a night in 1942 when a bat got into our Cedar Rapids apartment and started flying around. My mother was terrified so she barricaded herself in the bathroom and stuffed towels under the crack in the door, calling out instructions for Carolyn and I to hide under the covers of our bed until my father got home. "If Mother could only see me now!" I chuckled, glad that Bill had taught me enough about bats that I knew they wouldn't be landing in my hair, and thankful that I hadn't inherited that phobia from Mom.

The first two baby bats born in our house were named Albert and Jane, but we soon gave up trying to name the succeeding baby bats (which was good since we eventually had 74 bats). During this three-year *Count Dracula* period of our lives we turned a room at the back of the second floor of the house into a bat room. In addition to many cages of bats in that room we kept hibernating bats hanging in jars in our refrigerator right along with jars of pickles and jam.

Hoping to catch more bats in the late summer months when newborn bats are first zooming around, Bill would often leave the window of the bat room open in the evening while he lay in wait for the sounds of bats in cages to attract the inexperienced wild bats. One night while he was biding his time this way, his attention was diverted enough that he missed one of the incoming bats. Unfortunately, the bat sailed down the staircase from upstairs right into the living room where I was hosting our Crafties group. Pandemonium ensued when it began circling the room at knee level. The terrified women started screaming and throwing assorted sewing up over their heads. The combination of frantic screams from most of the them, and hysterical laughter from a couple of us brought Bill and his net tearing down the staircase.

Eventually he caught the culprit and order was restored, but the resulting word-of-mouth account of our winged house guests made it difficult to find babysitters brave enough to come to our house during those years. I did learn to cope, though, and Bill said that he knew I was over the hump when he came downstairs early one morning and caught me talking to the leaf-nose bat that resided in a glass cage on top of our upright piano. From the practically antiseptic environment of my childhood I was unobtrusively being tweaked into a more flexible and sturdy human being.

While Bill was engrossed in raising bats, I was engrossed in raising five sons and two daughters, and the children were absorbed in nurturing not only hamsters and guinea pigs but snakes, sparrow hawks, gerbils and numerous other critters...and plenty of mischief besides.

Since our first four children were boys who walked in their father's footsteps I had to work hard to hide my distaste for the gross things they brought into the house. I didn't want to dim their enthusiasm for things zoological so I had many opportunities to practice self-discipline. One of my worst incidents occurred one day as I prepared to do the laundry. Checking the pockets before throwing the boys' jeans into the washing machine, I came into contact with a live June bug! It could have just as well been an electric shock I felt! Ugh! Even the memory makes me shiver!

Our children continued to delight me with their curiosity about everything around them. I bought pads of paper from the local newspaper office and provided them with jars of bright poster paints, so the playroom was always a busy area of the house as they made a great mess of things. I taped their artwork to doors and walls all over the house. They went through so much clay, glue and play dough, I suspected they must have been eating it, and scissors and paper caused confetti-like blitzes ever so often. We had lots of fun with cardboard boxes, too, painting them into houses, trains, or boats.

All this activity was a bit dangerous for Anne-Marie when she was an infant so I had to put her in the playpen with the mat on the floor and the play pen upside down over her. Then, she could enjoy a stimulating environment without her siblings clobbering her with toys tossed on top of her in their well-meaning enthusiasm for sharing.

The older boys were a big help with the younger children. Any mother of multiple preschool children can tell you how much they can fetch and carry items, with big grins on their faces showing how proud they are to help, even if they can barely toddle themselves. One day when Joey was three, he may well have saved one-year-old Michael's life. I had foolishly left them in the tub to go get a clean diaper off the clothesline in the yard. Naked and wet, Joey came running out the door screaming for me to get Michael, who had slipped under the water and was too slippery for him to pick up. Michael was still threshing when I retrieved him from the tub and once he had vomited up the water he had ingested he was all right. I still tremble to think of what might have happened because of my carelessness.

I had been grateful that our very first apartment in Ames was furnished with a piano since I couldn't imagine life without one, so once we'd settled into our own home in Illinois we always had one. We started our marriage singing in the church choir and one day I came across piano music Bill had composed. Until then, I hadn't realized that he had been that involved in music. It was even years later before I learned he had played his grandfather's violin and carried it with him to the Philippines during the war. We started taking the children to recitals and concerts at the university, as soon as they were old enough to sit still for an hour. The Chicago Symphony's rendition of *Pictures at an Exhibition,* conducted by Sir George Soltis, was so continually the background music in our home that several of the children have spoken of how it seems to be woven into the very fabric of their childhood.

Bill put a lot of thought into what kinds of activities would be good for the children. Because of his long-time interest in chemistry he still had some chemicals around with which he concocted flares and smoke bombs, setting them off in our fire place occasionally to entertain the kids, but mostly he was oriented toward putting things into their hands that would help them to learn. A huge, brick-lined sandpile he built for them in the back yard was covered over with grape vines he planted to shade the area.

In preparation for Christmas one year, he took some eight-by-ten pieces of plywood and cut them into one-foot squares, and then cut one by one by twelve pieces to go with them, thus presenting the children with a huge set of building blocks that was enjoyed for many years. He bought them real carpentry tools before they were old enough to go to school, and a blow-torch with a supply of glass rods, when they were still in grade school. He didn't have much respect for the usual toys of the day.

I saw that he was growing passionate about his vocation as teacher, both at home and at the university. In fact, so much of his time was spent reading up on educational research during those years at Illinois, that I teased him about it. "Are your Sarcophagid flies going to play second fiddle to your teaching from now on?" He just smiled and shrugged, but I was happy to see this side of him. He worked hard to engage the interest of his students, assigning them bits of original research to work on and taking them on many field trips. He constantly challenged them to think.

In a book critical of the huge university, *The Multiversity,* Bill was described as a teacher who really got his students enthused, but because he didn't publish as many articles as the university thought appropriate, he became a casualty of the "publish or perish" practice. Although he had published some well-received papers, he was advised in the spring of 1965 that his contract would not be renewed for the 1965-66 academic year. This was the impetus that moved us to Michigan, where Bill joined the faculty of Michigan State University.

Approaching Real Life in Michigan

In June of 1965 Bill and I made a trip to Michigan to look for a house to rent but we were unsuccessful in finding one. "If you had only four children"...one man said to me and then paused, as if he was waiting for me to assure him I'd get rid of three of them. Later that summer our second trip resulted in the rental of a nice 1½ story house on Jolly Road in Lansing with a huge fenced-in yard. The street name made me smile. It was a good omen.

The children had been parceled out to the neighbors while we were house-hunting, so we gathered them up and began packing. Bill used his retirement money from the university to buy a new Chevy van, so once the moving van was ready to roll we headed in comfort to the site of our next adventure. We had always had to layer the kids in the back seat of a conventional sedan while I held the current baby, so it was wonderful to finally have a vehicle with enough space for us. I gave thanks to my Creator that we took only one pet with us—Barney, a sparrow hawk, which we had kept from a brood we found in our attic that summer. Our bats had been wiped out by a disease that swept through the colony and all the other critters were left behind, given to our boys' school friends, the ones with understanding parents.

This was a new beginning so I got my usual optimistic self into high gear and set out to learn my way around an unfamiliar city again. With Oldsmobile's corporate headquarters, the seat of government for the State of Michigan, and the university, our new environment would provide lots of opportunities for diverse activities and interests.

One thing that had attracted Bill to Michigan State was their new program of putting the offices of professors in the dorms so that interaction between teacher and student could be enhanced. We welcomed his students into our home every Sunday evening, giving them a place to discuss anything and everything while devouring freshly-baked soft pretzels and gallons of Pepsi. The pretzels were so popular with the students that they suggested to Bill that he could make more money hawking them in the dorms than teaching classes. They may have very well been right.

In the spring of 1966 Bill built a trailer that resembled the Russian Witch, Baba Yaga's house on chicken legs. This was towed behind our van so that we could take our first of many family camping trips. He carefully made it so that the two sides of light aluminum lifted off, revealing rows of drawers which were specific storage units for each of us, plus numerous cubby holes for camping equipment and entomological gear for Bill's scientific work. Our kitchen was built just inside the back doors of the van.

The day we were to leave it took us until 4:00 in the afternoon to get everything loaded, so our first day's journey was a short one. We went via St. Louis, where Bill's parents joined us in their station wagon in order to spend a month out west in New Mexico and Arizona with us. They were experienced campers, used to sleeping in the back of their wagon. I don't know how I would have survived without them.

Every night various kids would have to get up to go to the bathroom at different times and I would have to get up with them. Once I caught two of the boys just in time to keep them from heading out into the Sonora Desert west of Tucson.

Another night we arrived really late at a campground in Oak Creek Canyon in Arizona, so instead of putting up our two tents we just spread out our sleeping bags on top of our air mattresses on the ground and nodded off. A crack of thunder awoke us sometime after midnight as a deluge caught us by surprise. We stuffed all the kids and the wet sleeping bags into the van and watched our air mattresses float away in the lake that formed where we'd been sleeping. The next morning, our bedraggled group had to organize a rescue and retrieve mission in order to collect our air mattresses and wash them off at the campground pump. We had chosen to go to the desert because we had expected to be free from rain there but one night when we camped in the middle of Tucumcari, New Mexico, a cloudburst caught me with my girls in the bath house, and the streets became rivers which kept us stuck there for a few hours. We began to think about hiring out as rainmakers.

I loved seeing the country, but we seldom stayed more than one night in a campsite and the care of seven little kids under those conditions had me sympathizing with the early pioneer women. The trip exhausted me. Bill's parents were very kind to me and, at one point, Bill's mother said to me, "I sure hope he appreciates you!" All I could say was, "I hope he does too!"

At Apache Landing, New Mexico, we lost two-year-old Anne-Marie and suffered a frantic search for her that must have aged me ten years. (We had combed the beach for her but she had merely stepped into an empty tent next to us.) On the way home, when we stopped in the middle of the night for gas and bathroom visits somewhere in Kansas, eight-year-old Michael got left behind and we were a ways down the road before it dawned on us that he was missing. There were some tense moments before we successfully retrieved him.

Once we were back home and school was in full swing I settled down into a routine that was not very demanding. Bill continued to practically live at the university campus and I continued my busy life with the children and my women friends. With Julie now in school, I had only David and Anne-Marie at home during the day and since we were renting our house there were no remodeling projects I could indulge in.

I still enjoyed playing bridge with the university women but was more comfortable playing the game with Nancy, Jan and Jamie, whom I'd met through my church circle. Calling ourselves "The Judas Circle" since the other church circles were named after saints or apostles, we started meeting in each other's homes one afternoon a month to play cards once we'd put our little ones down for naps. But just having a game of cards occasionally did not satisfy my unmet needs for real adult companionship.

While other families watched TV together, we read together. I still have copies of some of my favorite Dr. Seuss books which I have read at least a zillion times. The Bookmobile lady said we had upped the Bookmobile's circulation quite a bit with our steady 80 books going out of there every two weeks when they came to our corner. That's only because I limited each of us to 10 books apiece each time we went. Bill frequently gave me a bad time about reading fiction, though. He detested it and didn't trust non-fiction much either, always feeling that you didn't know if those authors were reporting the truth or their own biases. But I persisted in devouring one book after another, needing to be able to go someplace in my mind to be distracted momentarily from the sadness of my relationship with him.

In the spring of 1967 we bought a house on Lansing's west side. It had four bedrooms, three bathrooms and a family room so it was good to have our own home again and more space. And when June rolled around, we once more headed out west for another camping/collecting trip. This time, I figured I was a veteran camper and the kids were a year older so I expected the trip to be less taxing for me than our first excursion. That was not to be the case.

Camping on the edge of the water at Conches Dam, New Mexico, a wild storm came up and blew the boys tent over on them. They are hardy souls though so it dampened only their bodies, not their enthusiasm for camping. We had some frightening moments out on the lake in a boat when another bad storm came up suddenly, and we barely made it to shore in an uninhabited area. A water patrol boat came to find us that time because they had gotten worried when we hadn't made it back to the marina.

At a rather desolate campground in Texas there were no signs of life except insects, in spite of the many cattle guards we had to traverse in order to arrive at our destination. Although Bill was happy with the insect population there, Anne-Marie definitely was not. She had unfortunately walked into the middle of a mess of fire ants, and her screams as they crawled up inside of her jeans and stung her, could surely be heard all the way across the state. To this day her only concession to camping is the Holiday Inn.

We did have a wonderful by-product of our stop in Corpus Christi, Texas, to visit my sister Nancy and her family. Early one evening when her husband had to work, Nancy, Bill, and I took our seven and her two children down to the bay to look at the big boats that hustled in and out of that busy port. We herded our group of little ones along a dock, gawking so intently at a huge container ship that we went right past a "No Trespassing" sign.

When someone yelled, "Ahoy there!" I thought, "Oh, Oh, now we're in trouble!" In unison, our twelve heads looked up toward the voice. Way above us, with his hands cupped around his mouth, a sailor yelled, "The Captain wants to know, would you like to come aboard?" Delighted, we scampered up, up, up a ladder and were greeted by the sailor, who introduced us to the Captain. He offered to show us around, he explained, because seeing us reminded him how much he missed his own family back in Liverpool, England. His ship was loading bitumen from Mexico as we spent a couple of hours in his domain.

We were introduced to everything from the pilot house, where we looked at the sonar equipment and other directional equipment, to the head. My boys thought it hilarious that the bathroom was called a head. We looked down into the cavernous hold, as heavy cranes lowered huge containers into it. Before we left, the Captain seated us at tables and served us refreshments as we watched night fall and gazed down at the sparkling lights coming on all around the bay area. It was a magical night! The next morning at Nancy's, we made a big batch of our soft pretzels and took them immediately to the ship for the enjoyment of the crew as they prepared to leave for England that day. That episode is a memory that still brings a smile to my face when I think of it.

By the time we were on our way toward home from the camping trip, I had a high fever and my feet and hands were so numb that I couldn't feel them. When I got to my doctor, the diagnosis was that some bacteria were circulating through my blood system, so I was given antibiotics and put to bed for a rest. Thankfully, some of my new neighbors pitched in to help for a few days while Bill rearranged our dining room bay window sill.

He removed the African violets that had been sitting there and replaced them with a dozen Mason jars, each housing a huge black live tarantula that he had caught out west. The kids were intrigued by them and had great Show and Tell material for school that fall. Our daughter, Julie, even adopted two of them. She named them Miles and Maximilian and let them crawl into her hands. I, however, had a phobia about spiders so I was uncomfortable with the new window arrangement in spite of appreciating the novelty of it all.

That fall, at our open house evenings for Bill's university students they sometimes played a form of "chicken" by sitting in a circle on the living room floor and letting a tarantula crawl out of its jar in the middle of the circle. As it crept toward someone, that person would pound their fists on the carpet until it changed direction and headed for someone else, who then did the same thing. I busied myself elsewhere in the house, whenever there was a tarantula loose.

Once, a sleepy trip to the bathroom in the middle of the night ended with me leaping on top of the toilet lid when I discovered that I was trapped between the bathroom door and our bedroom. Either Miles or Maximilian was meandering toward me through the doorway! Bill was out of town at the time so I had to yell long and loud before I finally awakened our son, Tom, who put it back in its jar. Another time I remember well, was when a water snake that the boys had in the basement, got loose and was not recaptured until after she had given birth to what seemed like an unending supply of babies. For the next month or so we kept finding what my boys called "cute little baby snakes" slithering out from under the washing machine or across the floor. I found it very hazardous doing laundry during that time.

Late in the summer of 1967, we met Ann and Walter Kron when they were going door to door in our neighborhood, inviting residents to a meeting at nearby Sexton High School, for the purpose of forming the West Side Neighborhood Association. This gathering to rally our mixed-race neighborhood to expose and end racial discrimination came about because of Ann's experience with racial prejudice. When she was in college, she had spent a summer in the Baltimore home of one of her African-American friends, and she was shocked when she experienced the extent, firsthand, that racial discrimination in that city affected her friend's life.

Walter's entire family had been wiped out in Germany because they were Jewish, so he and Ann felt impelled to take a stab at fighting the racial discrimination in education and real estate, that was going on right in our own neighborhood. More than 200 people from the 3000 households in our area attended that first meeting, and we began to form committees to tackle the problems in our midst. Bill got involved in the Education Committee and I ended up as the Secretary as well as a board member. Energized by my first real exposure to city politics and grass roots activism, I began to look deeper into what was happening in the world outside of my own family.

I hadn't really taken the time to pay attention to my spiritual or emotional life during the early years of my marriage. When my thoughts became heavy I redirected them to focus on the activities and experiences which were external. But in the fall of 1967, once the children were back in school, I was invited to a faith-sharing group composed of women in my new neighborhood and immediately felt at home. We were sixteen members of several different churches who referred to ourselves simply as the "Monday Morning Group."

We sat around a dining room table and took turns reading aloud from Keith Miller's book, *A Taste of New Wine*, which described his discovery that God wants to relate to us in a personal way. As we read the paragraphs, we stopped to discuss parts of it whenever anyone wanted to talk about it. The word "fellowship" took on real meaning for me as we grew close to each other by sharing our lives this way. I met Gerry Shaver, one of my dearest friends, in the group.

This was where I had my first opportunity to dialogue with women from other faith backgrounds. Bill and I had been living as cultural Catholics, going to church on Sunday and putting our children into Catholic schools, but I had not really examined my faith since my school days. I really looked forward to those weekly meetings and the stimulating ideas we tossed around. And even as my mind and heart began to open up to the possibility of a deeper relationship with God, a more personal relationship with God, my renewed faith was tested to the max when my world turned upside down in the fall of 1968.

Earthquake!

School was out for the summer mid-June in 1968 and we started on another camping migration out west. We stopped briefly at the University of Illinois so Bill could talk to someone in the Entomology Department office for a few minutes, and while he was there he was offered a job teaching a summer Entomology course. He decided to accept it so we found an empty old house in St. Joseph to rent. Instead of camping *out* as we had expected, we were camping *in*, with our sleeping bags and a borrowed card table.

The children and I enjoyed being back with our friends but my thoughts were troubled when I tried to go to sleep at night. Early in our marriage Bill had told me he had once considered taking his life, but he didn't, because the pastor of the Newman Center in Ames had talked him out of it. During the last few months, he had been so extremely remote that I wondered if he was again contemplating suicide.

Mid-summer, he began to talk about one of his students, a wonderful nun named Sister Hope, who seemed to be in love with God. The thought crossed my mind that he might be in love with her. When we took her camping with us one weekend I found her to be a delightful person, truly radiating an inner joy that was unusual, so I could understand his interest in her. I couldn't have known then, the powerful effect that she had on him.

With a week left to teach at the University, Bill drove us to Cedar Rapids so I could visit with my parents while he finished his class responsibilities at the university. On his drive back there, he started praying the Rosary, which is a series of prayers, divided into decades, said while meditating on various events in the life of Christ, and the life of his mother, Mary. Often, when Bill had meditated on The Third Glorious Mystery, which is about the descent of the Holy Spirit upon the Apostles, he had wished for that kind of power to talk to his students about God.

This time, as he prayed The Third Glorious Mystery he felt an overwhelming sense of God's loving presence in the car with him. He pulled off the road and sat there for two hours, being bathed in God's love, and crying like a baby. He phoned me and told me what had happened and said he realized that he had been a bad husband and a bad father. He wanted me to tell the children, that when he came to pick us up, they would have a new father. This man had always been unemotional, so I was concerned and apprehensive about what he told me, thinking he might be having a nervous breakdown.

His behavior *was* different when he rejoined us and we left to go camping in New Mexico for a couple of weeks. He said that Sister Hope had bawled him out for not spending enough time with his family. He seemed genuinely sorry that he had invested most of his time and energy with his students and research, at the expense of personal time with us. He made an effort to relate more to us.

He had a hunger to read the Bible and wanted to talk about Jesus. Scripture came alive to him and he sounded excited when he talked about it. Although none of us understood what he was experiencing, he was in love with God and wanted to find others who felt the same way.

Sister Hope had told him about a Christian community in the state of New York that she had visited, which, she said, was patterned after the early church as described in the book of Acts. And as we neared home from our camping trip, Bill told me he wanted us to go on to New York to visit there. Taken aback that he would even suggest such a thing, I definitely did not want to go! I just wanted to be back in my own home again after three months of traveling.

Bill still wanted to see what this place was like, so he phoned the man, Herbert, who was the leader of the community. He received an invitation for us to come but I told him to go without us if he wanted to go. Then Bill handed the phone to me and Herbert told me that the future of my marriage was at stake so I'd better come. Our relationship *was* in bad shape so I reluctantly agreed to go. A sixteen-hour trip brought us to a secluded farm surrounded by acres of woods where we experienced what I now would describe as a cult.

Although it was an unfamiliar word to me in 1968, by the 1970's the word "cult" became a very familiar word because of a lot of publicity given to the fact that many young people were being enticed into groups such as the Moonies or Children of God. Required to turn away from families and friends and isolated from all that was familiar to them, these unfortunate people were brainwashed and considered victimized to the point where they needed to be rescued from their plight, even against their wishes. Frantic parents around the country were hiring experts to kidnap their children from these cults and then de-program them, so that they could be returned to their families.

When we arrived at this community in the Catskill Mountains the people received us lovingly. We learned that approximately a hundred people of all ages lived there in several buildings on this tract of land near Middleton, New York.

Shortly after we arrived, we were taken to the big living room of a farmhouse where we were introduced to Herbert. An imposing figure, a bit heavy-set, he was presiding over a group of people who were jammed into the room to the point where some were even sitting under a grand piano. Plates of food were being passed around for our dinner, and someone took our children to a basement dining area where the children in the community were eating. Bill seemed very impressed with what Herbert was preaching but I don't remember anything he said.

My husband and older sons were assigned sleeping space on the second floor of a modern five-car garage. Our younger three children were bedded down on the second and third floors of the old farmhouse, with all the other young children, and I was taken to sleep in still another building that had just been built. It housed a new dining room which was about to be put into use, and two bedrooms that had been in use for some time. We were told that the children would be well taken care of and we were to concentrate on getting oriented to Herbert's teachings.

Although Bill seldom talked to Herbert, he spent hours visiting with some of the other men there and was deeply touched by the love and care that they showed toward one another and toward him. He was experiencing the euphoria of being in love with God and was predisposed to be impressed by the positive things he saw. My anxiety level rose as I saw that he seemed blind to things that disturbed me greatly, Things which would normally have disturbed him. I try to keep an open mind about new things but as each day passed I became increasingly uneasy being there. It was more than seeing that things were less than perfect; it was a growing sense that too many things just weren't right, as well as my growing antipathy toward Herbert.

Although the group was supposedly composed of people who loved God and each other, most of them seemed to be preoccupied with Herbert. At evening meetings, when Herbert was expounding on one theological point or another, I saw some of the women kneeling before him, swaying back and forth chanting, "Oh Herbert, we love you! Oh Herbert, we love you!" It made me sick, but nobody around me seemed to think there was anything odd about their behavior.

One woman told me how Herbert had cured her of hay fever, but her stuffed up nasal passages and itchy streaming eyes seemed to contradict her testimony. Everyone I spoke to told me how wonderful Herbert was, until my impression was that they were all worshiping him rather than God. Perhaps my experience there was so different from Bill's because there were a lot of unstable women there.

Herbert dominated the group. He explained to my husband that these people needed to learn to trust *him* to provide for all of their needs so that they could then learn to trust *God* to meet all their needs. But his role of mediator was a poor explanation of what I saw going on. Some of the women told me Herbert cared for them so much that he even went to the trouble to pick out the patterns, fabric and buttons for new dresses for them. Some of the men worked as professionals in New York City, but they gave Herbert their paychecks and then he doled out their provisions. The children who lived there were taken each day by car, into Middleton to attend a Catholic school there and when a Catholic priest came out on Sunday to say Mass, this veneer of Catholic legitimacy was confusing to me.

Our older boys were having a great time riding horses, driving go-carts around a track, swimming in a pool, and going hunting with a man who looked like somebody's grandfather. A beautiful 18-year old woman was in charge of the younger children but I didn't really know how their needs were being met. My daughters were four and seven then and not happy about being separated from me as much as they were. I mistakenly assured them that we'd soon be going back home.

I was concerned about our son, Paul, who was eight at the time, because he was having problems with his asthma. His allergy problems were always worse in the fall and this place was surrounded by woods, the worst place he could be at that time. Then I was really upset when we learned that he had been bitten by a dog and taken to a doctor for treatment without us even being informed about it until after the fact.

We had expected to stay only a few days, and at the end of a week, we really had to leave in order for Bill to get back on time for his teaching position at Michigan State. Our children were already late entering their schools in Lansing. However, when Bill went to tell Herbert that we would be leaving, Herbert acknowledged that Bill needed to fulfill his teaching contract, but he told him to leave the children and me there.

I was incredulous, when Bill came and told me that Herbert expected our residence there to be permanent, with Bill coming back to visit us during the Thanksgiving break and other holidays, until next June, when he would be able to stay there with us. And when he asked me to agree to it, I was absolutely floored! Of course I told him I just wanted to go home!

When Bill told Herbert that I didn't want to stay, Herbert accused Bill of abandoning the headship of his family and letting his wife run things. He told Bill to make the decision for the good of the family and to insist that I submit. I was terrified to see this husband of mine who had never trusted anyone's advice, now seeming willing to do whatever this man recommended! I was in the middle of a nightmare!

Bill took me off into the woods where we could be alone, and pleaded with me to try to stay for just another week. He promised to come and get us then if I still didn't want to stay. He said Herbert told him our marriage depended on me submitting to him. This was all so bizarre! There was no way I could believe this was right for our marriage. What marriage? How could this relationship even *be* a marriage?

Bill seemed sure that he needed to do what Herbert wanted, which made me worried that he might try to leave the children there even if I didn't agree to stay. As he was pleading with me to cooperate, I tried to think of scenarios which would get us all out of there without causing a major scene that would upset the children. I felt terribly afraid and helpless. This couldn't really be happening! But leave us, he did. He left without us.

I tried to control the panic I felt after he was gone but I evidently didn't do a good job of it. The day after Bill left, Herbert called me before him and announced that I could no longer see my children because it was disturbing them to see me so depressed. This was really, really scary. I tried to numb the anxiety inside of me and to act calm and normal around the other people so they wouldn't think I needed to be watched. Most of my remaining time there is a blank.

I do remember playing a game of tennis with three other people, once, and another time, I went into town with other women to do a pickup truck full of laundry at a Laundromat. And one day, Herbert took me into town and bought me an ice cream cone and a pair of tennis shoes for Julie. Julie told me she remembers one of the women telling her that Herbert had bought the tennis shoes just for her.

In a continuing state of desperation I kept trying to figure out how to get all of my children together so we could get away, all the while wondering if Bill would even return on the weekend for us. I just couldn't bring myself to imagine leaving without my children, even to try to get help. I was still in such a state of shock that I couldn't seem to think clearly enough to plot a way out of the mess.

I was given general housework to do that helped pass the time, but even then I was reminded of my sick environment. Once, when dusting furniture, I started to dust a grand piano and somebody yelled at me to stop. "Do you have a degree in music?" Hardly believing my ears, I replied, "No, but I took piano lessons for eight years." "That's not good enough!" I was told. "So don't touch the piano!"

Another time I was roused out of my bed shortly after midnight and told to go to the kitchen and wash tons and tons of dishes. But probably my lowest moment occurred late one evening when I sneaked up to the third floor of the main house, searching for my children. I found my little four-year-old Anne-Marie, filthy dirty, asleep with tear tracks down her grimy face. I had been praying desperately to God for help but I felt terribly abandoned.

Unbeknownst to me, our friends, Walter and Ann Kron, had become very concerned about me because when Bill returned to Lansing he had gone over to their house and told them about Herbert's place. Walter remembers Bill's enthusiasm as he came in their front door, describing the love the people there showed each other. As he expounded on the fact that Herbert was so wise, he seemed to fully expect that Walter would find it as wonderful as he did.

Then, when Walter asked, "Where's Laurie?" Bill told him that I had decided to stay there awhile. Walter thought he hadn't heard correctly. "You mean Laurie and the kids aren't here with you?" He still couldn't believe what he was hearing. "You see," Bill told him, "Laurie is possessed by the devil, and can't come home until they get the devil out of her." Walter was incredulous! He later told me, "I kept looking at him thinking, 'How could these words be coming out of this normally rational human being?'"

When he heard Ann coming in the back door with groceries, he scooted into the kitchen to apprize her of the situation. "We've got a problem here," he said to her. "Bill's left Laurie and the kids in New York because, he says, Laurie's possessed by the devil!"

Ann said that she will never forget walking into her living room and seeing Bill standing there. She felt scared for me and also wary. When she asked him what was happening, at first Bill started with the story that I wanted to stay there, and then that fell apart so he switched to saying I had to stay there because I had to get the devil out of me. She clearly expressed to him the thought that no matter what the problem was, it wasn't demon possession. As he repeated to her what he'd told Walter, she felt very afraid.

"Bill, all I can think of is I've been dropped into the plot of *Rosemary's Baby*! We want Laurie to come here and tell us that she wants to be there. We want to hear it with her own words." "That's impossible until they get her cleansed," Bill replied. Ann kept insisting I be allowed to come home. "Look, Bill, I'll pay her way back there if she really wants to be there. I just need to see her to be sure she wants to be there!"

Eventually Bill backed away looking heartbroken, and not believing what he had heard. He said, "I'm terribly disappointed. Even though you're Jewish, of all the people I know you're the ones I thought would understand." Ann thought, "There's something terribly wrong with this man. And what's being Jewish got to do with it?" She wondered what she and Walter had ever said that led him to think they'd understand what he was telling them.

As soon as he left, Ann wracked her brain trying to think of how to get in touch with my parents. She phoned around until she found a neighbor of mine who remembered my father's name and the city where my parents lived. When my father got through talking to Ann, he called Bill and wasn't satisfied with the explanation he heard. So he got Herbert's phone number from him and called there to talk to me.

Like most people there, I could only receive mail or phone calls after Herbert had first checked them out so I was cut off from contact with the outside world. Fortunately for me, though, Herbert wasn't home when Daddy called and since my father's name is Bill, too, the person in charge let me take the call. Maybe the person thought it was my husband calling.

"What the hell's going on!" I heard him say when I picked up the phone. "Oh, Daddy!" I blubbered! "Don't you worry, Darling," he said, "we're going to get you out of there!" I don't remember any more of our conversation but I began to hope to see an end to this fiasco.

My father called his pastor, who called the Catholic diocese where Herbert's community was located. Asking what they knew about the place, he was told that they really didn't know much about it although some of the children from there were in a local Catholic school. Then my father called Bill's parents in St. Louis and talked to his father, who decided to fly to Lansing to feel Bill out.

After his phone call from my father, Bill called me and said he had no idea I was feeling so desperate. As we talked, he assured me that he and his father would come the next weekend to pick us up. I remember how I wished he would come right away instead of waiting until the weekend. I didn't feel safe.

Shortly after they arrived we followed the sound of Anne-Marie crying hysterically and found her with two women who were trying to stop a nosebleed she was having. Even though we didn't say a word, they seemed angry when I reached for Anne-Marie. As they protested that they had been disciplining her but hadn't caused the nosebleed, I gathered her up, and we clung to each other as we went to find Herbert. I was not willing to let go of her until we were safely out of there!

One of the women ran ahead of us, complaining to Herbert of our interference. When Bill told him we wanted to take our children and our belongings and leave, Herbert became very angry. He told Bill that I was an evil woman who was going to hell, and that our Paul should stay because he had problems. After his tirade, though, we were able to gather up all of our children and most of our belongings and get out of there.

As we drove away, I thought, "Lord, whatever am I going to do now?" Even though we were leaving a place where I was terrified, I didn't see how I could feel safe with Bill any longer, either. I had been through bouts of his anger that had left me wondering how I could ever behave normally around him again but the acts of daily living would eventually bring us back to a routine that outwardly resembled an ordinary family life. However, this behavior change was so momentous that I couldn't imagine how I would get my shattered life together again. I had no faith in my husband at all anymore and felt that my marriage was definitely over.

It was the end of September when we arrived back home. I automatically ran through all the tasks needed to get the children cleaned up and off to school and get the house back in order. The first weekend that we were home, Bill flew back to Herbert's and when he returned he said that Herbert thought he should go back at Thanksgiving and take Paul with him and then leave Paul to stay there indefinitely. Bill's parents advised me to see a lawyer about getting a divorce in order to protect the children, especially Paul.

Bill's words regarding Paul scared me enough that I did go to see a lawyer about what I might do to protect the children. But I am uncomfortable if things aren't out in the open, so when I told him a few days later what I had done, he seemed appalled. "I feel betrayed that you would do such a thing!" he said, and continued to remind me of my perceived disloyalty on a number of occasions during the following years.

Bill's parents decided to visit us for Thanksgiving, hoping that their visit would encourage him to stay home from Herbert's place for the holiday. They did come and Bill didn't go to Herbert's again. Later he told me, "When Herbert told me you were going to hell, I knew that couldn't be right because only God has that kind of information." Needless to say, I wasn't much comforted by his statement.

For weeks after we settled back into our lives in Lansing, I was very apprehensive around Bill. Since he'd always been reluctant to talk of personal things with me, I still didn't know my husband very well, but uppermost in my mind after the experience at Herbert's place was the sense that he was really a stranger to me now. I felt a need to be constantly alert so as not to be caught off guard again. It was a time that was so dark within me that there was not even a hint of the dawn said to follow darkness, no hint during the next few months, of the birth of new life I was about to experience.

Interlude

As we continued our active involvement in our parish, I felt like a fraud. Outwardly behaving as if I was part of this good Catholic family, I felt like I was living a lie. I was truly committed to leading the exemplary life of a Catholic mother and wife, but inwardly I knew the wife bit was a shambles and I began to feel like I was existing as two people.

You might say I had disintegrated into two people. It felt like I was outside of myself, watching what I was doing. And from time to time I would say to myself, "I really am Laurie Downes and I really am in my kitchen preparing dinner." Or, I'd be in the car and hear myself saying, "I'm really Laurie Downes and I'm really driving to pick up some groceries at the grocery store." Or like at this moment, "I really am Laurie Downes and I really am sitting at my computer trying to write a description of this quirky mental behavior of mine."

When I'm aware that I seem to be observing myself from outside of myself, I always feel an aura of unreality around me. It's one of the lonely places within me and I had wondered sometimes if other people thought that way occasionally, too. But when I shared my weird behavior with my dearest friend one day, she seemed upset and told me not to do that again, so I have not mentioned my bizarre behavior to anyone else until now. Just recently I read in a book, an account of a woman telling of this same kind of experience, so I guess it is not that unusual or anything to worry about.

In spite of my busy external life, I passed through a long 1968-1969 winter of introspection, searching for answers, trying to picture a scenario that was feasible for me and the children without Bill in the picture, but I couldn't imagine any way out. Catholics don't divorce and Hogans live up to their commitments. I felt stuck.

I resorted to my tried and true technique of focusing on daily tasks in my home and enjoying moments of respite with my women friends in order to retain my sanity. The rhythm of life kept on going and the needs of my children kept me mercifully occupied, so the dark winter passed and spring finally arrived to greet me with the lavishness of new life. My spirit is always lifted in the spring, my favorite time of the year, and this year would prove to be even more eventful than the last.

In the summer of 1969, Bill would again be teaching a course at the University of Illinois. And this time we made arrangements to stay in the home of our St. Joseph friends, Jim and Bev Connell, to care for their children while they were gone on an extended trip. The home was comfortable and the children were familiar, so the weeks we lived there were pleasant, a time to visit old friends again.

My children presented me with a guinea pig for my thirty-fourth birthday so we had still another body on board when we made our trek out west to camp in tents and collect bugs. I was then an old hand at this, but it really didn't get any easier as far as the logistics of living rather primitively under less than ideal conditions. I still enjoyed the beauty of the Southwest, though, and we made it back to the Mid-west this time without losing anyone.

The children were getting a marvelous education on these trips, as Bill taught them about the flora and fauna around us. They learned to be very quiet on forays into the wilderness so they wouldn't disturb the animals around them. Using a well-worn library of field guides, their sharp eyes were trained to notice details that their father pointed out to them. They became adept at spotting insects and small animals, and I was glad that they heeded his advice about not picking anything up unless they knew it would not harm them.

Labor Day weekend, off I-80 west of Chicago, we broke camp early in the morning on the last leg of our journey home, and piled into the van with dewy-wet tents stored in the trailer. We drove until we pulled off at the Chicago Harlem Ave. exit in order to buy gas. Bill prepared to fill our thirsty tanks and I started to herd my group to the bathrooms, when a camper converted from a school bus, pulled in behind us. Bill started talking to the driver, who had gotten off to fill up with gas, too.

When his wife joined him, we learned that he was a high school science teacher and they also had been traveling all summer with their seven children. Their mode of travel, however, was obviously superior to ours. She invited us to come aboard the bus and see what they had done to it. Her children had just tumbled out of their beds and were still in their pajamas, eating bowls of Cheerios at a kitchen table. How I envied her! We ended up visiting for two hours with them before they left. And as we turned around to head back to our van and trailer, we noticed that there was a school bus parked behind the station with a For Sale sign on it!

We looked at each other, we looked back at the bus, and we looked at each other again. The same thought occurred to each of us, "It wouldn't hurt to ask." The owner of the station said that the bus (a 1960, 46-passenger, Superior coach with an International Harvester engine) had belonged to Quigley North, a Chicago boys' school, and had broken down on the freeway. They had towed it in and the school decided not to try to fix it. Bill talked to the owner for quite a while and then decided to pay him $1000 for the bus, with the stipulation that he would put a new motor in it. So the deal was struck. Bill gave him a check and would come back to pick up the bus in a month's time.

In October, Bill called the guy, who said the bus was ready. A couple of his students who were regulars at our weekly open house sessions wanted to go with us as a lark, so we crammed everybody into our van early on a Saturday morning and drove for four hours to the station on Harlem Ave. When we got there the bus wasn't quite ready yet, but the guy said he was sure it would be ready in the morning.

So, we called our friends, Joe and Joan O'Halloran, who lived northwest of Chicago, and received an invitation to bring our huge entourage for an overnight stay. Luckily they had a big basement family room where we could spread out sleeping bags. Since they had seven children, too, there were 20 of us in a little 3-bedroom house with one bathroom. We had a wonderful time in spite of a restless night and we all trooped off to the church together to attend Mass the next morning. Once we were settled in our pews, Joe O'Halloran started counting kids and came up with one missing. Sure enough, our six-year old, David, was not among us. Joe went back to the house and found him playing with some toys in the basement. With so many children around it was probably David's first opportunity to get a turn with the toys since we had gotten there!

After Mass, a call to the gas station brought discouraging news. The bus still wasn't ready. With promises that it would be ready the following weekend, we packed up and drove back to Michigan. When Bill called the following weekend, the bus still wasn't ready. Then Bill called Joe, who is a lawyer. Joe made a visit to the owner and outlined the trouble he would get into if the bus wasn't in good operating condition soon.

However, parts were difficult to find and then something else went wrong so we eventually realized that it would be spring before we could pick it up. In the meantime, while I began to consider floor plans for the inside of the bus once we got rid of the seats, and Bill started figuring out how to arrive at a plan that would optimize the space for both humans and bugs, another interest took over our life.

We had no sooner gotten back home, when I was introduced to the Baptism in the Holy Spirit, an experience that powerfully changed me forever. And as we became involved in the Charismatic Renewal in the Catholic Church, I finally began to understand a little of what had happened to Bill the previous summer.

Baptism in the Holy Spirit

What we hadn't known, was Bill was one of thousands of Catholics all over the United States who were being baptized in Holy Spirit at that time. There had been an outpouring of the Spirit in the United States at the turn of the century. People who began speaking in tongues and laying hands on the sick were often referred to as Pentecostals, or derisively, as Holy Rollers. These people were sometimes thought to be simple uneducated people. However, in the early 60's a number of Episcopalians began receiving the Baptism of the Holy Spirit and the "move of the Spirit" in that denomination took off.

Also, in the early 60's at the Vatican II Council, Pope John 23rd had prayed for a new outpouring of the Spirit "as at the time of Pentecost" and God answered that prayer in the fall of 1966. In the spring of 1967 thirty students from Michigan State University and the University of Notre Dame convened to seek the power of the Holy Spirit in their lives. The miracles that occurred that weekend fanned the flames of the movement, which became known as the Charismatic Renewal in the Catholic Church.

Unaware of this phenomenon, in the fall of 1969 I was dusting furniture in our living room when I paused for a moment and thought, "Is this all there is to life?" I wasn't referring to the fact that I was dusting the living room. I just had a sense of emptiness which I thought was more than the emptiness in my marriage. I certainly adored my children and enjoyed being a homemaker but it seemed like I was missing something.

Shortly after that episode, our friends, Gerry and Dick Shaver, phoned to see if we wanted to go to a prayer meeting that evening with them and Father Kieren Kay, a local Franciscan priest we knew. Bill had to teach a class but I was able to go with them to the home of Wayne and Dolores Wood where a dozen people had gathered in their living room to pray.

At this small meeting, most of the people there had been baptized in the Holy Spirit. Since I didn't know what that meant, someone picked up a Bible and showed me Acts 1:5 where I read that before Jesus ascended into heaven, he told the disciples: *John baptized with water, but within a few days you will be baptized with the Holy Spirit.*

Actually, this being baptized with the Holy Spirit is mentioned in the Bible many times. As the meeting progressed, we were exposed to some of the charismatic gifts of the Spirit which are described in I Corinthians, Chapter 12. The joyful people around me enthusiastically sang praises to God. I heard one person speak in prophecy and others spoke and sang in tongues. No one seemed to be orchestrating the meeting but the participation of everyone flowed. Even during a few moments when everyone was silent it was not an awkward silence, but meaningful. I was very impressed and asked a lot of questions. When I got home that night, Bill had questions about it, also, but I was ill equipped to answer them.

The following week, I went again to the meeting and Bill came after he was through teaching his class. Just as he arrived, one of the men, who happened to be a teacher, shared how he had been baptized in the Holy Spirit. Bill and I both recognized the similarity of that man's experience, with his own overwhelming experience of God's love the previous summer. We peppered the man with questions.

These new Catholic charismatic friends explained to us that, although we had received the Holy Spirit when we were baptized with water and received the power of the Holy Spirit when we were confirmed, we had not yet experienced the release of the Spirit in our lives. It was like all that grace was lying dormant within us. They showed us the verses at the end of Mark's gospel where Jesus says:

Signs like these will accompany those who have professed their faith, they will use my name to expel demons, they will speak entirely new languages, they will be able to handle serpents, they will be able to drink deadly poison without harm, and the sick upon whom they lay their hands will recover. (Mark 16: 17, 18).

I thought about that. None of those signs were visible in my life. Most of it didn't sound applicable to today's lifestyle but I thought it would be wonderful to be able to lay my hands on someone who was sick and see them get well because of my prayer. I did understand that something dramatic should be evidenced in the life of anyone who was a disciple of Jesus.

As the implications of the words of the scripture sunk in, I thought, "Why didn't anyone ever tell me this before?" All my years of religious upbringing and Catholic school had never suggested this possibility to me!

Although the apostles had experienced water baptism and had gone out healing the sick and experiencing some power in their lives, they were frightened by all that had happened and were ill equipped to build a church. As we read on into

Acts 2:2-4, we saw the dynamic intervention of the Holy Spirit in the lives of the disciples. From that upper room, the apostles went out with power, changed, in an instant, by the Holy Spirit. They had now experienced that fiery passionate awareness of the leading of the Holy Spirit in their lives.

In the Catholic church, the Sacrament of Confirmation which we receive as young adults is supposed to be the bestowing of the gifts of the Spirit upon us. But we are usually taught only about the spiritual gifts of wisdom, understanding, counsel, knowledge, and fear of the Lord, as mentioned in the 11th chapter of Isaiah. We are not usually taught to open up to the gifts of the Spirit described in I Corinthians 12:7-11. Knowledge, wisdom in discourse, faith, healing, miraculous powers, prophecy, discernment of spirits, the gift of tongues and interpretation of tongues are all mentioned specifically in that passage. This amazed me!

As I searched the scriptures in the book of Acts, I saw there were many occasions where the apostles laid hands on people who had already been baptized with water, praying for them to receive the power of the Spirit. The people immediately experienced new power, frequently accompanied by the manifestation of the gift of tongues. At the third prayer meeting I attended, I asked my charismatic friends to lay their hands on me and pray that I, too, would be baptized in the Holy Spirit. They did, and I was! The prayer of St. Augustine which I had memorized when I was fourteen and then forgotten, came flooding back into my mind, and I wept as the words flowed from my mouth because I knew that I really meant what I was praying. What I felt when they prayed over me was an intense sense of love surrounding me that changed me forever.

I was drawn to the Bible and found it exciting to read! Gerry and Dick had been baptized in the Spirit, too, so we were continually calling each other on the phone, sharing the wonderful things we were finding in Scripture! I marveled at the wisdom I read there. I was filled with joy and praise as I asked God to open me up to his gifts so that I might be more useful to Him. I had a keen awareness of listening for a sense of God leading me as I went about my ordinary tasks. I woke in the night with songs of praise running through my head. I kept sensing God speaking to me, encouraging me, teaching me.

For the first time in our marriage, Bill and I were excited about the same things and shared what we were feeling. "Surely," I thought, "we would be entering a healthy new relationship through this shared experience." The sky was the limit! Although this new awareness of God's presence in my life began thirty-four years ago it has never faded away. I had been merely existing until then, and since receiving the Baptism of the Holy Spirit I have felt keenly alive. My whole life's focus and direction changed.

I found that there is all the difference in the world between knowing *about* Jesus Christ and actually knowing him *personally.* I knew all about Jesus but it hadn't occurred to me that I could know him the way I know my family and friends. Now I realized that Jesus had died upon the cross in order to give us his Spirit that we might be empowered to lead lives of joy, holiness and productivity. I was determined to hang on to this new awareness of God's presence and power in my life, no matter what it cost!

After Bill realized what had happened to him and consciously sought the Spirit's leading, his students often talked to him about their personal struggles and he was able to share scriptural wisdom with them, wisdom that he was just learning himself. As a teacher of Natural Science courses, he had always tried to be available to help students outside of class. He had spent many hours working with individuals who needed personal attention in that vast university setting but they had never before shared personal things with him.

When we got into the habit of reading and studying scripture every day, it seemed that, often, what a student needed for encouragement was the exact scripture Bill had read that morning during his quiet time with the Lord. It reminded us of the time when Bill was teaching an anatomy course and was learning the stuff, himself, just one class ahead of his students. He discovered he was given knowledge through the power of the Spirit, knowledge of personal things in the lives of students who came to him for counsel. He could quickly bring root problems out for discussion, much to their amazement (and his)!

As we began to pray for his ministry to students, the number of them coming to him, increased from an average of one per day to three per day. We had entertained students in our home on a weekly basis for years and had even welcomed some of them into family activities but we had never before discussed spiritual matters with any of them.

Sharing with the women I met gave me great joy. Similarly to Bill's experience, it was uncanny the way I would be intrigued with a certain scripture during my morning prayer time and then find out later in the day that it was exactly what someone I came in contact with needed to hear. So it wasn't just that I was excited about what I was learning from the scripture, I could encourage someone else with it too! I was constantly reexamining the way I looked at my daily life, gleaning new ways to approach my role as mother, daughter, wife and friend.

We began to share our exciting new life with other couples and friends, and soon prayer meetings became our regular Friday night activity. One of the marks of a genuinely charismatic gathering is that it is all-inclusive, so it was my first in-depth experience of worshiping with people from other denominations and persuasions. Some of the African Americans from the Morning Star Church of God in Christ on Leslie Street were coming regularly on Fridays.

One night after a prayer meeting, some of them invited us to come and worship with them, so Gerry, Dick and I decided to do that. Their little church on Leslie Street was very modest but their worship, praise, and singing was exuberant. We joined right in and I will never forget seeing a tiny fragile, elderly woman clapping, singing and dancing up and down the aisle with vigor that was hard to believe. Then, when everybody settled down for a quiet spell, we visitors were in for a big surprise.

The leader announced that there were visitors present (as if we could have been missed, being the only white people there) and the visitors were going to begin the meeting by each giving their testimony! Well, I had never given a testimony in my life but I did that day and so did Gerry and Dick. We were not given an option. I loved being in that church with those brothers and sisters in the Lord. I always look forward to worshiping with people of different denominations because it gives me a deeper understanding of the larger body of Christ.

The prayer group meeting we first attended in the Wood's home grew into a meeting of two-hundred fifty people so it moved to a gymnasium at the Church of the Resurrection on Lansing's East Side. Early on, we had been thrown into leadership responsibilities in the group so we were highly motivated to study and learn all that we could as fast as we could. Delving into Bible study guides, Bible history texts and concordances as well as the latest writings about the Charismatic Renewal and the gifts of the Holy Spirit, kept us excited and hungry for more.

In my letters to my mother, filled with the exuberance of the love I was feeling for our friends who were also involved in the charismatic movement, I made the mistake of writing that I loved some of these people like they were members of my own family. When I learned that she was threatened by that comment I tried to assure her that what I felt for these friends took nothing away from my love for my biological family.

When she and Daddy made their next visit to us we took them to a meeting of the Full Gospel Businessmen's Association where they heard Colonel Carruthers give an extraordinary account of what his life was like before and after being baptized in the Holy Spirit. He ended his stirring testimony with an invitation to come forward to be prayed with to receive the Baptism of the Holy Spirit, and my parents got right up and went to the front of the room for prayer. I remember the astonishment I felt when they did that because it was such a surprise but I was overjoyed!

Once a month, a weekend leadership meeting was held in Lansing for people in leadership positions in the Charismatic Renewal. Most of them came from nearby states and Canada. We usually housed people from out of town and it was exciting to hear what was happening in the Catholic Charismatic Renewal in other places. The first Saturday that we were part of this group, and were gathered around the altar at the Church of the Resurrection for the celebration of Mass, the worship was so beautiful, it transported me to a place of such joy, I was incapable of words adequate enough to express my experience to anyone else.

I remembered the scripture from II Chronicles 5:13-14,

When the trumpeters and singers were heard as a single voice praising and giving thanks to the Lord, and when they raised the sound of the trumpets, cymbals and other musical instruments to 'give thanks to the Lord, for he is good, for his mercy endures forever,' the building of the Lord's temple was filled with a cloud. The priests could not continue to minister because of the cloud, since the Lord's glory filled the house of God.

One of my high school nuns had once described heaven as a place where we would praise God all day long. I had thought that it sounded pretty boring. But that morning at Mass I began to look in a different way at what she had told us.

The leadership weekend always ended on Sunday afternoons with a prayer meeting attended by fifteen hundred people. The first time we took our oldest son, Joe, who was thirteen, he plucked my sleeve when he heard the beautiful polyphonic singing in tongues and excitedly whispered to me, "Mother, when do you practice?" Of course, we didn't practice. The singing was all quite spontaneous as led by the Holy Spirit.

We were constantly learning more about how God could work among us as we opened up to sensing him in new ways. One type of prayer that was new to me was identified by the phrase, "healing of memories." As I stepped out in faith, laying my hands on an individual's shoulders, while asking God to reveal things from the past that were a present source of pain for the person, I experienced a new phenomenon. The first time it happened I was praying over a young mother who was in deep depression and suicidal. Her husband and a couple of other people were praying with me.

As we prayed, I saw what is best described as a Technicolor movie. In it a young girl was swinging in a swing which hung from a high branch of a tree in front of a white two-story house. As I described what I was seeing, she became agitated and then she told us that she was the girl in the swing. She cried out,

"Every day, I would come home from school and swing in the swing. I didn't want to go into the house because my father was in there. Sometimes he made me go into his bed with him."

Her husband was stunned! He mentioned that he knew nothing about her family because she had refused to tell him anything about her past. As she sobbed, we asked her to picture herself back there again, this time with Jesus's arms around her protecting her from harm. We asked God's Spirit to lead us in our prayer as we prayed for him to heal those memories and to free her from her pain so she could share her whole life and her whole self with her husband.

This new world of mine was pregnant with possibilities now. What relief I felt from the bleak place I had been! And God's constant presence with me was the seed of my joy!

A New Way of Living

One of the things we had been told was when you seriously surrender your life to God you become a threat to Satan. There is more to supernatural life than just God and his goodness. We read about spiritual warfare in Ephesians 6, where the apostle Paul talks about what we need to do to stand firm against the tactics of the devil. It made sense to me, but it hadn't been brought home to me until one night when I had an extraordinary experience with supernatural evil.

As we returned home that night from one of our weekly core group prayer meetings, it was late so Bill went right up to bed. I wanted to spend some time thinking over one of those Technicolor pictures I had seen in my mind at the meeting so I sat down on our living room sofa for a few minutes to think about it. After some time I must have dozed off, but I suddenly awoke, terrified! Our living room seemed full of boiling rolling black malevolent clouds and I was in the midst of it. A fierce wind was coming from my left, blowing my hair. I felt a horrible hissing snarling evil spitting in my left ear and instinctively I covered my head with my arms. I was so full of terror I could only cry out, "Lord, Lord, Lord!"

The maelstrom continued as I struggled to stand up, cowering against the strong force against me, continuing to cry, "Help me, Lord! I laboriously put one foot in front of me and then another as I began to move, bent over with the weight of the evil, continuing to cover my head with my arms as if to defend myself. In this posture I made my way slowly up the stairs toward our bedroom with this horrible cloud whirling around me.

I slammed our bedroom door shut as I hurled myself against the solid outline of Bill's back on our bed. The evil cloud stayed outside the door. Bill awoke as my shaking body struck him. When I was finally able to speak well enough to tell him what had happened he didn't seem unduly alarmed. In fact, he ventured the thought that the evil force could come right through the door if it wanted to. He went back to sleep and I laid there still terrified. I remembered how we were told that we had the power to rebuke Satan and tell him to leave, so I did that, but I didn't feel much better. Finally, I began to say the Lord's Prayer over and over until I calmed down enough to go to sleep.

The next morning as the memories of the experience flooded back, I was afraid to open the door to call the children to get up for school. But I screwed up my courage and when I opened the door there was no sense of evil in the hall. Then, I paused at the head of the stairs as I was about to descend to make breakfast. I was afraid to go down through the living room. But I made myself do it and everything seemed normal, although, I still felt a residual nervousness as I saw the kids off to school and Bill to work.

I called Gerry to tell her what had happened. As we mulled over the whole episode, she told me that if it happened again I should call them right away and they would pray with me. As it turned out, a few weeks later at their cottage on Lake Huron, her husband, Dick, had a similar experience one night, so they weren't caught off guard as I had been.

Before the day was over, though, I figured out the reason for the experience. That afternoon a woman came to see me. She was new to the weekly prayer meetings so I barely knew her. When she arrived and sat down with me, she told me she was full of fear and afraid she was losing her sanity. She had gone to a psychiatrist but that didn't seem to help. When I asked her what the problem seemed to be her answer astonished me.

She said that frequently when she was on her way home from work at night, at a certain point of the country road she must travel to get to her house, she felt a terrible evil presence in the car with her. As she began to describe an evil cloud around her similar to what I had experienced, I thought I knew what was happening. I believed that God had allowed Satan to attack me so I would be able to help her. When I told her what had happened to me the night before, we looked at each other, hardly believing what I was saying. "You mean I'm not going crazy?" she asked. "I don't think so," I replied.

I told her what the Bible said about Satan roaming about the world seeking someone to devour, and how we are more likely to learn first hand about Satan's power in the world when we get serious about serving God. "So you must be doing something right," I told her. We prayed together, rebuking Satan in the name of Jesus, and before she left I referred her to the many scriptures about this type of thing. The next evening I was a little apprehensive again but to this day I have never again experienced anything like that evening of terror.

In the midst of all this activity I became a mother for the eighth time. A year previously, a friend who worked for the Michigan Department of Social Services had told me that there were eight hundred hard-to-place children in the state available for adoption. When he saw how dismayed I was at the thought of so many children being unwanted, he encouraged us to consider adopting one of them.

I was still uneasy with Bill and thought we weren't a stable enough family to take on another child, but over a period of a few months we looked into it and went through the interview process which included a few counseling sessions. The sessions consisted of only a superficial glance at our life so we were cleared to adopt without dealing with our relationship problem. And in March of 1970 we brought home our new daughter, Amy, when she was four months old. She had been born to an eighteen-year-old Michigan State student of Armenian/Iranian descent and all that was known of her father was that he was an African-American from Lansing.

All of our children went with us to pick her up. When we got home, I spread a blanket on the living room floor, and plunked her down in the middle of it since she could already sit up unassisted. She sat there solemnly gazing at all the kids hunkered down in front of her as they looked her over.

"Well, what do you think of her?" I asked. At first nobody said anything but then seven-year-old David hesitantly spoke up. "Well, she looks different than I thought she would." A bit puzzled, I said, "What do you mean, David?" "Well, I thought the top half of her would be white and the bottom half would be black," he explained. At the stunned look on my face he defended himself, "I mean, you said, Mom, that she was half black and half white!"

She was a delightfully precocious child whom we all enjoyed tremendously. And the strong loving relationships we had developed with other people in the Charismatic Movement, meant that Amy was received into a family much larger than our ten-person nucleus. She was baptized at a special Mass at Holy Cross Church attended by our friends and relatives, and instead of the priest baptizing her, Bill was the one who poured the water over her, giving her spiritual life even though he hadn't been able to give her physical life. We had a deeper understanding by then, of her being adopted into the family of God, something we had never fully appreciated with the arrival of our other children.

In May of 1970, Bill was again told that the school bus was ready. Wisely, he decided to go to Chicago alone this time, using a Greyhound bus to get there. By the time he got back to Lansing with our bus it was 4:00 a.m. the next day. I was awakened by this awful *Whump* Whump Whump Whump, *Whump* Whump Whump Whump sound from outside!

Peering through the darkness as I looked out the window, I saw something resembling a giant beast panting and wheezing at the curb. Bill had needed to be towed three times along the way home and was not very happy with his purchase.

It obviously needed more work, so Bill followed a friend's suggestion that he hire a man who was a Vietnam Army Veteran and an ace mechanic. This turned out to be a mistake because the guy took a blow torch to the radiator and cut it into pieces before we learned he was mentally ill and had never been near Vietnam or the Army! But after many false starts and a trip to Detroit for a used radiator, Bill thought he had it in shape for us to drive that summer.

He found an awful shade of green paint on sale which he bought to apply to the outside of the bus. I thought the green was worse than the orange but at least we wouldn't be accused of masquerading as a school bus any more. After dubbing it "The Great Green Gas Gobbler" we set off again in June for the University of Illinois with plenty of seats for everyone. This time we rented an empty house in Champaign which had a mural of a huge jet plane going up the wall in concert with the stairway to the second floor, and a 7-up bottle from floor to ceiling in the living room.

While we camped out there, Bill spent his spare time removing most of the seats from the bus. I sewed curtains for the windows and used canvas to make double-decker, litter-like beds slung from wooden poles attached to the sides of the bus. Bill built three bunks for storage space and sitting/sleeping, and also a counter to use as a cooking area. I upholstered cushions for the bunks and tacked carpet to the floor. He built shelves near the ceiling on both sides of the length of the bus and another counter with storage place underneath it for his entomological gear. With a space for Amy's playpen we were set to go on our annual camping trip when he got through teaching that summer.

The trip west that year was the same and not the same. It was noisy because the three oldest boys had just received brass instruments to practice on during the summer. The cacophony of sound created by coronet, french horn and trombone in the hands of novices, definitely disturbed the peace of the Davis Mountains of Texas during our stay there. Traveling on into New Mexico, our outside environment continued to be noisy but my inner being was still quiet.

New spiritual awareness begets the ability to see all things new and I was moved to tears by the stark beauty of the desert. I had to settle for a local desert instead of the Mt. Sinai area of the Holy Land but I felt like Moses may have felt when he saw the burning bush. I was delving into the Bible every chance I could, and realized for the first time that the way God was telling us to live was for our own happiness, not just to please him. So many new thoughts whirled around in my mind, with hope for the future if I could but put into practice what God was telling me to do.

An episode with Amy precipitated baby steps in faith regarding physical healing. One day on the way back from our camping trip, Amy began crying frantically, throwing herself and screaming as if in terrible pain. Nothing I did could calm her until several minutes that seemed like hours had gone by. Then her pain seemed to stop abruptly and she collapsed against me and slept.

This happened again a couple of times before we reached home so I took her to our pediatrician as soon as we arrived there. He could find nothing wrong with her but told me to bring her in immediately if she had another episode. I did take her back a couple of days later as soon as she doubled up in pain. The pediatrician thought that she might have an intoussusception, which means a portion of the intestine has telescoped into another part, causing excruciating pain. Repeated incidences of this would cause scarring and possible blockage, so he talked about the possibility of her needing surgery to remove the area that was causing the trouble.

As I left the doctor's office, I stopped at Dolores Wood's home and asked her to pray with me for Amy to be healed of this affliction. We placed our hands on her and prayed that the physical problem would be healed. I didn't have any sense that she was healed but Dolores said she felt confident that Amy was healed and this proved to be so. She had no more pain after that. It seemed too simplistic to believe that we could pray for healing with a real expectation that it would occur. Dare I believe that? I was beginning to.

We had another faith-building experience when God showed us more about the power of parents praying for healing for their children. An incident with David, when he was ten, was a case in point. He began having episodes of stomach pain several days in a row, with pain so intense that he doubled over each time it hit him. It wasn't like he had a stomach ache after eating. It happened randomly and I couldn't make any sense out of it. We prayed over him for God to heal him but the episodes continued so I took him to our pediatrician.

The doctor felt that something was definitely out of the ordinary so he ordered David into Ingham Medical Hospital for tests. After three days, David seemed no better but the tests were not revealing what was wrong. Wednesday afternoon before Thanksgiving, David had been taken to another department for still another test so I sat down on his bed to pray and to read from my little Revised Standard Bible while I waited for him to be brought back to his room. I randomly opened my Bible to Luke 9:43, and began reading with growing amazement.

In front of my eyes was the story of how a man begged Jesus to heal his son because a spirit seizes him and he suddenly cries out. Jesus told the man to bring his son to him and the spirit again seized him and caused another convulsion. But Jesus rebuked the spirit and cast it out of the boy and gave him back to his father.

I was shocked by the similarity between my David and the boy in the story, so when David came back to his room and climbed into the bed, I read the passage to him and said, "I think we should rebuke Satan like Jesus did. Don't you think so too?" David thought that was a good idea, so we did pray, and I told Satan to leave David alone in the name of Jesus, knowing I was calling on the authority of Jesus when I prayed.

The doctor came in later and said they still were puzzled but thought it would be okay for us to take David home for the holiday weekend and re-admit him for more tests on Monday. We went home and when David had a peaceful weekend with no episodes of pain, we called the doctor Monday morning and told him that David was fine now. Since he never did have any more attacks of pain, the incident left us with lots of food for thought.

Growing in the Spirit

We settled into the fall routine with all the kids except Amy, in school all day. When a member of a group of women in De Witt, Michigan, asked me to take them through a Life in the Spirit Seminar, I looked forward to doing that. I was taken aback, however, when one of the men in leadership of our prayer group objected to me doing that when he heard about it because he thought I should teach just within our prayer group.

Bill saw no reason for me not to teach the women, though, so once a week I grabbed my Bible and Amy and drove the ten miles to De Witt. There I put her down for a nap while I shared with these women all the wonderful things I was learning about the power of the Holy Spirit. She went with me to my Monday morning women's fellowship and to my work on the West Side Neighborhood Association projects, also. She was a good little traveler.

A lot of our discussion with others who were experiencing this exhilarating new walk with God, centered around the question: How fundamental do we get with believing what the Bible says? Were we in danger of being fanatics? The people we knew personally who were attempting to learn more about this walking in the power of the Holy Spirit, seemed like sensible, stable people. We all simply had a sense of being called to serve others and saw the gifts of the Spirit as empowerment to do what God asked us to do for him.

Bill posed the question to me one night, "What would you say if God told us to sell our house and go live on the bus?" "Surely he wouldn't ask us to do any such thing!" I retorted indignantly. "But what if he did?" Bill persisted. The next morning I went to early Mass still pondering the question. After Mass I sat in my pew and randomly opened my Bible to II Corinthians 5:1: *For we know that if the earthly tent we live in is destroyed, we have a building from God, a house not made with hands, eternal in the heavens.*

I was scared to death when I went back home and reported to Bill what I had read. He just laughed. However, two days later someone knocked on our door and asked if we would consider selling our house and a couple we knew mentioned to us that they were looking to buy a house like ours, so I continued to be anxious about it. But God wasn't asking us to sell the house yet; only making us think more seriously about this supposed surrender of our will to his.

Another year raced by. With school activities, prayer group meetings, and West Side Neighborhood Association work woven into our family life, there was not much time for me to spend worrying about God asking us to sell our house.

In the spring of 1971 we gathered a number of people from the area and took them on our bus to the National Catholic Charismatic Renewal Conference at Notre Dame, which had become an annual event after the first gathering of thirty people there in 1967. There were three thousand people there this time and Bishop Joseph McKinney of Grand Rapids, Michigan, began his address to us by expressing his amazement at the large number of us gathered there. "People," he said from the podium. "Where did you all come from?" And we all roared back with laughter and rejoicing.

It was thrilling for me to see and share with so many people who had this same reverence and enthusiasm for God that I was experiencing. Also, there were many workshops available which were the source of sound teaching about the historical background and emerging aspects of this movement, so I attended as many as possible in order to grow in my understanding of this new life.

We lived that summer of 1971, in a second floor unfurnished apartment next door to the fire station in St. Joseph while Bill taught his class at the University of Illinois. Lots of good visiting ensued punctuated by occasional blaring sirens calling us to watch the local volunteer firemen drive up in their pickup trucks and hop aboard the fire truck. Our annual trek west was familiar and uncomplicated that year and Amy continued to be a good little camper.

By the end of the year, many of us from the West side of Lansing were going weekly to the gathering at the Church of the Resurrection on the East side of Lansing, so our pastor at Holy Cross Church asked us to begin a Charismatic prayer meeting at our own church. Therefore, in January of 1972, we held our first prayer meeting in the school gym with thirty-five people present.

Over the next few months the group grew to more than a hundred people and we developed a community life of our own. All of the people who came regularly to the weekly prayer meeting were invited to be part of a small sharing group. These groups met during the week in each others' homes and the people in them began to relate to each other as if they were an extended-family.

Bill had instigated some new ways of our relating as a family when he was first baptized in the Holy Spirit. He started making it a point to be home for the evening meal instead of allowing himself to be detained at his office. He instituted the family dinner hour. We not only visited with each other as we ate but once we were through eating, he read aloud to us from books about vibrant contemporary Christians who had led exciting lives. He began with *The Hiding Place,* which acquainted us with the life of Corrie Ten Boom, and then David Wilkerson's *The Cross and the Switchblade,* and Brother Andrew's biography, *God's Smuggler.* These books held our children's interest from the youngest to the oldest.

As we began to seriously search out God's instructions for our lives, we asked him for help in guiding our children. I asked the Lord to help me be a better wife and mother by showing me ways I needed to change my thinking or my behavior. One attitude change in me came with the realization that I needed to respect my children as my brothers and sisters in the Lord. I needed to see them as people, not just my children, and to look for ways to encourage them in their gifts, thus preparing them also to be used by the Lord. I needed to be very careful in my correction of them so I didn't wound their spirits, but encouraged them to change things that needed to be changed.

We adopted as our own, the commitment of Joshua, recorded in Joshua 24:16b: *As for me and my house, we will serve the Lord.* Both the Old and New Testaments are full of advice about human behavior and relationships, so correcting and guiding the children was simplified for me. I didn't get into a clash of wills in a disagreement because we could look at what God said to do for our peace and happiness in the matter and come away satisfied.

A major scripture we all worked to be generous and brave enough to act upon, was from Matthew 18:15: *If your brother should commit some wrong against you, go and point out the fault, but keep it between the two of you.*

So we discussed the need to talk things over with the person with whom we were upset instead of telling everybody else how upset we were with that person. I refused to be a mediator unless the offended one had tried to talk to the offender without reconciliation. By the time other people came to live with us, our family was trying to following what God's word said, with pretty effective results, so we were united in showing new people a more peaceful way to live than most of them had experienced.

What I found hard to understand, though, was why my attempts to tell Bill about something he did which caused me pain, usually resulted in him being angry with me. The scripture from Matthew goes on to say you should bring another person with you and approach the offender again if you can't work things out together, but I felt it would be disloyal of me to expose the reason that I was so unhappy in my marriage. Being in leadership was a very lonely place where I had no one to talk to about my own problems. Bill refused my request for us to go for professional counseling so I just kept praying for God to do something to help us, thinking that since this was a spiritual problem, it would surely be God's will to fix it.

Our life as a family changed dramatically as the children also entered into this adventure with God, and one by one, they were baptized in the Holy Spirit. The first time 11-year-old Paul stood up and prophesied at a prayer meeting Bill was very nervous about it, but the prophecy was confirmed by others and Bill learned to relax with that. By then our whole family participated in our weekly prayer meeting, even Amy, and three of our children joined me in the music ministry for the prayer meeting. At this point, our spiritual life as a family had never been healthier but our sense of security was about to be sorely tested.

God's Provision

The first inkling of a shaky financial future occurred in April of 1972, when Bill learned that his teaching contract was not going to be renewed. He had again fallen victim to the "publish or perish" policy of the university. In spite of being let go before because of that policy, he had stayed with the decision to be available to his students and to do careful research which would be published only when it was really something helpful in his field. Although we knew he was jeopardizing his teaching career because he hadn't published many papers, I understood his decision not to short-change his students. And they were coming to him for after-class counseling to the point where it seemed as if God was stacking his classes with spiritually hungry people.

Bill had no heart for fighting the university's decision to let him go, in spite of a great hue and cry from his students. He was so frustrated with the politics of the big university setting! So he sent out nearly 300 queries to Christian colleges across the nation, looking for a position where he could have an impact on students as a Christian role model, hopefully in an environment where he could share God's love more freely than in the secular university.

He received a number of replies from colleges which were interested in him but couldn't pay him enough for us to live on, and then, in August he received a phone call from the President of a Christian Brothers College in Memphis, Tennessee. Bill's concern for the spiritual state of students had led him to suggest in his query letter that our family live on campus in order to facilitate a close relationship with the students. That possibility excited this administrator and he made arrangements for us to come and bring our children with us to his campus in order to see if this was what God had in store for us. It sounded like it was a situation planned by the Lord.

We climbed aboard our Great Green Gas Gobbler and went to take a look at what might be our new home. As we approached the city, I sat down on a back bunk and flipped open my Bible to read for a few minutes and these words leapt out at me: *Up! Let us return to our own people, to the land of our birth, away from the destroying sword. Memphis shall be a desert, an empty ruin. (Jeremiah 46:16 and 19b)*

I was shocked! I hadn't remembered that "Memphis" was even mentioned in the Bible, and I certainly hadn't expected to be confronted with words like these as we entered the city with high expectations that it would be our home. Also significant to me, was the fact that Michigan was the land of our spiritual rebirth. If this scripture was the Lord speaking to us it sounded like we were to go back to where Bill now had no work. I didn't like the sound of this at all!

During the next three days we met with the President of the college and some of the faculty. We looked at possible living quarters on campus and at schools the kids would attend. And as we earnestly sought the Lord's guidance, we came to the conclusion that we had to go back to Michigan. My heart was full of questions as we journeyed northward. Where would Bill find work in Lansing? How could we survive?

Friends and neighbors had joyfully decorated our house with balloons and banners to welcome us home. Members of the prayer group told us that they thought we should stay and help develop this new community instead of seeking work in another city. It was good to be among these dear people but I had moments of panic when I tried to imagine living with no paycheck, knowing that our savings account was practically nonexistent by this time. But the next nine months were a very special time for us.

Bill looked for any kind of work he could do but he discovered that his forty-six years and Ph.D. were definitely a disadvantage in the labor market. He checked with lots of prospective employers but couldn't find anyone who would even let him pump gas because they figured he'd be looking for something better and wouldn't last. He might have omitted his educational history from applications if he hadn't felt it would be dishonest. I learned another side to him as I watched him patiently looking for work, keeping at it when I would have been very discouraged. I discovered a deep humility in him that I wouldn't have expected from his normal behavior.

It wasn't until December that he was given a chance to earn money by selling home fire alarm systems on commission. Then, for five months his sales visits to people's homes usually resulted in either fire alarms sold or in his sharing about God. His boss was upset with him, once, when he had spent eight hours on a call and sold no fire alarms, but that particular sales call resulted in a healed marriage for a troubled couple and their new life in Christ. One month Bill was the top salesman in the company even though his personality was not the type usually associated with that of an outgoing salesperson. In fact, a scientific study of personality types has the scientist at one end of the spectrum and the salesperson at the other!

By the end of March the sales dried up rather abruptly and Bill then was given work with an investigating firm owned by George Brownell, the husband of one of the members of our prayer group. While working for George, Bill had quite an effect on some of the other personnel. George said that the other guys cleaned up their rough language when Bill was in the vicinity. By the time Bill left there, he had encouraged both his immediate supervisor and George to come to the prayer meetings and those two families joined our prayer group fellowship.

In June at a Full Gospel Businessmen's meeting, Bill was approached by John Rogers, a friend we had met when he and his wife were working hand in hand with Teen Challenge in 1968. John was also a foreman at Schafer Bakery and had heard of Bill's employment dilemma. "I have a job opening at the bakery, Bill, but with all your education I doubt if you would be interested in it," John said. "I need to feed my family," Bill told him, so John gave him the job. At the bakery he was able to earn enough money to support the ten of us, although by then we had learned that it wasn't Bill who was supporting us.

During those months of unpredictable income and depleting savings God stepped into our lives in an incredible way and saw to it that we were taken care of as well as, or better than we had been when Bill was employed at the university. On several occasions during those months Bill found $20 bills among his papers in one or another of his many file cabinets. He was always bewildered because he couldn't imagine when or why he would have put any money in those places.

Our friends, Gerry and Dick, phoned in November to tell me they had purchased a plane ticket for me so I could fly to Houston with Gerry, who was going to visit her son there. While Gerry visited her son, I would be able to visit my sister, Nancy, and her family who lived there also. "As long as Bill is home to take care of the kids, you might as well take advantage of it," they pointed out. We had a wonderful trip and a good time in Houston. I learned that God not only met our needs—he provided extras!

Sometimes friends would call and ask if we had a utility bill that needed to be paid. Then they would pick it up and pay it for us.

Once a friend brought me clothing her oldest daughter no longer wanted and I pounced with delight on a wool *Bobbie Brooks* coral-colored skirt. It fit me perfectly. A week later a neighbor returned from visiting relatives on the East coast and brought me some used clothing. An item that immediately caught my attention was a *Bobby Brooks* sweater the same color as the skirt I had just received via the other friend! It also was my size! Evidently God has an eye for fashion!

Our mail one day included an envelope that contained a one hundred dollar bill wrapped in a sheet of paper on which was written, "PTL" (shorthand for "Praise The Lord!"). I had never seen or touched a one hundred dollar bill before.

Friends, Theresa and Esther, showed up at our front door one afternoon, loaded down with food from a warehouse owned by Theresa's husband, who was a food distributor. As they went back and forth between their car and our kitchen bringing more and more boxes of food and canned goods, Theresa told me, "I just couldn't stand the thought of all that food sitting there when your kids might be hungry!" Actually, we were never hungry. My children weren't that thrilled with powdered eggs someone once gave us, but often we were given food more luxurious than I would usually buy. And besides—powdered eggs were fine when used in recipes for cakes and cookies!

One Tuesday in April, about the time we realized that there was no money for my usual Wednesday grocery-shopping trip, the mail arrived with a letter addressed to Professor William Downes, with no return address on it. I remember making a flippant remark as I handed it to Bill. "What is this? Hate mail?" It was not hate mail—it was love mail!

The letter said:

"Dear Professor Downes, Two years ago I was a student at Michigan State and you led me to a commitment to Christ, and last October I was baptized in the Holy Spirit. I just want to thank you for all that you've meant in my life."

Included in the letter was a quotation from Nehemiah 8:10: *Eat, drink and be merry and share a portion thereof.*

Also with the letter, was a fifty-dollar bill, which was exactly the amount I usually spent on our weekly grocery trip!

Ten years later, when we went to hear a new minister, Ed Reynolds, speak at Spirit of Christ Church, we encountered this former student, Ed's wife, Cindy. As we visited with her after the service, she mentioned that she had written to us once, and Bill immediately thought of the letter with its timely money. When he asked her about it, she admitted that she had impulsively sent it right after she received the money from her mother. She said, "I had just gotten engaged to marry Ed and was realizing that if you had not talked with me about God, I would not have been the type of woman Ed was looking for in a wife. I had no idea you had a financial need when I stuck that fifty dollars in with the letter." She was thrilled when we told her how God had used her to help us.

Our old faithful Chevy van collapsed several times. One day we heard an awful *Bam! Bam! Bam!* which indicated that the engine was throwing a rod. I felt a little silly as I laid my hands on the motor between our front seats and asked

God to either provide us with money to fix the van or heal it, but the engine purred like a kitten for a while. Another time, the water pump broke and we didn't have money for a replacement. So I again laid my hands on the motor, and the water pump stopped leaking. But finally it reached the point where our prayers for healing didn't work. Then a friend loaned us her car until another friend arranged for us to drive a brand new nine-passenger Oldsmobile station wagon for a year.

The very day that Bill got the job with the bakery, I remember sitting in our living room with Marilyn, a friend who had come to pick up our electric bill so she could pay it. As we chatted, John came to the house and joined us. (He was the same man who had cut up our bus radiator) Then our garbage man knocked at the door and asked to be paid. "That will be $6.25, Mrs. Downes," he said. I went to my purse and scrounged up $5.00 in loose change. Marilyn said, "I've got a dollar." Then John piped up "I've got a quarter!" And we looked at each other and giggled as I paid the garbage man!

Applying for food stamps was another way God provided for us during the last two months before Bill started working at the bakery. The money allotted to us was more than I was used to spending each month, so we were well taken care of through that program. I was well aware of how incongruous it was that I was driving a new Oldsmobile to the Department of Social Services to pick up food stamps.

We believe in tithing, and during those lean months we experienced another aspect of God's wisdom. By giving ten percent of what we received, we enjoyed the pleasure of giving every time something came our way in spite of our tenuous financial position. The constant giving enabled me to retain a sense of dignity and helped me avoid the danger of feeling impoverished. We never felt like someone's poor relation with such concrete evidence of our relationship to the King of the entire universe.

During those months, we knew the main thing each one of us needed to be concerned about was being obedient to God, and God chose to provide for us to live in about the same way we had lived when Bill earned a good income. We learned, deep in our hearts, *who* was providing for our needs, and since God never changes, we expect that he will continue to provide for our needs. That doesn't mean we will always have what we want or that there won't be a time when we are hungry but we have a peace in the knowledge that God knows our circumstances and is with us.

What many onlookers thought was a terrible trial for us was actually a time of challenge and excitement. God's faithful care of us made a deep impression on our children. I remember our oldest son saying one time when God had dramatically provided for us, "Mother, we need to write this down!" Our time of financial strain was also a good lesson in humility. We cannot provide for ourselves. While we can be industrious in preparing for employment and diligent in seeking it, only God can open the door to work which will earn sufficient money for our needs.

God mercifully brought us through a difficult time, teaching us to know him as our Provider. He met our daily needs in ways unmistakably his, building our faith and enabling us to be bold enough to move on to the next phase of our life. Those months of experiencing God's provision in an unusual way gave us a marvelous sense of freedom from worry about money. I think that this freedom was instrumental in our decision to take another person into our family, even when Bill was still without a decent-paying job. Of course, we had no idea of the ramifications of what we were doing when we made that decision. Not in our wildest dreams could we have imagined where God was leading us!

Acceptance and Rejection

As the weekly prayer meetings at Holy Cross grew from thirty-five, to one hundred fifty participants, the fifteen of us who provided the practical services formed a core group which met weekly to prepare for each meeting. Certain people took responsibility for setting up chairs or organizing the food to be available after the meetings. Others provided music. Some took turns leading the prayer meeting or giving teachings, and a few people formed a team to pray after the meeting for people to be healed. We also had a team of people who taught an eight-week Life in the Spirit Seminar that explained the Catholic Charismatic Renewal.

One energetic young woman who was part of the core group began spending more and more of her time at our house. She had committed herself to prayer group functions four nights a week and we also got to know each other pretty well from working together in music ministry. Since she lived twenty miles away, she often had dinner with us and sometimes stayed overnight.

Frequently she came for lunch, too, as she worked to teach me new skills on the guitar. We joked about how she practically lived with us and an idea began to take root. We began talking about the possibility of her moving in with us. And even though she had to share a bedroom with our three daughters, Sharon moved into our home on May 4, 1973 and would stay for three years. She paid us $50 per month for household expenses and was a blessing to have with us.

Although we didn't know it at the time, her move was the beginning of our extended-family household. We could not possibly have anticipated that over the next fifteen years, ninety-five people would live with our family for varying lengths of time, ranging from a month to ten years.

When Sharon moved in, the number of remarks made by close Christian friends was disconcerting to me:

"How can you stand having another woman in your kitchen?" (It's great! She helps with cooking and washing dishes!)

"Won't having another person in your home take time away from your children?" (She doesn't *take* time, she *gives* time. She pitches in to help in many different areas and her musical ability has been especially helpful.)

"Won't this arrangement interfere with your privacy as a couple?" (It's nice having another adult in the house to talk to since Bill's in another world so much of the time.)

"How can you possibly afford another person in your family?" (Putting another potato in the pot is no big deal and besides, she does contribute some money each month.)

I think those questions were coming from their own fears, although it was good to know they were concerned about us. Perhaps most people with a healthy marriage would not care to have a non-family member sharing their home. But when Bill thought it would be fine to have her come, I really looked forward to the companionship she would bring with her. She would prove to be a bulwark for us in an extremely difficult experience that began to brew that fall.

Bill and I were very involved in the prayer group. My main responsibilities were the music ministry and sharing my faith with the women, counseling them and encouraging them. Bill regularly gave teachings at the prayer meetings and we both helped teach the ongoing Life in the Spirit Seminar, as well as courses on growing in spiritual maturity. Bill was one of several men in leadership in the prayer group and he had a passion for exhorting them to begin their days in prayer and get their lives in order, financially as well as spiritually.

Occupying a leadership position in the prayer group was a mixed bag for me. While some people tried to put me on a pedestal, you can imagine what an uncomfortable place that would be. (Foremost would be the difficulty of maintaining my balance in every sense of the word.) Then there were always a few discontented people who found fault with the choice of music played during the prayer meeting or the brand of coffee served afterwards. Although all of us in the prayer group were trying to grow in holiness and maturity, evidence of our contrary human nature would pop up regularly.

Still, I was a bit dismayed when some of my friends told me to beware of Ethel, a woman in the prayer community who seemed to have a grudge toward me. She said to me one day, "I wonder why people come to *you* for counsel. Can you tell me why?" I felt vaguely uneasy as I tried to understand where she was going with that question. All I could tell her was that I didn't know why. We talked for a while longer and then she walked away leaving me a bit puzzled.

Not long after that encounter, Carol, a regular member of the prayer group, prayed for a miraculous healing for her little daughter, Linda, who needed surgery. She told everyone she knew, that God had told her he would heal her daughter. Over time though, there was no miraculous healing so she finally agreed to the surgery that Linda needed. After the operation was successfully completed, Carol stopped by our house to talk to me, weeping copiously, frantically upset. "What have I done!?" she cried. "What about all the people that I told God would heal Linda?! I might have damaged their faith!"

I assured her that she was not responsible for other people's faith and she calmed down eventually. As we visited, I opened my Bible and showed her Chapter 38 in the book of Sirach, which tells us to understand that God heals us sometimes through physicians and sometimes through the use of medicines which we should not neglect. We prayed together until she became peaceful and thoughtful about what she was learning about God's ways.

That same night at our weekly core group meeting, Carol got up at one point and said, "Thank God for the Downeses," and proceeded to tell about what had happened, and our conversation that afternoon. Then Ethel jumped up and said, "I'm sick to death of the Downeses, Downeses, Downeses. You'd think nothing ever happened around here except at the Downeses!" I was horrified and felt sick at heart. I thought, "How can this be happening among a group of people who love the Lord!" I was being faced with the fact that we are all vulnerable to sin given the right set of circumstances, no matter how sincerely we're trying to follow Jesus.

Meanwhile, Bill was having a rough time with the men in leadership. One of them had let people know that there were certain hours when he would be available to members of the community but he reserved the rest of his time for his family. He was critical of Bill for not doing the same at our house. We had people dropping in on us all the time and we were usually glad to see them. This same man also expressed disapproval of Bill working at a bakery instead of utilizing his education by working at a professional level.

And on January 4, 1974, at a meeting of the men in leadership, one of the men became upset with Bill and asked him to step down from leadership. Another man who was there told me later that he was shocked when this happened, since he had no knowledge that it was coming, but most of the men told Bill that they wanted him not only to step down from leadership, but to not even speak at the prayer meetings. They felt he was too harsh in dealing with the failings among the men in the group and they were frustrated by his unwillingness to be more flexible.

I understood very well the type of behavior the men were referring to because of my own struggle with it. I had hoped that in Bill's participation in the men's group he would be helped to deal with his inability to relate well with people. I had also hoped he would learn to show me the warmth and affection that I so desperately needed from him. But that was not to be. My spirit sank when I realized that he would receive no help from them in any area. I don't think any of them had a clue as to how to relate to him although they did offer to meet with him to counsel him. He was just too different for the rest of them to cope with him.

We were asked not to tell anyone that Bill was out of leadership because the men were afraid if the community knew he had been asked to step down, it would sow division. One of the men met with me and told me that they thought Bill might have a nervous breakdown because of their decision. He said the men wanted me to know that they would take care of the children and me. They hoped the children and I would still lead the music ministry because we comprised most of the group and it was very important to the worship of the prayer meeting. They wanted everything to seem the same to the body of people gathering there each week. Secrecy was something I abhorred so I was appalled! It seemed totally opposed to the Bible's injunction to live in the light.

While Bill withdrew within himself, I struggled to keep going. It was a dark, dark time for us. One of the women who belonged to the prayer group came over to the house to comfort me one morning and said to me, "It's like somebody has died!" And she was right. Bill reverted back to his distrust of others and during his prayer time he pondered what had happened. He told me God had told him that all the men would be scattered. That did come to pass. His hours at the bakery changed to evenings about that time, so when people asked about him, they were told he had to work.

Of course the truth of what had happened did get out and the prayer group as we knew it changed. Some of the men in leadership left to join The Work of Christ Charismatic Community in East Lansing and others took over leadership of the Holy Cross group. I kept busy at home with the children and with my friends, still participating in the prayer group with the children each week, even though I dreaded going. And I really appreciated having Sharon's companionship and support in the house. Although I didn't know it then, she was tangible evidence of the window that was opening for us even as a door had been closed.

320 N. Sycamore Street

During the course of her work, Sharon met Lucy and started bringing her to the prayer meetings and to our home. After Lucy achieved her Masters Degree from Michigan State University in June of 1974, and had been back in her home in New York for about a week, she phoned us and asked if she could come back for a visit. People were frequently popping in and out of our house so, of course, we told her to come. She slept on a sofa in the living room and when she found a good position in her field in Lansing that July, she decided to stay in the area. Then, she asked us if she, too, could live with us.

We thought about it for probably two seconds before we told her she could stay. We really liked Lucy, who was fun and energetic like Sharon and had already spent a lot of time at our house, but the sofa was not adequate for a more permanent stay with us, so we started praying for God to find us a bigger house.

It was our family custom to gather for prayer every evening after dinner, so now there were twelve of us praying for a house with another bedroom so we'd have some privacy for Lucy. I did the practical thing by reading the real estate ads and going to see a few houses. Because our means were modest I began to think we would have to find an old house that needed a lot of work in order to find something big enough.

Then, one evening in August as we were gathered for our usual prayer time, we heard Bill praying, "God, please find us a bigger house no matter what it means." Immediately Sharon jumped up off the living room couch and shouted, "Now, wait a minute!" After a lively discussion, we realized that we were deliberately giving God a blank check. We had a sense that we would be taking a step forward into the unknown. We could identify with Abraham when he left his homeland, not knowing where he was going but having the sense that God was leading him somewhere specific. So in spite of feeling a bit insecure, after talking it over, we decided to give God the green light, praying in unison, "Lord, please give us a bigger house no matter what it means."

Lucy, Sharon and I went back to looking for a five-bedroom house but on the 20th of August, our realtor, Mrs. Brewer, wanted to show us an enormous house at 320 North Sycamore St. that had been converted into six apartments. I told her that we wouldn't be interested in anything that large and we couldn't possibly afford it. But she continued to urge us to at least take a look at it, saying we could live in part of it and rent out the rest of it for the extra income we would need. So more or less as a lark, we agreed to look at this ridiculously large house on Sycamore Street.

As we walked through the house my heart leapt in excitement. It was exactly what we needed only much more. We had started examining the rooms on the third floor and slowly worked our way down. I got more and more excited as I saw the possibilities, and when we got to the huge kitchen my heart was pounding. "A community-size kitchen!" I exulted. "Who would have thought it would have such a huge kitchen!" Lucy saw a room on the third floor that she wanted and Sharon found one she claimed for herself on the second floor.

We were all excited as we tried to describe it to the family that night, but I still didn't think for minute that we could afford it. At one time, a few families in our community had talked half-seriously about living together, or at least near each other, but nothing had come of it. This seemed to me like just another dream that wouldn't materialize.

When Bill came with us the next day to see the house, we had cause for amazement. He had seen this house earlier that year and had told us about it because he had been strongly drawn to it. He had described how it stood out from the other houses on the block, with light shining from all the windows as he walked past it. He had even attempted to show it to us one day but he wasn't able to find it again and had eventually forgotten about it.

While we took our second look through the rooms, he examined the furnace, plumbing and electrical boxes and looked for termite damage and all those things responsible buyers are supposed to check out. Bill was very impressed with the quality of construction, such as steel beams in the basement, and didn't seem put off by the fact that the exterior stucco was crumbling in spots. We all went home chattering excitedly about the unusual coincidence and the electrifying sense that God might be up to something.

We have always been very conservative in matters of finances and buying the house on Sycamore Street didn't seem financially wise. As we talked about the house with some of our friends, they thought we were crazy to even think of buying it! But we had a strong sense of the Lord leading us to buy it anyway, so we sat down and prayed about the situation with a sense of expectation, saying, "Lord, this is beginning to look like it is something you want for us so please help us to know your will in the matter."

Because of the enormity of the responsibility, as we prayed earnestly to know if we should try to purchase this house, we remembered the Old Testament story of Gideon putting out his fleece when he was looking for guidance (Judges 6:37), so it occurred to us to seek God's guidance by asking him to sell our present house within one week if he wanted us to buy the house on Sycamore Street. We knew that we couldn't possibly buy the new house unless we sold our present home, and since houses usually take a while to sell, it seemed like a reasonable thing to ask. If it didn't sell within one week of being listed, we would know we needed to keep looking for a different house.

When our house sold after only a couple of days on the market, I was in a state of shock! As I stood on the sidewalk in front of our house watching our realtor drive away, the reality of the fact that we had signed a contract to sell was beginning to sink in. Sink or swim, ours prayers were answered and we were moving to a larger house.

Back when Bill was actively looking for a teaching position at a Christian college, someone in our prayer group prophesied that we would move east. We finally did—eight blocks east. Our new home was situated on a quiet street just two blocks from the state Capitol complex in downtown Lansing. Being so centrally located would prove to be very convenient for us.

On October 1, 1974 the house was actually ours. After we first learned that our offer to purchase was accepted, Bill felt the Lord telling him that he hadn't called us to be landlords. So we approached all the tenants to give them 30-days notice to leave their respective apartments. That was no problem for four of them but when we met Alice, who had lived in an apartment on the second floor for eighteen years. She really didn't want to move. She told us she had cancer and had been unable to work for the past five months.

As we listened to her, we learned that she was from my hometown in Iowa, had attended the church I was raised in, and had been baptized as an adult by the same priest who had baptized me and married us. She had lived across the street from my father's business and knew several of his employees. It was too much of a coincidence! We knew we couldn't ask her to leave. And since I had spent months helping to care for a friend who had recently died of bone cancer, I figured I'd eventually be helping to physically care for Alice.

Another person who didn't want to give up his apartment before we moved in, was State Representative John Engler, who later became governor of the state. He was up for re-election on November 4th and wanted to wait until he knew if he would be staying in Lansing. We agreed to move in around him when the time came.

Then I was surprised by a phone call one day from 23-year-old Faye, who asked if we had an apartment for rent. She explained that she was still living with her parents, working for the Tri-County Community Mental Health Board and doing volunteer work with Youth for Christ, a ministry to teens. Another Youth for Christ volunteer, Catherine, was in the same situation, so they were thinking of getting an apartment together. Someone at Youth for Christ told them about us, and they liked the idea of living with Christians because they thought that would help them grow in their faith walk. I knew we weren't in the business of renting apartments and I filled her in on where we were coming from. But I invited her to bring Catherine and come to dinner with us later that week so that we could get acquainted and get a sense of what we might do.

On the heels of that phone call, came one from Allison in Hillsdale, Michigan. She was a high school graduate just entering Lansing Community College and she wanted to live with a Christian family. She belonged to the Church of the Brethren, whose minister had referred her to us, so we invited her to dinner also. The evening of our dinner with the three of them, we all seemed to get along well and have the same goals. And after that encounter, although they weren't ready to become part of the extended household, the three of them wanted to be near us, so we felt fine about them sharing an apartment on second floor.

Although the inside of our new home was in pretty good shape, the outside of the 6,000 square feet of space needed attention. We couldn't deal with the crumbling stucco exterior right away but we could begin working on the trim and the eighty-five windows that needed glazing and painting. Our firstborn had a part-time job in downtown Lansing that year and that enabled us to buy a forty-foot ladder with his employee discount. I liked the bird's eye view of the neighborhood from the top of the tall ladder as I started the outside repair work.

It was balmy that fall, so once the kids were off to school I would climb to the third floor level and busy myself scraping, caulking and painting the ornate white eaves. I had lots of time to speculate about what this new situation was all about. One day when I was up there, I pondered over the concern some of our well-meaning friends had expressed about us taking our children to live in the inner city among drug dealers and other unsavory characters. Then I remembered how God loved our children far more than we could possibly love them and I was again at peace.

For our children, the move made the biggest impact on Anne-Marie and Amy because we took them out of their Catholic school and put them in Genesee Elementary School near our new home. This meant a change in school friends for them, but since God had put us in that neighborhood for a reason we thought we should participate with the life of the people around us. Joe was off to college that fall with full funding for Michigan State University that included a dorm room and the rest of the kids would go to the same schools they had been attending.

We had prayed every step of the way as a family so the kids were as excited as we were when, among other things left behind by the previous owners, we found a set of dishes in the attic that matched our dishes! We saw that discovery as another small coincidence that seemed to be God's way of assuring us that we were where he wanted us. We needed reassurance as we looked closer at the dubious condition of the monstrous ancient furnace. It was easy to imagine expensive trouble with it in the future. Hopefully it would be the far future!

The house was a rectangle thirty feet deep and fifty feet across the front, with another rectangle at a ninety degree angle to the back. On the main floor, the living room with its large fireplace, and the dining room, were at the front of the house with a ten-foot foyer in between. Eight French doors off either side of the foyer could be opened to unite both rooms and provide a comfortable area for entertaining large groups. In back of the living room was a library/den with two walls of tall casement windows and another wall of built-in bookcases with glass doors.

The dining room had been turned into a bedroom which we decided to leave that way for the time being. The enormous kitchen had lots of counter space and cupboards. It was large enough to accommodate our huge oak table that seated up to fourteen people. The walk-in pantry was the full length of the kitchen with floor to ceiling shelves and it had its own window overlooking the back staircase. There was a large bathroom off the kitchen, and attached to the rear of the house was a two-car heated garage with a sink and additional work space.

There were nine rooms and three bathrooms on the second floor, and the third floor had two enormous bedrooms, two baths, a large living room, a small prayer room and three attic storage areas. In addition to the central staircase, a glass-enclosed staircase along the north side of the house was a second access to all four floors of the house.

The basement ceilings were high and large windows let in plenty of light. Seven rooms there took care of all our extra stuff, including miscellaneous furniture that came with the house. We had parking space in the back for as many as ten vehicles in addition to our big school bus. It was perfect for us! Now all we had to do was figure out how to live together in it!

Extended-Household Beginnings

November 1, 1974 was an unseasonably warm sunny day and the house was swarming with friends of all ages. Bill was supervising the loading of the trucks at the old house as I directed where to put what at the new house. The fact that there were thirty rooms made it difficult to direct people accurately, so it was weeks before we found some of our things. At noon we dined on food brought in by more friends, and as the moving activity slowed down a little, some of the people picked up putty knives and started working on the window panes that were practically falling out of some of the windows. That evening our friends joined us for the first of many prayer meetings in our living room.

After we all got settled into the big house, Faye, Catherine and Allison were in and out of our living space frequently. By the end of December, Allison was so homesick that she moved back to Hillsdale, but Faye and Catherine said they wanted to be integrated into the rest of the extended family the way Sharon and Lucy were. So they converted what had been their living room into a bedroom for Faye, and Catherine expanded her stuff to fill up the bedroom she had been sharing with the other two women.

With Joe living in a dorm, we were a household of nine Downes family members and four women. In addition to our household, Alice maintained her separate apartment but visited with us and often joined us for our evening prayer time. She was a Catholic, as was Sharon and our family. Lucy was a Methodist, Faye belonged to a Nazarene church and Catherine was a Congregationalist. We were getting a good healthy dose of different perspectives of Christianity.

Our first household crisis occurred when Lucy and Sharon decided to invite a few friends over for a New Year's Eve Party and Faye learned they planned to have wine available for their guests. Because Faye grew up with an alcoholic father she was adamant about not having alcohol in the house and her church background supported that stance.

It was rare that we had so much as a beer in the house. Neither Bill nor I had any experience with misuse of alcoholic beverages, but he felt that if it was disturbing to Faye we should all love her enough to defer to her and not have it in the house. I disagreed with his reasoning and would have pointed out to Faye, the

Gospels that tell of Jesus changing water into wine and Timothy's exhortation to take a little wine for your stomach.

Passionately debating the various pros and cons, we barely had enough grace to stay civil with each other. Bill finally decided to ban the wine for Faye's sake, and no alcoholic drinks were served in our house that New Year's Eve. Such a little thing—such a big thing—this living together with our differences. Most of us usually think that differences are fine unless they infringe on what we want to do. Obviously there was more to living together than all of us doing our own thing.

Alice had been having physical check-ups every six weeks because of the aggressive nature of her type of cancer. In January she was told that the disease was making new inroads, necessitating more surgery. Our relationship was such, at that point, that she responded gratefully when we asked her if we could lay hands on her and pray for God to heal her. Then I went with her to the University Hospital in Ann Arbor where she submitted to surgery followed by a course of radiation treatment. The radiation caused her only minimal discomfort and subsequent check-ups showed her to be in remission.

That first January, as big bills came in we prayed for God to help us pay them. Bill was called to work an unprecedented amount of overtime (one day he worked twenty-three hours straight) during a period of the year when temporary lay-offs were routine. Finally one night he prayed, "Lord, I thank you for helping me to earn all this extra money so we can pay our bills but I am very tired. Couldn't you find some other way to pay the bills?" Right after that prayer, all the overtime opportunities dried up and several people came to us with gifts of money, enabling Bill to get a well-earned rest.

After receiving our first monthly gas bill for $423, Bill started putting big pieces of Styrofoam between the drapes and the windows. Nobody else in the household liked that solution because it made the house darker during the winter months, but big heating bills were a terrible drain on our finances. Somehow, we had enough money to make it through the winter and we realized that living together really was cheaper for all of us in the long run. There was no way of ignoring, though, that so many people from diverse backgrounds attempting to live together presented other problems.

The assimilation of Sharon and Lucy into our nuclear family had required a bit of adjustment but with the advent of still more people we had to get a little more organized. Bill and I recognized that the other adults would be leading their own busy lives, but to retain a family sense we still needed to participate in some specific shared activities. Lucy and Sharon were used to our family dinner hour which we still viewed as a critical necessity. When Faye and Catherine joined us, we told them that they needed to be committed to being with us for dinner and the brief prayer time that followed, on Mondays through Thursdays each week. On weekends the women were free to meet social and familial obligations elsewhere. This didn't mean that there weren't exceptions but those times were rare.

One of the cornerstones of the household was from I John 1:6: *If we walk in the light as he is in the light, then we have fellowship with one another and the blood of his son, Jesus, cleanses us from every sin.*

We understood that the scripture meant we must keep our lives open to one another in order to know each other and could therefore offer love and encouragement when needed. We would share both the good and the bad, the sorrows as well as the joys of our life. By living in the light that way, God could work in us and through us, to show us what true fellowship is.

So we asked them to meet with us for a household meeting every Monday night. It was basically a time for the adults to look at any problems we might be having and to work together for solutions. We might talk about the phone bill, a leaky faucet in one of the bathrooms or the pot hole in the driveway. Sometimes we listened to a spiritual teaching on tape or discussed a good book. We might spend the evening listening to and encouraging someone who was going through a rough time. Sometimes we just did something fun together. This household meeting commitment kept our communication open and provided more glue to bind us together.

The women had said they'd help us clean up the yard, which was untidy from winter debris, on the first Saturday of April in 1975 but we awoke to find 16 inches of snow on the ground. So after giving the shovels a workout as we uncovered the driveway and the sidewalk, we abandoned any other ideas about outside cleanup. Instead we took up paint brushes and painted pictures and proverbs on some of the inside doors of the house. We had so much fun together that day, we decided to make the first Saturday of every month a regular commitment to be used to do whatever maintenance jobs that needed doing around the house. We knew we could count on some part of the house falling apart regularly. The first Saturday in May we took all the Styrofoam off the windows and got them washed. We were very enthusiastic about getting that big job done so light could stream in all the windows again.

My parents had been following all of our activities, but my mother, especially, was concerned about so many people living with us now, in spite of my trying to allay her fears. The next time she and Daddy came to visit us, she found it, in her words, "A pleasant surprise."

"When our daughter first wrote and told us about the household we were hesitant. First thoughts were—No use to go there to visit anymore; she'll be too busy. I couldn't imagine anything else. The time came for that first visit—the situation had to be tested. It was a very pleasant surprise. Our daughter was just like she always was—a joy to visit. We were there, her parents, and every minute counted. Even more, it was an enlightening visit, a learning experience. When I mentioned my first concern, she laughed. She said, "I just told people, 'My folks are coming. Forget I'm here. My time is their time.'" We never hesitated to visit again. To see the respect and sharing of these people was interesting."

My parents continued to visit us once or twice a year and we all looked forward to their coming. My father's Irish wit and mother's loving ways made their presence in the house greatly valued. When they were around, our whole household gravitated toward them in order to take in the nuggets of wisdom interspersed throughout their conversation and to enjoy their ever-present sense of fun. A number of people in our household called them "Grandma" and "Grandpa."

Daddy loved all the activity and thrived on being in the middle of so many interesting people, but his main comment to me was always that he was humbly amazed by the work God was doing with us. "Indeed," I replied, "Remember all the times when you brought people who were down on their luck home to stay with us for a time? I am only following your example!"

My parents had laid a solid foundation for my life, training, encouraging and loving me into a place where I could stand before God and man, even though I struggled at times. Bill's parents, too, were always supportive of us and had done a good job of raising their children to be responsible adults. Parenting is an awesome task and I respect and honor our parents for their faithfulness in executing that responsibility. Their good work was one of the things that enabled us, in turn, to function as parents ourselves.

By the summer of 1975 we were getting used to this way of living and I was really enjoying the other women who lived with us. My daughters, especially, seemed to enjoy the older women and Amy had a ball with all those people to talk to. I enjoyed sprucing up the rooms, painting and wallpapering where needed and rearranging furniture.

Sharon had tried college once before and dropped out but she was back in school and working too. Faye said one of her high school teachers told her she wasn't college material but we could see that she was smart. So she began going to Lansing Community College to work on an accounting degree. The college was only six blocks from us, so many of us used its convenient location to take classes.

I was just beginning to feel well settled into this household living mode when another door opened for me.

In August of 1975, I was asked to begin serving as one of twelve Directors of the Tri-County Community Mental Health Board, which was responsible for mental health services to the 325,000 people living in Clinton, Eaton and Ingham counties. With no formal education or training to prepare me for the work ahead, I was flabbergasted that I had been appointed to the position. The work was interesting and it opened a whole new world to me. One of the positive things about it was getting to know the mental health professionals in the city. Also, it was a new experience for me to be respected in an intellectual setting.

This was the beginning of a valuable learning environment for me, almost like I had gone back to school. I did not enjoy all of the paper work I had to absorb each month, but my extended-family living situation was a good basis for understanding what the expenses should be in the group homes we supervised. It must have been the combination of my experience with the West Side Neighborhood Association and the managing of what looked to mental health professionals as a group home, that prompted my appointment to the board.

Our first male household member arrived late in the summer of 1975. Robert, a Political Science major at a college in Grand Rapids, had heard about us from his Catholic Charismatic group there. He wanted to live with us because he was coming to Lansing to work for a state legislator during the fall term. Even the geography was perfect for him since we were practically in the back yard of the State House. Robert was a good role model for our teen-aged sons while he was with us that fall. It happened that his family's business was a Christmas tree farm so he also brought us our Christmas tree that year.

One afternoon that October, Lucy called from work to ask if she could bring home a social worker visiting from England, Gillian, who desperately needed to stay with us. She had been awarded a Winston Churchhill Fellowship to enable her to study how child abuse is handled in the United States. However, she had been forced to go directly from the hospital where she had been recuperating from a nervous breakdown, to the plane bringing her to this country. The poor girl had been traveling for eight weeks already and Lucy could see that she was exhausted physically, mentally, and spiritually. Gillian was involved with the charismatic movement in the Anglican Church in Oxford and we found her to be a delightful person as she canceled the rest of her tour and spent ten days with us before returning to England. She came back to spend a few weeks with us in 1978 and again in 1983.

Sharon and Lucy left in January of 1976 at the same time that the household bills were the highest so it looked like we might have financial problems again but that didn't happen. What did happen was George, who showed up at our front door one day saying that he had heard about us from someone in the First Assembly of God Church. He had been lured into a cult called "The Way." He worked for Manpower, but was mandated by the group, to hand over his paycheck each week. He said he didn't like that nor the fact that he wasn't allowed to drive his car, and besides that, he said he was always hungry. I believed he was always hungry because he was well over six feet tall and painfully thin. We took him in and started putting some meat on his bones and some cheer in his spirit. George stayed with us for several years and usually seemed appreciative of the household.

Shortly after George moved in, a non-denominational, charismatic church referred Kelly to us. She was a strong-minded, attractive, young woman who had been in a drug-rehabilitation program down in Texas. Looking for a place to receive some stable teaching and common sense, she was a new Christian, embarking enthusiastically but not very realistically, on a 40-day fast. We asked her to pray for direction regarding her desire to live with us and we would do the same. She came back and told us she felt God had confirmed her desire to live with us for a while and we welcomed her into our home.

Jody, a social worker for the State of Michigan, moved in that February also. She was a member of Faye's church and wanted the fellowship of the household for support in her Christian walk since none of her family were Christian. She stayed with us for three years until she got married. With all of them contributing financially to the household we made it through the second winter on Sycamore Street.

The advent of these new people gave us cause to pause and ponder what the future of the household might be. We also were beginning to be uncomfortably aware of some of the personal problems in the people we were living with. Our discomfort motivated us to start confronting these problems in spite of our reluctance to do so. And since recognizing problems and confronting them is the beginning of a solution to problems, we made our first feeble steps toward the real work of the household. Our place of refuge for new, troubled, or lonely Christians was not meant to be a place to stagnate but to grow into maturity. We began to pray seriously for God to work in us and make us into his people.

Extended-Community

That same winter of 1975-1976, the Lord began to build a community around us that was broader than the household but inseparable from it. This began when Bill's work hours at the bakery changed from nights to days, enabling us to accept a request to teach another Life in the Spirit Seminar. We had taught the seminar many times while involved with the Resurrection and Holy Cross prayer groups, and found it to be a very effective way to introduce people to the basic truths of Christianity and to lead them into receiving the Baptism of the Holy Spirit.

This group meeting in a home in DeWitt, was composed mainly of married couples who had recently attended a Marriage Encounter Weekend, a retreat designed to enrich a marriage and to help couples experience the love of God the Father. These people were hungry for more of God and were seeking ways in which to grow spiritually. It was a time of joy for all of us as they soaked up the teachings in the seminar and explored ways of living the Gospel more radically.

When the eight weeks of the seminar were completed, they had such a strong desire to continue relating to each other that they began to meet every Friday in our home for a prayer meeting and more teaching. As we began to grow closer to each other, we shared more and more of our daily lives with each other. Some members of the group wondered aloud, if we should become a formal community and endeavor to live closer to each other. So about thirty of us decided to spend a weekend praying together at our house in order to ask God for guidance regarding this matter. We sent our children to spend the weekend in the homes of some of our other friends and we settled in to pray. At the culmination of the weekend retreat we received what seemed like a word from the Lord that we were to become a community known as The Lord's Delight.

That leading began during the retreat when a number of the people suggested that the attachment we were feeling for each other might be something God had given us for a reason—to use us for a corporate witness. We considered some serious name suggestions and some as silly as The Sycamore Street Saps. Finally, we prayed for God to give us a name if he wanted to identify us as a certain body, but nothing came to light until we concluded the retreat with a special Mass said for us at St. Mary Cathedral on Sunday evening. Father Douglas Osborn was the spiritual director of our household and he had agreed to celebrate the Mass for us.

Our babysitting friends brought our children to join us for the Mass, so there were eighty-five of us gathered there when God answered our prayers for a name. During the liturgy when time for the scripture readings arrived, Father Osborn entered the pulpit, looked out on those of us gathered before him and said, "God is surely pleased with you tonight." And although he had no idea of our earlier discussion about a name, Father chose to speak from Isaiah 62. He began to read the first three verses of the text and then with the fourth verse these words jumped out at us:

You shall be called by a new name pronounced by the mouth of the Lord. You shall be a glorious crown in the hand of the Lord, a royal diadem held by your God. No more shall men call you 'Forsaken,' or your land 'Desolate,' but you shall be called 'My Delight.'

Then Father looked up at us. "You shall be His delight," he said. "Your name shall be 'His Delight'. You shall be known as 'His Delight!'"

There were scattered gasps from among us as we recognized that God was answering our prayers for a name and confirming that he had a corporate work for us to do. Chattering excitedly about it later that evening, it seemed uncomfortably presumptuous of us to think of being known as the Lords *delight.* But Bill was quick to point out that the Lord had said, "You *shall* be my delight. He didn't say that we already *were* his delight. That most assuredly meant that the Lord would be doing a lot of work in us.

During the retreat we had felt God speaking to us through Isaiah 54:2-3, also: *Enlarge the space for your tent, spread out your tent cloths unsparingly; lengthen your ropes and make firm your stakes. For you shall spread abroad to the right and to the left.*

During the next three years, five families sold their homes elsewhere in the Lansing area and bought or rented homes adjacent to our house on Sycamore Street and also across the street. Some others in the community rented apartments on the street and around the corner. We became a visible sign of Christ in the midst of a very transient neighborhood.

Because we lived right near each other we were able to share our lives on a daily basis in very concrete ways. We were running in and out of each others' homes, hauling furniture back and forth across the street or next door as someone needed something, sharing cars, and eating many of our meals together. Once when we were given a pick-up truck full of corn, we were able to share it with all of the neighbors, not just members of The Lord's Delight.

Our behavior did not go unnoticed by other inhabitants of the block. We got acquainted impersonally with Magic Man, the drug dealer across the street, because his CB system interfered with some of the television reception in other houses on the street. He soon organized back-to-back drug pickups to take place during our Friday night prayer meetings when there was a lot of legitimate traffic on the street.

Amy's fascination with people propelled her into the role of roving ambassador in the neighborhood. She'd go from house to house up and down the street acquiring new friends as she visited with the elderly people in their rocking chairs on their front porches and the little kids playing with their toys. She reported back to us that some of the neighbors thought at first that we were a group home or an orphanage, a fact that she indignantly protested! I guess in some way though you could say they were right. There were a number of professional people inhabiting our block in addition to college students, people on welfare and drug dealers. I loved the richness garnered from the variety of people I came to know there.

In May of 1976, Sandy Lee moved in with us and stayed nine years. Recently she wrote and told me about an occasion when her son asked her to read him the fairy tale, *The Ugly Duckling.* As she was reading the story she identified with the ugly duckling because she too grew up feeling unlovable and out-of-place. Because she had scars on her face due to surgery for a birth anomaly, she was very reserved and self-conscious. Growing up she experienced children making fun of her and calling her names. With few friends and little self confidence she stayed within her own protective environment as much as possible, adverse to trying anything new.

When Sandy Lee was sixteen she had more surgery on her face to try to correct some of the difficulties. She was going to make things right! What she had hoped to accomplish was that by changing the outside of herself other areas of her life would also be changed. She hoped she would be more acceptable and better liked by herself and others, but that didn't happen. She never went to any class proms and was never part of the popular group at school. She still had her poor self-image and still felt unacceptable.

Her attitude toward herself had a profound influence on her attitude toward life, as well as her relationship with God. She felt, "If what I see in the mirror, and the rejection I experience, is an example of God's love for me, then how can I trust him?" She was pretty angry at God, and although she went to church regularly, praying when she ran into difficulties, she didn't really feel like it made any difference.

Some of Sandy Lee's friends persuaded her to accompany them to a prayer meeting one Sunday evening. But meeting new people, being in large groups or being in unfamiliar situations always made her uncomfortable, so although her friends encouraged her to come again the following week, she didn't want to go back.

As she drove home from a shopping trip a few days later, she was considering what excuse she could give for not going back, when suddenly her rearview mirror fell off her car windshield and plopped onto the seat beside her, interrupting her train of thought. As she continued to drive she realized how much she needed that mirror. Then it occurred to her that just as she couldn't see what was going on around her without that mirror, she might not be able to see what God had for her if she didn't keep going to the prayer meetings. Was God trying to tell her something?

She kept going to the prayer meetings and went through a Life in the Spirit Seminar. She had prayed and talked to God before but had never thought of listening for an answer to her prayers, so she prayed for God to speak to her and work in her life like he did in the lives of the people who shared with her during the seminar. God, being faithful, did indeed lead her into a vibrant relationship with him.

One of the first areas she prayed about was finding a different place to live because her roommate was moving. People at the prayer group recommended that she come to see if our home might be the right place for her. But after that first visit with us she said to herself, "Only as a last resort would I live there!" She was still very timid, so it was very threatening to her when she thought about living with twenty people she didn't know. "Then all the other doors seemed to be closed except living with you," she wrote to me, "so I started considering whether this might be God's answer to my prayer."

The years she lived with us brought tremendous changes in her. God began to heal and change the inside of her. She started to realize that he didn't form her the way she was to make her miserable. Rather, he had a good plan for her to serve him through her sensitivity to the needs and pain of others. His Spirit made it possible for her to open up her life and allow him to do a work in her that made it possible for her to serve him today in ways she never could have otherwise.

"God brought me to people who loved and accepted me no matter what I looked like or how much crud was inside of me," she wrote. "I began to experience that God loved and accepted me. He wanted good things for my life. In the Ugly Duckling story the swan discovered that it doesn't matter about being born in a duck yard as long as you are hatched from a swan's egg. The Lord taught me that what happened to me growing up didn't have to keep me from becoming what he wanted me to be because I was his daughter. With the knowledge and acceptance of God and his love for me, I started to grow in confidence and self-worth, to be able to reach out to others, to not be so wrapped up in myself. I was able to hear from him."

One area of her life that she really experienced God working through prayer was when she was getting close to thirty and reminded the Lord that she had always wanted to be married even though she was pretty happy being single. She told the Lord that if he wanted her to get married he could bring someone to the front door. She didn't have to go looking for a husband. She felt the Lord wanted her to write down the scriptures about husbands and wives and to use that as a guide in praying for a husband and in acquiring qualities she needed to grow in.

The Lord heard her suggestion and her future husband, Ken, came through our front door one morning after being invited to have breakfast with some of the men in our household. It was interesting to learn that Ken had also written down the same scriptures about husbands and wives, and used them in his prayer time. They've been married for 17 years now and have two sons. When she asked Ken, recently, what attracted him to her, he replied: "Your being governed by what the Lord wanted, and doing it. Proverbs 31:30 says: *Charm is deceptive, and beauty is fleeting; but the woman who fears the Lord is to be praised.*"

Sandy Lee finished her letter by saying, "I want to be faithful to a God who has been faithful to me. The reconstructive work that God does inside us is workmanship that no one else can match. He is forever faithful, he is forever trustworthy, he is forever loving me no matter what mistakes I make or how often I fail."

Sandy Lee decided to live with us despite her fears because she felt that was what God wanted her to do. When she first moved in, she would sneak down the back staircase and avoid having breakfast with us because she was so afraid of people. But as she got a little braver and began to let us know her, we delighted in her wit and humor. She kept making decisions to try new things and to go to new places.

Because of her terrible self-image, it was especially hard for her to confront people who were taking advantage of her. She'd tell us about an incident in her work place when someone had treated unkindly or unjustly, and we'd insist that she needed to confront the person. She'd cry and storm around about it, but she would eventually do it and feel better for it. We admired her courage in confronting her fears until they no longer ruled her.

Lifelong habits of relating to people are hard to change, but they are well worth the effort put into it when change leads to personal freedom and happiness. She eventually let down her barriers and was one of the most loved people in the household.

Sycamore Fellowship

Throughout the summer of 1976 several more people came to live with us. We reached a point where Bill and I sat down and took a hard look at what seemed to be developing in our midst. We evaluated what had been happening in all of us thus far and how we were handling it. Our children seemed to be relating well to most of the extended family members and really enjoyed some of them. We were seeing some good fruit in all of us, encouraging us to look at what was working and noting what seemed to be consistently leading to sound decisions. Some basic guidelines we had adopted seemed to be working well. We began to recognize our extended-household way of life as "Sycamore Fellowship."

Although we took in almost anyone for a brief stay if they were in a crisis situation, we only accepted on a more permanent basis, those people who were willing to follow the teachings of Jesus. They didn't have to be Christians when they came but they had to be willing to learn to live as Jesus said we should. The only way we knew how to help people was to point them to what the Bible recommended. Our experience and confidence in the practical wisdom of the Bible was the foundation for our life together. The accounts I have read about other community living situations all cite the necessity of a common focus in order for any group to hang together. We stayed together because Jesus was our focus.

When someone asked to live with us, no matter how sad or how bad the person seemed, I was always optimistic about what God could do in their life. I had already seen him do so much for others and for myself. So if we could possibly make room for another household member, we prayed for God's will in the matter together as a household.

Some household members did not want to accept anyone new. Usually it was because they felt threatened by change, so we would gently remind them that each of them had once been that new person. After discussion and prayer together, Bill and I had the ultimate responsibility to decide whether to receive a new person into the house.

When anyone asked to join us, we met with them to try to understand their reasons for wanting to live with us. People presented many different reasons, but we tried to discern God's reasons for bringing them to us—the sense that God wanted them with us for a time. We asked God to give us an uneasiness in our spirit if we were to refuse the person's request to join us. Our home was not a place to eat and sleep—it was a place in which to grow spiritually.

Although we tried to explain our household living routine to potential members, we knew it was impossible for them to really know what it was like until they had actually lived it. So we always suggested that new people come for a thirty-day trial period and, at the end of that time, to reevaluate their decision to join us. Sometimes at the end of thirty days it would be apparent that a person was unable or unwilling to receive what we had to offer. Then we would suggest that they find another living situation. One such person was Javier.

When his therapist brought him to our house for an interview, Javier appeared to be an affable, Hispanic, young man who suffered grand mal seizures because of epilepsy. He had been living with his family but they were unable to cope with him anymore. Although many people with epilepsy lead normal, productive lives, Javier hadn't been able to hold down a job because he regularly refused to take the medication he needed to keep from having seizures. He didn't follow through with the simplest tasks we gave him and did not take responsibility for himself during the six weeks he was with us. It really scared the little kids in the house when they saw him fall all the way down the main staircase of our house one day during a seizure. When I met several times with him and his therapist, she made excuses for his behavior at every turn, so I didn't see any way of making any progress toward growth for him in our home. We finally had to ask him to find other living accommodations, and we were relieved when he left.

Perhaps we made a mistake when we took Javier in, or perhaps we didn't. Maybe God was giving him another chance for change which he didn't use. God is so merciful that he gives us many opportunities for repentance. Maybe Javier truly couldn't be held responsible for his actions or his inaction. We did the best we could to correctly discern God's will in the matter and that was all we could do. With some who came and stayed only a month or two, perhaps God was planting seeds.

We heard about Bobby one day in May when a woman who worked in the state office complex phoned me. Bobby was working in her department part-time while finishing up his degree at Michigan State and she'd just discovered he was sleeping in his car because he could afford no housing. If he took on more work in order to pay for a place to sleep, he would have no time for classes and studying, so he was limping along on his meager funds in a most unsatisfactory way.

Bobby was a likeable Irish chap from the East Coast, who was industrious around the house and had professed to be a follower of Christ. As he shared about his life though, we learned that he was regularly having sexual intercourse with his girlfriend and didn't even seem to regard her very highly, since he said he planned to leave her behind when he graduated and moved back East. As Bill talked to him about this relationship, Bobby began to realize that he really wasn't living as a Christian and indeed, he knew little about the Christian walk. In spite of this realization he seemed unperturbed and was not interested in staying with us after the school term ended. He returned to New Jersey with a jolly good-bye to us and we've never heard from him since.

Seed-planting is not nearly as rewarding as harvesting, but it is a necessary part of God's work. I used to worry about what we had done wrong when people didn't seem to follow through to a more mature spiritual life, but God eventually gave me a peace about letting the results of our labor rest in his hands.

When new people moved in, everyone else in the household had to rearrange themselves in order to try to include the new person into their lives, and we all began to get to know each other in a new way. A person sent to us by God would have an impact on all of us. Some of the people were blessings and some were afflictions. If the new person was especially difficult to live with, it caused us to see clearly our weaknesses in the areas of compassion, confrontation, tolerance, etc. If the new person had gifts of thankfulness, appreciation and encouragement we could see ways in which we could improve those virtues in our own lives.

Usually, when people first came they were on their best behavior for a while. Later we would see the need for repentance or healing. We found that many people would experience tremendous grace from God in the beginning, especially if they were new Christians. Then when God had firmly established in their minds and hearts the fact that he loved them, he would begin to show them areas of their lives that they needed to clean up. Some would balk at that point and be unwilling to change. Others dug in and worked on the areas that God brought to their attention and they were a source of blessing to all of us. Our main task seemed to be to encourage people and to point out to them what God's word said about their present situation.

One person who comes to mind was Christy. She was seventeen years old when she crossed our threshold after living a hand-to-mouth existence for two years in Chicago. She was a buxom girl with curly, red hair, whose past was revealed in the wary look in her beautiful dark eyes and a pouting demeanor to her pretty face. She had come to Lansing to be near her mother. The baby-sitting job she had accepted here turned out to be too difficult for her. One day when she poured out her woes to one of her mother's friends, that woman referred her to us.

Christy had once been told that God loved her, by a man who had befriended her when he found her crying in a booth in a Chicago diner. But she had never had the opportunity to learn much about God, since she never stayed in one place long enough to experience Christian teaching and fellowship. We talked with her, trying to give her a vision of a stable living environment, but she was hesitant to make a commitment to the routine of a daily schedule that included such things as going back to school and being home at meal times. As we sat there at prayer with her in our den, a scripture from Sirach 51:23 caught her attention: *Come aside to me, you untutored, and take up lodging in the house of instruction.*

She was intrigued with the thought that God might really be speaking to her, and opted to stay with us for a while. She went back to school to finish her high school education and she experienced God blessing her by bringing her into genuine friendships with people who cared about her. She found part-time work and was able to have a sense of peace and purpose that comes from moving along with goals and plans for a future.

After one year, she had been with us longer than any place she could remember, and she was beginning to be attached to some of the people in the household. At the same time, God seemed to be speaking to her about her unwillingness to let down barriers and to begin to really trust some of us. That frightened her so much that a week before she graduated from high school she hurriedly moved out of the house rather than confront the feelings welling up inside of her.

We attended her graduation and talked to her afterward, encouraging her to examine what was going on inside of her, in order to overcome her fears. But Christy soon fled back to Chicago and the anonymity of that big city. We had a couple of letters from her about her new apartment and new job, but the day eventually arrived when a letter I had sent to her was returned with no forwarding address. We have not heard from her personally since then, but we learned through friends that she had married and subsequently divorced an abusive man, and is still searching for the healing she needs. I still hope that she eventually finds a place of peace.

People who were under psychiatric care or meeting regularly with a therapist while they were living with us, were expected to allow Bill or I to work in conjunction with their professional care-givers. After a person had been with us for a time, we were better informed of their daily functioning level than the therapists who saw them in an office setting once a week or once a month. It was critical that we and the professional counselors worked as a team toward the same goals in the person's life. Also, there is a tendency in many people to be less than candid with their counselors, but with good communication with therapists I felt we had a better chance of really helping the people who lived with us. And when someone as sick as Karla came to live with us, I knew I needed to have professional help close at hand.

Karla was a young woman whose petite beauty hid a mind tormented by the voices of schizophrenia which emerged when she was a twenty-year-old university student. She came to us after being hospitalized for a couple of years and then living in a custodial situation where she was quite isolated. When she was thought to be well enough to try interfacing with the larger community again by taking a college course or two, she met one of our household members in class and eventually asked if she could live with us. I asked her to place herself under the care of a psychologist, a man I knew and trusted, and she was also under the care of a psychiatrist, since she needed medication which had to be monitored.

Whenever she went into a catatonic state or began to withdrawal from reality, I could call my psychologist friend for advice and help. Together with Karla, we planned activities and strategies which might help her to achieve her goals. The psychologist watched in amazement as she functioned in a part-time job and completed her university education despite the hurdles she had to overcome.

We discovered ways to get around her handicap. To circumvent the voices she heard drowning out the voice of the lecturing professor, she took a tape recorder to class and then listened to the lecture at home at a time when her concentration level was good. When she was very upset, I spent hours reading to her from the Psalms because that seemed to calm her. When she was in such a state of fury as to want to physically harm herself, we took long walks to help dissipate her anger enough that she could talk about the feelings she had been repressing.

Karla's struggle with her affliction was so courageous that we felt honored to be part of her life, and the whole household was inspired by her perseverance in spite of many setbacks. She was a gifted musician and composed music which we sang in four-part harmony. One of her musical creations we all loved was a grace that we sang before meals at dinnertime.

After living with us for several years, she received her university degree and then got a job in her field near her parents' home in the Atlanta area. I would never have attempted to help someone as sick as Karla, without knowing I had expertise a phone call away. Even with the professional help, it was scary for me to assume responsibility for her. It kept me on my knees.

Bill and I understood our role in the household to be one of helping each person with their spiritual walk. We first looked at their relationship with God and encouraged them to set aside some quiet time each day to talk to God, and then to listen for a sense of him speaking to them. Secondly, we looked at their relationship with their parents. Since that is one's primary relationship, it sets the tone for all other relationships, and when that relationship is out of sync whether we are aware of it or not, it brings pain into relationships with other people.

We always began our counseling sessions with people by working toward healing that parental relationship. We stressed the necessity of giving up bitterness toward parents and to replace those negative emotions with the honor and respect God requests. We had to consider that their parents might have been in a great deal of pain themselves and needed to be viewed with compassion rather than judgement.

Such was the task that faced Erica, who lived with us for about a year. When she was fifteen, Erica came home from school one day to find a note from her mother saying that she had left for good and the rent was paid up for only another week. Since her father had been in a mental hospital most of her life, she was on her own.

She managed to survive, spending part of her young adulthood in the armed services where she had a place to belong and receive some stability in her life. When she learned that her mother was dying, she set aside her anger at being abandoned and moved out west to be with her, physically caring for her during her final illness.

While she lived with us, she tried to develop a deeper sense of compassion toward her parents and she began praying earnestly for her father. Right after that she received an opportunity to begin a new relationship with her father, who was now living nearby and seemingly stable, due to new medication he was taking. As she spent time with him, God was able to bring emotional healing to her and free her from some of the bruises left from her painful childhood. She became affiliated with a church and left us to live with some of the people there, eventually marrying and raising a son.

Some parents were suspicious of our household and disapproving of their child's decision to live with us. Others were indifferent and never or rarely came to the house even though their child might have lived with us for several years. But there were also some parents who were very appreciative of our work with their children and were still very involved in their lives. Most of the people who lived with us had problems with one or both parents. We seemed to function as substitute parents for those whose own parents had not been able to give them the nurturing they needed in order to grow up to be healthy.

On the other hand there were some people who showed up at our door who seemed to be spiritual parasites simply looking for a place to eat and sleep. These are really good at conning well-meaning Christians. They go from church to church and group to group, looking for a hand out. Frequently they have an avocation of spreading disunity among Christians. We were on guard against those people.

Bill was concerned about protecting household members, and we tried to be very careful about who we let live in the house. Some persons had to be refused simply because we already had the same type of serious problem in a present household member. We found for example, that having a second drug addict or alcoholic in the house was asking for trouble. They would gravitate toward each other and usually brought each other back into their addiction instead of helping each other to overcome it.

It is true that some of the people we took in could have been considered dangerous to us because of their hostile behavior, but we always looked for that sense of inner peace regarding those who came and then trusted God to take care of us. Once when Bill was counseling a man, who was not a household member, he sensed an urgent command: "Leave—now!" He dashed outside as the man threw a machete at him that struck the door as he closed it! We had a few things stolen and some furniture broken and walls damaged by someone acting out their anger, and we were yelled at, but no physical harm ever came to any of us.

When we first started to take people into our home, I prayed for God to give me immediate feelings of love for whomever asked to come, as a sign that he was equipping me to care for them. I thought, "How can I minister love to people unless my behavior toward them is motivated by feelings of love?" Eventually I learned that love is more of a decision than a feeling, and that I didn't need to depend on feelings.

God did equip us to care for those who came to our home. There were some people who lived with us that I never did develop feelings of love for, but I still knew words that would encourage them, and God showed me many loving things that I could do for them to show them that he loved them. God's love was what they needed to receive, not mine. More than once I was told by someone that they knew I loved them, and I knew that I did too, even though I didn't have gushy feelings for them. I loved them by serving them, praying for them, hugging them, and spending time with them, whether I felt like doing those things or not. It's just easier to do those things when you feel like it.

Our first Saturday of each month work days were well established and fruitful, but one of our first Saturday household work days was remembered as being very special. It was a day we did no exterior work on the house, but a deep interior work was accomplished in our hearts. After our breakfast together and a brief prayer time, we instructed each person to go somewhere quiet where they could be by themselves. There we asked them to give some thought to the rest of the household members and to write a love letter to each one, describing to them the things about them that they liked the best and appreciated the most. Our house had many nooks and crannies, so eventually everyone settled down somewhere and wrote their letters.

In the afternoon, we gathered back in the living room to exchange all the letters; then we went back to our quiet places to read them. When we gathered for dinner that evening, there were smiling faces and tangible evidence of joy everywhere we looked. Our eleven-year-old Anne-Marie said to me later that evening, "Oh Mother, I'm going to save my letters always so I can take them out and read them when I'm having a bad day!"

I could identify with her, since I was still aware of being in the mode of avoiding my broken places by keeping too busy to think. And God was gentle enough to allow me to stay there yet as he kept bringing new people and new challenges to our door.

Multi-Family Mix

A significant household change occurred in 1976 with the arrival of a newly divorced woman, Bernadette, and her four children, who came to live with us in order to receive support while she tried to establish a new life. Confident in her cooking skills, it was a blessing to both of us for her to take over a lot of the meal preparation. By serving that way in the house, she felt more a part of it, and with my encouragement to make our home her home, she redecorated her children's room and even put new carpeting down in our living room.

The tricky thing about having another family unit living with us was the need for the parents to remain responsible for their children. All of her family came with the baggage of rejection and were struggling to make sense of what had happened to them. I quickly learned that her kids were used to staying up late. They were also used to getting into the refrigerator and eating anything they pleased whenever they pleased.

Amy was still young enough that she had a specific bedtime and I didn't allow her that much food freedom, so we had to work out a compromise, with Bernadette reining her kids in a little and me letting Amy be a little more venturesome. And because there were some discipline problems, especially with her oldest child, we had a really difficult time working through some of them. The struggles, though, were far outweighed by the good things we experienced, and Bernadette's children thrived on all the attention they received from the adults in the household.

As I look at my photo album of all the fun activities that took place with the household and the community in 1976 it is full of happy events. There was the Saturday when many of the Lord's Delight community showed up to help us lay a new driveway to the lower parking area in back of our house. One of the families came from a town south of Lansing to help us. As they arrived they were all excited, waving a tool used for spreading fresh cement, something called a "come along." It was a T-shaped tool, a sort of rake without tines, consisting of a long pole with a four or five foot wide piece of board attached at one end. While driving to our house they had noticed it in a ditch by the side of the road and stopped to bring it along, considering it to be a coincidence too good to pass up.

Children and adults alike were impressed as the huge cement truck delicately backed through our narrow driveway alongside the house, threading its way to the site in the back yard. The men had begun the project earlier in the week by making a wooden form for the driveway, and once the cement was poured and distributed by the "come along," the children finished the project, eagerly drawing their names in the fresh cement along the edges and in the corners. It was a very satisfactory day.

In July we took a bus full of the Lord's Delight members to Kemper Arena in Kansas City to attend a huge interdenominational conference of people involved in the charismatic renewal throughout the nation. All of us had experienced times of being misunderstood by friends or relatives concerning our participation in this new way of living in the Spirit, so we felt a sense of comfort being among the fifty thousand people gathered there. If we were crazy, we had lots of company and the fellowship was wonderful. One workshop I attended there dealt with spirituality and mental health, and the presenter, Bob Mumford, said something I took to heart. "Sometimes the most spiritual thing you can do is go to bed." Aware of the endless busyness of our household it did me good to hear the common sense in that advice.

The household and community people whom I had grown to love, continued to sustain me with their generous hearts and joyful communion with me. Life seemed good and it was still possible to dream that my relationship with Bill would be healed someday.

We took the family to Missouri for a visit with Bill's parents late that summer. His father was now in a nursing home because his senility had made him unmanageable at home, but we were able to spring him and take him on a bus ride to a nearby state park for the day. Then we went on to Texas to camp for a bit. As usual we brought home an array of bugs and snakes, but this time we also acquired a young armadillo we found wandering around during daylight hours where he had no business being.

Intrigued by the armadillo, we figured he probably wouldn't live long on his own, so we dumped the ice out of our Coleman ice chest and made room for him there until we got home. He was named Sherman because he resembled a tank. He took up residence in the basement furnace room which doubled as Bill's computer room. Our basement was a busy place of seven rooms, so he had lots of company. While David practiced his drums in the paint room he'd let Sherman snuffle around in there, and people walking through the furnace room to get to the photography room would chat with him a bit as they went by. He curiously explored the big all-purpose room while people used washers and dryers, providing them a bit of welcomed distraction from the boredom of folding laundry.

First thing in the morning and again in the evening, Sherman enjoyed a meal of cat food in the kitchen and he was frequently taken for walks when the weather was warm. David made a sort of leash for Sherman, and created a stir when he took him for walks in downtown Lansing. One morning we discovered that Sherman had littered the furnace room with paper he had shredded from a pile Bill had left by his computer. Bill was dismayed by the destruction, but still couldn't help but admire the animal's prowess. However, when Sherman learned to climb on top of the water heater one night, by squeezing his back between the heater and the rough cement wall, that was, literally, his downfall. We found him one morning at the base of the heater with a bashed-in proboscis, an injury from which he did not recover.

Another household experience begun that summer, was to host groups of musicians from other countries who were attending Blue Lake Art Camp on Michigan's western shore. As part of their summer workshop these talented tourists made trips to cities around Michigan, spending a few days in private homes and giving concerts in those cities. Usually each summer seven groups came through Lansing, and the taste of their visits in our home was sweet.

We had some great jam sessions in our living room and their visits were a wonderful way for all of us, especially the children, to learn about other cultures. During those years some of the people we entertained were from Belgium, Japan, West Germany and the Scandinavian countries. Choirs, flag dancers and the Belgium National Orchestra, to name a few, made music in return for room and board with us, and we certainly felt that we had the better part of the bargain. We were always careful to clarify with them, that they weren't experiencing the typical American home while participating in our household.

Music was always an important part of our family life and in the life of the household. At one time we had six guitarists living with us. When Paul and Mike bought a grand piano, we became a two-piano family. Other household members brought a harpsichord, a marimba and a hammer dulcimer into the house. My husband had his grandfather's violin which had fallen apart when he had it with him in the Philippines during World War II, refurbished when a woman moved in who played the violin but didn't currently have one. Of course David's drums were a constant presence in our midst, and during their teen years, David and Julie joined several household members entertaining as a Christian music group called "The Light" and later another one called simply "Children."

My father had always modeled for us a deep respect for the elderly people around us, so I was happy when our two older daughters decided to volunteer some of their time at the Senior Citizens Center located near us. When they became aware that some of the people had no families at all, we set aside each December first Saturday work day for them. We'd get their names and sizes beforehand, buy gifts for them, and have them over for dinner and entertainment. It was a very good way to live out the spirit of the Advent season.

We went caroling as a household for several years, visiting local senior housing buildings and centers as well as caroling for our neighbors. Being blessed with a number of voices that blended well, we enjoyed making music together. When we first started caroling, Bill and our three oldest sons backed us up with their coronet, trombone and two french horns, but when the boys got older and moved on, I just accompanied us with my guitar. I had some stiff fingers to deal with when we were caroling outside! But God was dealing with more than stiff fingers in me. He was busy warming and softening a heart that needed to be more malleable too.

Personal Growth

I had so much to learn about the ordinary human condition, about myself, about people unlike myself, and about the strength available from God in every situation. Neither Bill nor I felt we had any special gifts for this work, and we certainly had our own problems. But everyone who came to live in our house with the intention of growing closer to God, experienced him healing their hurting places and dealing with their self-defeating behavior, and I was no exception. God used the household living years to really work me over!

I knew God loved and cared for me, but my self-esteem was still very low. I couldn't get rid of the conviction that no one could possibly love me except my parents. I thought my husband, children and friends valued me only because of the service I rendered them. I felt lonely despite having people all around me.

One Saturday when Sharon and Lucy first lived with us they went to a healing service and came home talking about how wonderfully God had touched them. Sharon particularly, exulted in how much better she felt about herself, what a release of anger and hostility she felt when people laid hands on her and prayed for her to be healed. That night, with a very bad attitude, I cried out to God, "You heal everyone else. Why don't you heal me?! Then he answered me as I opened my Bible, and began to read: *If you repent, so that I restore you, in my presence you shall stand; if you bring forth the precious without the vile, you shall be my mouthpiece. (Jer. 15:19)* I considered myself thoroughly chastened, and asked the Lord's forgiveness. I also asked him for the patience to let him work out his own timing for my healing. I had much to learn.

When Sharon moved in with us, it was pleasant having her to share with and I easily accommodated her. I certainly felt that I gained as much from her as she did from me. When Lucy came, it was much the same; sort of like when you get the hang of having a child the first time around and the second baby is not as much trouble nor as life-changing as the first.

But the first year we were in the larger house, with more physical responsibilities as well as more human relationships, the Lord began to insist on some significant changes in me. I had prayed for the mountain of my pain and self-pity to be cast into the sea, but I learned that some mountains are for climbing. It would be very nice if my problems always disappeared with prayer but I wouldn't necessarily have grown any wiser. I needed to work through some problems in order to grow in wisdom. That's what God was after in me.

One afternoon when I was indulging in self-pity, sure that I had nothing worth giving to anyone, a former neighbor phoned to tell me she was coming over because she was upset and needed to talk to someone. Instead of telling her that I couldn't cope with my own problems that day, let alone hers, I hung up the phone in a panic. I looked wildly around and then ran up to the third floor into a bedroom and on into a closet in that bedroom and then on into an attic storage room off of the closet. There I sat for a good long time until I was sure that the woman had come and gone. This was more than a bad hair day!

A lot of the tension and difficulty I had the first year or two in the big house was because of my unwillingness to confront problems. I had no trouble talking about the few difficulties that people asked us to help them deal with—those problems were out in the open. The problems I had trouble confronting were the ones I began to see once people had lived with us for a while. These were things people were either unaware of or unwilling to deal with. This was where I was a big chicken.

I would pray, "Lord, if I'm supposed to talk to so-and-so about a problem I see regarding them, let them bring it up." And in the beginning, the Lord would sometimes do that. But he eventually expected me to wake up to the fact that my job was to help people to grow up to be sturdy Christians. That meant confronting every area of their lives that was an obvious trouble spot, even if it meant experiencing their rejection and anger.

One day I was ironing a blouse up in the second floor sewing room when Elizabeth, a tall, red-headed, nursing student living with us, came bouncing happily in from the adjacent living room to tell me that she was on her way to buy a new bicycle. Since this happened when I was fairly new at confronting people, I made polite noises while she excitedly described her anticipated purchase, and it wasn't until after she left that I noticed I was pressing my iron down a lot harder than was necessary to get the wrinkles out of the blouse.

One facet of our calling people to responsibility was in the area of finances. Each month I figured out what it cost us per person to handle the expenses of the house and everyone had access to that information. Since I knew that Elizabeth was not putting enough money into the household account to cover what it cost us to have her with us, I was more than a little irritated at the thought of her buying a new bike.

So I pulled the plug on the iron and tracked her down. Then I sat down with her. Firmly, but as gently as possible, I gave her a practical financial lesson. "I too, would like a new bicycle, Elizabeth, but I cannot afford a new bicycle, and neither can you." Before I went back to my ironing, we communicated well enough for her to understand that before she purchased any extras, she needed to be contributing to the household the amount of money it was costing us to house and feed her. The money she had thought she was saving by living with us was not hers to save at that point. As I went back to the ironing I felt good for her and good for me that my reluctance to confront had been overcome and nobody died.

On the other hand, I still seesawed a little, feeling presumptuous confronting someone else's problem areas when I had so many problems myself. The real turning point for me in this issue of confronting, though, came late one night when Bill was working and all the household members were in bed except a woman I was talking to in the living room.

Lydia had been with us since a suicide attempt several months earlier. Now she was complaining with copious tears, that nobody loved her. After trying for a while to reason with her and mindful of the late hour and my own fatigue, I eventually became so frustrated with her that I said, "I am sick and tired of hearing that nobody loves you! What is love, if not providing housing food and clothing for you, as we have these last few months! You need to stop this pity party and start being thankful for all that you have been given!" (Obviously, patient endurance and mildness, those lovely fruits of the Spirit mentioned in Galatians, were far from me at that moment.)

In response to my outburst, Lydia rose and ran screaming and crying loudly up two flights of stairs, waking everyone as she traveled through the house. In defeat, I went to my own bed on the first floor. Sometime later I became aware of her standing in my bedroom doorway, saying, "You shouldn't talk to me like that! My therapist doesn't talk to me like that! You don't even know what you're doing! You've ruined me, so now I'll never get well! I can't even walk now! I'm paralyzed!"

Well, I figured that she couldn't be terribly paralyzed if she had made it back downstairs to my bedroom, but I *was* worried. "Lord," I prayed, "she's right. I don't know what I'm doing. I have no psychology degree and I don't want to hurt anybody. Maybe we shouldn't even try to address these problems. Maybe we should give up taking people in to live with us."

But then a thought went through my head as if the Lord was speaking to me: "Look, if you know in your heart that you're trying to do what I've asked you to do, then you have to trust that what you instinctively feel to do in these situations is from me. Trust that I am leading you in what you say and do."

With that, I told Lydia that she could stand there all night if she wanted to, but I was tired and I was going to sleep. She gave a pitiful cry and fell in a heap at the foot of my bed but eventually she got up and went to bed herself. The next morning she acted like nothing had happened and had a much better attitude for a while. I ventured a guess that although part of her wanted to get well, she really didn't want to give up all the attention that she got by being sick.

We had a number of emotional scenes with her during the years she lived with us and I didn't back off from dealing with her emotional blackmail anymore. She hadn't died on me and didn't seem any the worse off for my candid advice, so I didn't need to be so long-suffering with behavior that was obviously not cool.

Experiencing this bit of drama and the fruit of it, I began to gain confidence in my discernment with people and it was easier for me to speak of concerns I had for them as we went along. Of course, the more experience I had, the more I began to see some good fruit from my labors which made it easier to rest in my spirit. I knew that I might be mistaken, but I also knew that if I waited to be absolutely sure of a thing before I acted, I might miss an opportunity that wouldn't come again. I didn't want the fear of making a mistake hold me back from being of any earthly use.

God also used the household to work on my need for neatness and order around me. I was trained by my mother to be a meticulous housekeeper and that wasn't always appreciated by my family. To have your mom on your back all the time about picking things up is no fun. But eventually I gave up going around angry half of the time because of people leaving their belongings all over the downstairs rooms. I had prided myself on keeping a neat attractive home as if it were a reflection on me. Pride had to go. We all lived a lot more peacefully when I decided that I could live with some clutter.

Each person who lived with us had something to teach me about myself or about human nature in general. The abrasive ones wiped off my veneer so that my lack of loving was apparent to me if not to others. The more I saw my own areas of sin, the easier it was to feel genuine compassion for those struggling with theirs. Each morning, I looked into the mirror and saw a person in need of resurrection, in need of supernatural help. Each morning I reminded myself of God's promise in Philippians 1:6: *I am sure of this much: that he who has begun the good work in you will carry it through to completion, right up to the day of Christ Jesus.*

During my daily prayer time I was still confronted with another issue that seemed really stuck in nowhere land. My relationship with Bill. Why wasn't anything changing for the better? What was I doing wrong? Over and over I would ask God to change me so Bill would like me and not be angry with me. One spring, for a period of six consecutive days during my prayer time, I kept running into scriptures that talked of God breaking down the barriers of hostility between us and building bonds of love, so little kernels of hope would take root again; hope for our relationship to be healed.

Sometimes Bill would relate to me congenially for a few weeks, even affectionately calling me "Dearie," and I would feel very encouraged and happy. Other times, I'd feel pressed to the floor with the weight of his anger which seemed to come out of nowhere. At one of the annual National Catholic Charismatic Conferences at Notre Dame, we had taken a large group of people there on our bus. After getting parked we were all walking along the sidewalk together toward the main conference arena. At one point some of us toward the front of the group crossed the street to where the arena was located. Later that day when I was alone with Bill, he lashed out at me, saying I deliberately led everyone across the street! When I protested that I didn't know what he was talking about, that I wasn't leading anyone, it was no use. "You always try to defend yourself!" he continued angrily. As usual, I had no clue to what set him off.

Back in Lansing the next weekend, as we approached St. Mary Cathedral to attend Mass, he instructed me to walk behind him from now on, instead of going in first. I knew his behavior was unhealthy and my response by obeying him in this instance was sick, too, but I kept trying to do anything to keep the peace. It didn't feel good though, and reinforced my tendency to loath myself. I hated behaving like a wimp!

Perhaps if I could have removed myself physically from Bill for awhile I could have seen more clearly how to cope better. The demands of so many people around us were a mixed blessing. Although I was distracted from my own pain and got some satisfaction from my role in the household, I had no time to really dig in and try to find a more sane and comfortable way to exist. I had been taking courses in counseling techniques at Lansing Community College since the late 1960s in an attempt to figure out how I could change myself, and I read tons of self-help books, but I never seemed to be able to help myself as much as I helped others. So I headed into 1977 none the wiser as to solving my dilemma, but still having a deep sense of God waiting for me to understand at a deeper level the things he was trying to teach me.

1977

In addition to the continued growth of the household, we began a significant outward movement toward the larger community of Christians in Lansing through John and Sue Rogers, whom we had known since 1968. They had made a radical decision to serve Christ, and they felt particularly drawn to serve the students at Lansing Community College. As they roamed the campus environment, talking to students about God, they befriended a number of young people who were looking for something more in their life than drugs, sex and material goods. Before long Sue and John opened their modest home to young people, laying many sleeping bags on their basement floor in order to house them overnight when that need arose.

Similarly to us, they were led to a big house. For them, it was through a dream John had one night. In his dream he clearly saw a certain farm house and when he awoke he was convinced that the farm was meant for them. So from then on he spent every spare minute he had, driving around the outskirts of Lansing, up and down the country roads until he found the exact house he had seen in his dream. Then he went up to the door and met the owners, told them about his dream and asked them if they would sell their farm to him.

They agreed to do that, and by scraping together all the savings Sue and John had, including John's retirement money, they were able to buy 72-acre Bethel Farm. All that acreage was much more than they had bargained for when they saw the house, but it was part of God's plan for them. At Bethel Farm, people who came to them addicted to drugs, would learn a new way of living removed from the temptations of their former environment, and working around the farm gave them healthy, physical work that was important during their period of recovery.

We had developed a close relationship with them, drawn together by our similar situations. They referred people to us who were ready to get back in the mainstream of life, and we sent people to them who needed the more secluded environment. And every fall we took lots of people out to Bethel Farm to pick the fruit of four hundred fifty apples trees on their beautiful property. It was always a special time of fellowship, often with people from other Christian groups, as we gathered in the crop that would be sold to pay the annual taxes on the farm. We spent the day picking and sorting apples, with a break at noon for a picnic lunch. And later, when the work was done, we'd have time for more fellowship and a prayer meeting in the barn.

One evening John invited Bill and me out to the farm to meet Dr. Lewis Moncrief, Chairman of the Department of Parks, Recreation and Tourism at Michigan State University. Lewis was a big, exuberant Texan, quite a contrast to Bill, but John felt they had much in common because they both had experience witnessing to students at the university. Lewis held a prayer meeting in Wells Hall each week which eventually developed into the Spirit of Christ Fellowship, a non-denominational, charismatic church. He had been an ordained minister in the Church of Christ, but was asked to leave when he received the Baptism of the Holy Spirit and started preaching about the power of the Holy Spirit.

In 1977, Bill accepted Lewis's request that we teach a marriage course to a Sunday School class in his church, which was then meeting Sunday afternoons in a place near us called, The Master's House. I felt deeply, the irony of being asked to teach about marriage when ours was such a failure in my eyes. I was not enthused about this assignment but I couldn't very well refuse to participate with my husband in this endeavor.

So as not to overburden ourselves or neglect our own people who were meeting on Sunday evenings, we arranged for the Lord's Delight to worship on Sunday afternoons with the Spirit of Christ after their Sunday School class during the few weeks that we taught there. The joy of that joint worship experience was so special that we continued to fellowship together for many years in several types of meeting arrangements. Spirit of Christ members became brothers and sisters with us. Some of them moved into our household from time to time and some of the Lord's Delight members joined their church.

Martin, who lived with us for several years, first met us at the Sunday School class. He arrived a little late, just in time to hear us talking about our honeymoon experiences. He thought, "Any man who would drag his wife around collecting bugs, let alone collecting them from mounds of excrement, had to be an unusual character indeed!" Martin told me the fact that we found humor in difficult situations impressed him to want to live with us.

Because we had such similar desires to live a life more patterned on the principles that Jesus taught, our community and the Spirit of Christ members came together in a variety of fellowship situations. The women in our community who were at home during the day with children, met with similar women of Spirit of Christ for fellowship one morning a week. In a setting like the Monday Morning

Group I had belonged to when I first came to Lansing, we were all yearning for a deeper relationship with God. As we came together, each of us could ask for prayer about things we were concerned about as we encountered glitches in our spiritual journeys.

I was candid to a point as we gathered each week, but I was conscious of inner reticence, choosing carefully which of my struggles I revealed, feeling a need to skirt areas that would include my marriage. The position of leadership in this kind of environment comes with a certain unavoidable loneliness. I experienced this problem in other ways too.

A major source of separation from others came from the counseling sessions we had with the people who were associated with us. And many of the intimate things we knew about them caused us to be judged harshly. A case in point was that of a beautiful young woman who lived with us and asked for our advice regarding the problem she had with promiscuity. She seemed helpless to refuse any man who pursued her, so we explored with her the spiritual, emotional and physical circumstances that led to each of her indiscretions.

When we suggested that she just not date anyone at all for a period of time, she quickly accepted the idea. This would remove temptation from her while she sought help to change the inner pain that caused her to be so vulnerable. Feeling relief at that prospect, she vowed to refrain from dating for a year.

But her problem of having a hard time refusing anyone led her to tell prospective suitors, as if she had no choice in the matter, that she wasn't allowed to date. So a few months later we learned that word was going around the larger Lansing Christian community that we were control freaks who wouldn't allow single people to date.

The other aspect of being privy to intimate information about others, was the added burden of trying to be so very careful not to ever reveal any of that privileged information. I have to rely on the Lord to keep me faithful to those who trust me with their confidences, and it helps me to pray regularly, from Psalm 39:2*: I will watch my ways, so as not to sin with my tongue. I will set a curb on my mouth."*

The meetings with the women were held either at my house or at the Moncrief's house in Haslett, MI, where Lewis's wife, Delzene, offered her hospitality. After we had been meeting for a few weeks I noticed a pattern was established, that the women from The Lord's Delight Community would always have lunch at my house when we returned to Lansing after the meeting. People dropped in at our house all the time and I liked that, but I wished that they also would be moved to open their homes for fellowship in their own homes sometimes.

One day when we got back from a meeting at Delzene's and settled down for lunch, I told the women how I felt. "You are always welcome to this house, but have any of you ever considered that I would enjoy going to one of your homes for lunch sometime? I've wondered why none of you have invited us to your house for lunch after our meetings." After a shocked silence they all started talking at once.

"We just never thought!" said one. "Your house is always the gathering place!" said another. "We just always love coming here" chimed in still another. Each woman expressed regret that she hadn't thought to suggest we come to her house for lunch, so from then on our lunch location varied from home to home. My friends hadn't realized I was feeling a bit weary of always being the hostess, until I told them. I have always hoped that people, including my own children, would learn from my example. But it isn't necessarily so.

Speaking to my friends about some of my wants and needs, opened the door for me to receive loving words and actions from them which were a source of healing for me. By the fall of 1977, the constant ballet of people coming and going kept me contented with my lot in life despite my inner struggles. Since Bill still seemed to distance himself from an intimate relationship with me and spurned my efforts to relate in that way, it was a blessing that my tendency to nurture people could be spent on people who appreciated it.

Meanwhile, our Joe had finished two years at the university and moved to Texas to pursue music with some people he knew there, Tom was working as a security guard to pay for his classes in commercial art at Lansing Community College and Michael was in the honors program at Michigan State. The younger kids were busy with their school activities so I was contented with my life. Then, as1978 rolled around, I was even more thankful, because God had provided the answer to our prayers for a maintenance person who could handle some big physical changes that were needed in the house.

1978

Charlie was an out-of-work alcoholic and a dry-wall expert, who would beautifully demonstrate that gift in our midst. And in February, the stage was set for reformation, when Polly and George moved into the house with their two offspring. Both Charlie and George had lots of construction experience they were eager to expend, so we vacated our downstairs bedroom that had been the original dining room and moved to a bedroom on the second floor.

This enabled them to begin work that would restore the dining room to its former splendor. The men also added a pass-through window in the wall between the kitchen and the diningroom. This was wonderfully appreciated, since we had twenty-four people in the house at that time, necessitating seating ten people at a round table in the dining room as well as the fourteen at our big table in the kitchen.

Two of our six bathrooms had shower pans that had leaked into the ceilings below before we had bought the house, so we had those replaced and then Charlie re-plastered those ceilings. We were intrigued when he donned a pair of shoes on springs which raised his height to the level needed to put new plaster on the dining room and living room ceilings. He was the Pied Piper all over again, as the kids in the house and in the neighborhood, followed him around, applauding his antics with his special springing equipment. Since he really needed a place to live, it was a win/win situation as we admired his work throughout the house during the year he was with us. I was very happy to have so many annoying things repaired properly!

During the early spring, another big change for us and for the community was being set into motion when one of our household members, Susan, bought the five-apartment house across the driveway from us. Since community members would be renting parts of the house from Susan we would be losing one of our more colorful neighbors.

On the third floor of this house, there had for many years, resided an elderly man and woman who lived in a constant alcoholic stupor with accompanying problems. We usually saw only the woman and caught the brunt of one of her errors in judgement the first winter we lived there. A heavy snowstorm had inspired our younger kids to bundle up and build a snowman in our backyard. Midway into their creative project, our house was surrounded by policemen with guns at the ready, looking for the masked gunmen she had reported. She had misinterpreted the kids ski masks they wore to protect their faces from the cold.

And every spring we witnessed the result of their winter's inebriation, a noisy event that occurred when she had a pickup truck pull around to the back of the house so they could throw tons of whiskey bottles down into the bed of the truck from their third floor apartment. It was evidently her attempt at spring housecleaning.

So, because of the bizarre behavior of these particular tenants, we cautioned Susan to insist that they be gone from the premises before she closed on the deal. It was good that she did that. When the owner made attempts to visit them to terminate their thirty-day lease, he was met at the top of the stairs by the elderly gentleman, who was aiming a shotgun at him. The owner wisely retreated. Later we learned that instead of going the legal route to get them out, he found another apartment for them to live in and hired a firm to move them.

In May, Susan officially owned the house, and some of us worked hard to clean it up so that more people from The Lord's Delight could live there. The third floor was so filthy that we had to practically gut it and start over. In the midst of the clean-up, we got up one Tuesday morning and found a note from our 20-year-old son, Michael, telling us to give certain of his belongings to some of his siblings. Stunned and filled with dread, we searched all through the house but didn't find him.

After a careful check of his belongings we could find nothing missing, but we did discover some writings which indicated that he was very depressed. Such a gentle, quiet, young man was Michael, and he was very much loved, but none of us had a clue as to where he had gone or why. Michael had seemed to be his usual normal self at our household meeting the night before, but depression is a sneaky and dangerous illness, and often not apparent to others. We were very afraid.

Our Tom started checking the airport, bus depot and train station to see if anyone resembling Mike had been there. I called the prayer chain for help but couldn't thing of anything else to do. The helplessness we felt was terrible. When your child hurts you want to *do* something! You *need* to do something!

My mind was racing with recriminations. "Was I so busy helping others that I neglected my own child? Why is it we can help other people and we can't even help our own son? Why didn't I sense that Michael was struggling so? I thought I was being led by your Spirit, God. Why didn't you alert me to this danger he was in?" All through that day and night, I was terrified! Praying for God to protect him, calling on all the saints and angels to surround him, I was appalled with my powerlessness to help this dear son whom I loved so fiercely.

How we thanked God profusely later the next day when Michael phoned from a gas station somewhere in central Indiana! I told him how distraught we all were; how much we loved him; how his father was driving around like a madman trying to find him. He sounded pretty miserable, but promised he would wait where he was, until Bill could reach him and bring him home.

Later when Michael was safely back home, we learned that he was so depressed he had stopped going to classes at MSU early in the year, and simply went out of the house each morning as if he were going there but spent all his time in the library instead of going to classes. When he had left our house that Tuesday, he had set out walking and hitch-hiking, taking nothing with him except his Bible. After spending the night out in the pouring rain, he finally was so exhausted he called us.

In my daily prayers I thanked God for watching over Michael, asking him to heal his spirit and build him up as only he can do. Throughout those days in May my thoughts went frequently to Michael and his sadness. Although we asked him to seek professional help, he declined to do so. Emotional pain can be excruciating, especially with no distraction from it. He found work with a builder that filled long hours every day and he was a big help as we moved into another phase of fixing up our house.

The transformation of the house moved to the outside with a vengeance once winter was over. Mike Walker, another community member, got us a good deal on some narrow, slate-blue aluminum siding. He also arranged for the loan of metal pipe scaffolding for several months as we refurbished our grand dame of a house, with many of us working throughout the summer whenever we could. We first used hammers and chisels to dislodge all of the stucco from the exterior, and the day finally arrived when she stood there with her lath fully exposed.

You had to admire the dignified look of her, even when she was naked as a jay-bird. With George and Charlie guiding us and urging us on, we proceeded to drill holes and blow her full of insulation. It was only then, when she was full of her underwear, that we were able to dress her with the siding. We had already painted the exterior doors cherry red and given all the trim and window frames a fresh coat of white paint, so we were quite pleased with the result of our months of endeavor.

I was thankful, too, that none of us had been injured during all the time we amateurs spent climbing around on ladders and scaffold. We would sometimes be so weary it was easy to make silly mistakes. I remember climbing down the ladder one evening, when a can of putty I had forgotten on the top step, glanced off the side of my head on its way down to the ground. It just might have knocked some sense into me, but I was glad it hadn't hit squarely on the top of my head.

During the months that George and Polly lived with us that year, it was apparent that they were extremely devoted to each other; a graphic contrast to the relationship between Bill and me. One afternoon when Bill and I were talking with them, the subject of my underlying sadness came up and they asked if they could pray over me for healing of memories. I assented and they began to pray. Soon I felt like I was in my father's bookkeeper's office, hidden between the open door and the wall. I was a young child. I heard the bookkeeper telling someone, "Marge and Bill are so attractive I don't know how they ever managed to have a kid as ugly as that Laurie. It's a shame, really. One of those kids only a mother can love." Hearing the words, I deduced that nobody could possibly love me except my parents.

Later as I talked about it with Polly, George and Bill, I recognized that the scene may have never taken place, but it surely could account for the reason I've felt all my life that no one could possibly love me except my parents. We prayed for me to be healed of that self-image, but I still have times when those feelings come back. Then I have to take my own advice and turn my attention from myself onto the Lord and his known love for me.

On July 18, 1978 we received word that Bill's father had died, so we gathered the children and went to St. Louis to honor him for the last time. He had suffered a series of small strokes a few years previously, which had resulted in aphasia, and we had agonized with him as he had struggled to communicate with us during the last time he had been able to visit us. He was eighty-five years old when he died, and had experienced a good life, so all of us at the wake celebrated the man he had been, appreciating how good it was to be part of his family system.

He had always been kind to me and I hold all of his family very dear. We enjoyed visiting with all of Bill's siblings and their children as we gathered for the wake. And afterward, when everyone had left except family members, Bill abruptly announced that our family would sing for them. We were all startled, and I thought this was all very awkward, wondering what had come over him. But when he drew the children and I together and asked us to sing "Hallelujah, my Father" with him, we understood. We had sung that hymn together for years and immediately complied, blending our four-part harmony in such a lovely way that everyone was in tears. My husband had certainly been led by the Spirit at that moment.

One of our first Saturday household days that summer was devoted to an in-house talent show. After much hustle and bustle, as individuals organized themselves into entertainment units or polished special individual talents, the evening was devoted to enjoying each others' efforts.

Exposing hitherto unknown gifts in household members, Susan, known to be very introverted, wowed us with her rendition of a western ballad. Other entertainment included joke monologues, mime, musical instrument performances, poetry recitation, and a mouth-to-mouth resuscitation demonstration by Elizabeth. From the children to the eldest member of the household, we all participated and enjoyed each others' antics. A skit depicting some of the many mix-ups encountered when answering the telephones in our kitchen, brought down the house!

Everybody could have told a personal anecdote about household communication!

Communication

There is a plethora of communication information available these days, and many self-help books spur us on to better dialogue with one another. Since our house had so many more people than most, it stands to reason we had more opportunities for misunderstandings, so I put my organizational skills to work to try to minimize the confusion.

On one of the kitchen walls, we installed a three-by-five-foot bulletin board. Across the top we stapled the picture of each person in the house and put their name under it. At our household meeting each Monday night, I would assign duties for the week to each person and post the assigned duties in written form under the appropriate picture for all the world to see.

So if you found the kitchen trash overflowing and wanted to do something about it, you could look on the bulletin board and see whose job it was to empty the container. Then you might try to find that person and give them the opportunity to perform their designated duty or you might decide that it was just easier to serve your brothers and sisters by emptying it yourself. (Needless to say, there were plenty of opportunities to serve!) Or, if you were tired and cranky, you might decide to do nothing.

Our bulletin board was like any other, in that important messages under appropriate names were but a small percentage of the clutter. On any given day it might be filled up with things like it was one day when I made note of this inventory: a red mitten, cents-off coupons for pizza, a thank-you note to the whole household, Campbell soup labels for our school kids who were collecting them for a project, a comic strip thought relevant to someone else in the household, a wedding invitation, a white gym sock that had been mixed up with somebody else's laundry, an advertisement touting upcoming stock car races, and a bracelet found under a living room chair. To discover the smiling faces at the top, I regularly had to clear off and discard outdated material.

We had two private telephone lines to the house and seven telephones scattered throughout the four floors. Two wall phones hung side-by-side next to the kitchen bulletin board. Ideally, phone messages could be taken on one of those phones, written on a memo pad located next to the phones, and then transferred to the spot under the picture of whomever was called. However, if you answered a phone on the third floor and had no paper handy to write on, it was quite possible your message never made it to the bulletin board. Also, some people seldom looked under their name for messages, and, therefore, didn't receive them promptly. No system works perfectly when people are involved.

My attempts to insure that each household member paid for their long distance telephone calls usually fell short of 100% compliance. By stapling a large piece of paper next to the kitchen phones, with headings that read: Date, Name, City, Number, I tried to make it easy for people to be responsible for their charges. People making long-distance calls were supposed to record those calls on the paper when they made them.

It quickly became apparent that this communication attempt was really a monthly puzzle, challenging my wits and my patience. And since our phone bill was in the neighborhood of $200 every month, I was playing for high stakes! Without fail, the system I had devised broke down, and calls turned up on the bill that had not been noted on the piece of paper. Not only were they not on the list, they were not in the memory of anyone in the household either! I had to resort to calling the phone company for help in tracking down the guilty parties, and from time to time, I threatened to add a charge for my tracking services to anyone who had to be tracked. However, I realized that we're all forgetful at times and this inconvenience was simply part of the cost of living the way we did.

Sometimes we experienced communication problems that were not mechanical. Knowing that Satan would want to disrupt the redeeming work God was doing in our midst, it made sense to me that he was at the bottom of some of the things that happened.

An example of that occurred, once, when we were trying to encourage a very shy newcomer to do things with other people in the household. For the first few weeks with us, she had been too scared to respond positively when she was invited to go shopping or to a movie with some of the other women in the house. Then, one morning as I was talking to her about her reluctance to socialize, she agreed to go to a shopping mall later in the day with two of the other women and me. I informed the other two that she would be going with us, and they were glad that she was finally attempting to come out of her shell.

And yet, when it came time to go, all three of us forgot that she was coming with us and left without her! We had only gone a few blocks when we realized the fact, horrified at what we had done! How could all three of us have forgotten her, when we had tried so hard for so long to get her to do something with us? We rushed back to the house and found her crying in her room.

In spite of explaining to her that things like this had happened before, and who we suspected was behind it, we had to practically physically drag her from her room. and then double our efforts to counteract that hurtful experience, with many more invitations and lots of patience.

We tried not to give undue attention to the Evil One, but we knew that the Bible does warn us about spiritual warfare. Words spoken and not heard, words not spoken but assumed, messages sent and not received; scowls and smiles misinterpreted—all these can provoke misunderstandings in any relationship, unless the parties know each other so well that they don't misinterpret things. With people moving in and out so often, there were usually at least some people in our household who hardly knew one another, and others had relationship problems before they came. They expected to be offended or neglected so we provided Satan with fertile ground for raising havoc.

Our best defense was being obedient to God's word regarding misunderstandings, and double checking when something that happened didn't add up. As we had done with our children, and from the earliest days of extended-family living, we continued to strongly urge people to do the Matthew 18:15 thing: if you're upset with someone, for heaven's sake go talk to them!

So many misunderstandings were cleared up when one of the persons involved took the initiative to talk to the other about it. I have to admit, though, that it doesn't always bring about reconciliation, as was the case whenever I approached Bill. Although he said he was sorry a few times, when I told him of my distress because of something he had said or done, he still usually reacted in anger or just walked away.

The 16th verse of Matthew 18, says to go bring another person with you to talk to your brother if he won't listen to you. But because Bill and I were in leadership, I didn't feel like I could do that. However, it was apparent to Sandy Lee, after living with us for several years, that we had a problem which needed to be solved, so she talked to Bill about it. But she didn't get anywhere either. Maria Post and her husband spent a lot of time with us and were also concerned about our marital relationship, so they and Sandy Lee asked Father Osborn to come to the house and sit down with all of us one evening. They were following the advice of Matthew 15:17, which says that if he still ignores the problem, take it to the church.

The evening's meeting was very uncomfortable for all of us, and bore no discernable good fruit. As each person expressed to Bill their concerns about our relationship, and I reiterated my need for him to relate to me more personably, he became intractable. He stuck to his stance that all this intimacy and romantic love stuff was Hollywood junk. Finally, Father Osborn appealed to Bill one last time, saying, "Christ described his desire for intimacy with each of us by comparing it to the intimacy between a man and woman in marriage. He chose that allegory, because he knew people would understand what he meant." Bill couldn't find anything to say to refute that so he simply clammed up and wouldn't say anything more. With that, our meeting broke up and all we could do was get back on our knees and continue to pray.

When we went into that meeting with Father Osborn, I hadn't had high expectations for a breakthrough, so I wasn't surprised when Bill went into his mode of punishing me with silence for awhile afterward. I turned again to the Lord for comfort, distracting myself, renewing my courage, and driving resentment far away from me the way the book of Sirach says in Chapter 30, Verse 23, and I kept myself occupied with the affairs of the household and the community.

No matter how much emotional pain I experienced because of my marriage, though, I continued to expect God to heal it. Part of that expectation was my natural optimism and the other was my knowledge that God still does perform miracles in our midst. And there were times when we worked together well, productive times that would give me reason to hope.

Ironically, we were still counseling couples who came to us for advice because they were having marital problems. Certainly communication is one of the biggest problems in that relationship. Usually we were able to help couples by focusing on those things which we knew were important in any relationship. Since the basic teachings of Jesus tell us to love one another, we could remind these couples of those specific things which would bring about change for the better, if they would put them into practice. I never could figure out why Bill would counsel others but wasn't willing to do anything for our own marriage.

We had gone to seminars, workshops and conferences that had taught about ways to communicate better in relationships, but Bill couldn't seem to get past merely analyzing the information he was given there. A few things did happen though, which gave me a glimmer of hope. Fresh from a seminar on marriage communication, Sandy Lee talked Bill into getting me a present for Christmas. He actually picked out an attractive blouse for me and I enthusiastically expressed my pleasure and thanks for the gift, when I received it. He told me he had carefully looked at my wardrobe to see what kind of things I liked, and seemed pleased with himself and the result of his efforts. Now *that* was really an exciting Christmas for me!

There was also another time that Bill applied himself to doing something for me. One Valentine's Day he was walking by a nearby florist shop, and he decided to take Sandy Lee's advice by getting some flowers for me. He bought a few roses and walked on home with them, telling himself, "This is all pretty silly. It's just a ruse by florists to make a ton of money. I certainly can't imagine getting all excited if someone gave me roses!"

When he came in the front door, he saw Anne-Marie in the dining room and thought, "Gee, maybe she would like a rose!" So he gave her one and she seemed very pleased. He learned that I was doing something on the third floor, so he started up the stairs. There he ran into one of the women who lived with us and he thought, "Maybe she'd like a rose too." So he gave her one. She, too, was pleased with the attention. He stopped in Julie's room on second floor to give her one and then ran into a few more of the women, so by the time he got to me, he was out of roses.

He seemed amazed at the reaction he got as he kept giving roses to the various women he encountered. "I just don't understand it," he mused, as he explained to me what had happened. "It's a beautiful reminder that you were thoughtful of them," I explained to him, "and I appreciate the thought, even though I didn't get any roses. I guess this is one of those ways in which women think differently than men." And even though I was encouraged by his gesture, I was still ornery enough to be disappointed when he didn't go back to the flower shop to get me a rose of my own. I had so much yet to learn about acceptance and letting go of what I thought was important. The next twelve months were rife with roller coaster life-changing moments.

Fallout and Fun in 1979

During the early months of 1979, four young men had moved in. Some of them were occupying the two bedrooms on the third floor of our house and we also rented the third floor of Susan's house, which provided two bedrooms, a bath and a living room for two of our sons and two men from our household. Maria and David Post had sold their house and were now living with their children on the first and second floors of the north side of Susan's house. Clark and Carolyn Broadbent, who had also sold their house to join the community on our street, were living with their children on the south side of the first two floors. By the summer of 1979 there were twenty-five of us living together as a household.

Then an upsetting incident occurred which brought home to me, again, how precarious a path we trod, living our unorthodox life. Tough times were not necessarily easier just because we knew that going through difficulties from time to time is to be expected in the Christian walk.

The Broadbents sent a hurried message, one day, for everyone in the Lords's Delight Community to assemble at their apartment. Once gathered there, they told all of us that they were uncomfortable with Bill's leadership. They said it made them feel like we were a cult, so they were leaving Sycamore Street and the community.

I felt a terrible sense of rejection, again, as I stood against a wall in their dining room, listening to them voicing their fears and urging others to leave the community also. Intellectually, I reminded myself that I knew that their parents were upset about them being part of the community, and that they might be overreacting to the horrific Jonestown massacre, but I felt terrible that these people whom I had grown to love dearly, would put being associated with us in the same light.

Although some of the other community members tried to reason with them, I understood that they needed to go, so I wished them well as the meeting concluded. Some of the others who were there attempted to comfort us, but when I went back to our house I went up to our bedroom and had a good cry. We had tried very hard to be on guard against cult-type stuff, especially me, because of my horrible experience at Herbert's place. I had to really struggle to come to a place of peace again and put the incident behind me.

We had encountered that "fear of us being a cult" attitude, once before, when a young woman living with us called her father and asked him to come and rescue her. This occurred a few days after she had called us and asked us to come and get her from a fraternity house at Michigan State, where she had spent the night. Since we had spent the night worrying where she was, we asked her, specifically, not to do that again, and, also, to keep us apprized of her whereabouts when she left the house. I guess she didn't want to be restricted that way.

As her father observed household members helping to carry her belongings to his car, he could quickly see that she did not need rescuing, and he obviously was not thrilled to have to come and get her. We were relieved to have him collect her and move her on to some other place and someone else's responsibility.

Sometimes, we were questioned about how we handled sexual activity in the household. I always responded, "There is no inappropriate sexual activity in our midst, if that is what you mean." Many people would scoff at such a reply and simple refuse to believe me. But it was really true. We all related to each other as brothers and sisters, except for those of us who were relating to our spouses.

We were aware that there were some people who came to live with us because they had a romantic attraction toward someone already in the household. That didn't necessarily disqualify them from living with us. God can be pretty tricky. Sometimes I think he used that attraction to get them to an environment where they could see that there was more to life than sexual fulfillment. And certainly there were some cases of sexual attraction between certain household members, but it didn't mean the attraction needed to take priority in the persons' lives at that time. We had two similar situations in 1979, but they each ended differently.

When we learned that a fairly new household member, Kevin, was attempting to get a romantic relationship going with Susan, we knew things about each of them that waved a red flag, so we did some serious talking with each of them for a couple of days. Susan saw the wisdom of keeping her distance, but Kevin was not so agreeable. We finally had to tell him that he would have to leave if he insisted on continuing to relate to her in a romantic way, and he did leave.

In the other situation, Dick, a member of the Spirit of Christ Fellowship, had moved in with us early in the year. He was such a free spirit that he felt stifled having to be at the dinner table regularly, but he loved the fellowship of so many kindred spirits and he truly had a heart for the Lord. His contributions to the musical component of our household were considerable, since he wrote music, as well as playing the guitar and singing, so we enjoyed his presence with us.

After he had been with us for a few months, Jody, one of the women in our household, sat down with me one day, wanting to talk about the more than sisterly feelings she was having for Dick. She said she was concerned about dealing with those feelings in the right way, so we prayed that God would remove her attraction to Dick if it was not appropriate. A short time later, Dick told Bill he was interested in marrying Jody and he wanted to court her if she would be willing.

We advised them to start spending time together exploring their relationship in appropriate ways, and that same night, when Bill asked during the dinner table if anyone knew of a romantic relationship going on in the household, nobody had a clue except Amy, who blurted out, "Jody and Dick?" Amid much laughter we expressed our hope that everyone would be respectful and give them a bit of space.

Of course there were a number of incidences of household members getting romantically interested in people outside of the household. There were thoughtful discussions about what to look for in a spouse, and the whole marriage preparation arena. One scripture we brought people's attention to was from the book, "Song of Songs" which exhorts us to not stir up love before its own time.

Our children had not been allowed to date until they were sixteen, and then only in group activities. We counseled them not to get into a steady relationship until they were ready to marry. This is what we taught in the household also. We encouraged the single ones to do things in groups until they were ready emotionally and financially to marry. One of the women gave a testimony at one of our community meetings, telling about a serious relationship she had been in five years previously which didn't end in marriage as she had hoped. She had just learned that the man she had loved had married someone else and she was still struggling to deal with it. The pain of a broken relationship can do a lot of damage and last a very long time.

As Jody and Dick started going together, some of the other household members observed the courtship process with somewhat ambivalent feelings. Many of them felt the lack of that kind of relationship in their own lives and had to struggle with feelings of sadness for a time. But we were all happy for them, and celebrated their official engagement that fall.

In the meantime, a Hogan family reunion occurred late in July at Fairfield Glade, a resort situated halfway between Knoxville and Nashville, Tennessee. It had been many years since all of Marge and Bill Hogan's progeny had been in the same place at the same time. Bill had announced on July 9th that he would withdraw from all of us for a month to seek the Lord so he wouldn't be going with us, but the rest of us awaited the reunion with great anticipation. Tom, Mike, Paul and I could all drive our bus so we headed out, looking forward to seeing Joe, who was joining us there from Texas.

And we did have a wonderful four days, staying in some condos my parents had leased for the occasion, playing lots of tennis, singing all the old favorite songs, eating, playing games, eating some more, and just visiting up a storm with each other. Anne-Marie had spiked a high fever while we were there, necessitating a trip to a health clinic when we couldn't get it down without an antibiotic, but she was the only physical casualty that long weekend.

Early on the morning of the day we had to leave, we Downses hugged everybody for the last time, boarded our bus and started for Michigan. But before we had even gone a mile, the engine sputtered and died. Fortunately we were going down a hill when the engine quit and there was a gas station at the bottom of the hill, so we coasted into it to find out what was wrong. Remembering how my dad had often voiced his dread that any of us might have car trouble away from home and get cheated by an unscrupulous repair guy, we thought of that possibility. We were in the midst of nowhere, so it was definitely a time to pray for the motor to be healed.

Paul had recently started working on the line at Oldsmobile, so he got out to take a look under the hood, and the station proprietor (later identified as Hank) came out to see what the trouble was. Paul said it was obvious to both of them, that the fuel pump had gone bad. Hank didn't have a fuel pump to replace it, but offered to drive Paul into Knoxville to see if they could find one. And, though it was not exactly the kind of auto part you'd find easily, the first place they walked into had only three fuel pumps on its dusty shelf, and one of them was the pump we needed. Paul could hardly believe it!

And although he had expected to be charged an arm and a leg for it, the price was only $17.95, so he came back to the bus in good cheer with expectations of us soon being on our way. In the meantime, the rest of us had been saying goodbye again and again as each family group leaving caught up with us and stopped to see if we needed help.

Even after the fuel pump was installed, though, the bus didn't start, so Hank called another guy over to work on it with him. I've always heard that two heads are better than one, and with Paul hanging in there, we now had three men searching for the reason that the engine still wouldn't start. When we told Hank that Bill had worked on the engine for years, he finally called him for advice.

"Dang, Bill," I heard him say, "We cain't get no fire to the coil!" Bill did not know what to tell them so they continued to work until evening, when they finally discovered that the problem was a $2.00 capacitor that had evidently blown at the same time the fuel pump failed.

Hank felt really bad that it had taken them so long to get us on our way, and apologized profusely for delaying us. We were amazed by his kindness and concern, and we thought the $20 he asked for payment was way too low, so Paul slipped him another $20 as we left again for home. We felt that God had taken care of us very well in spite of the delay.

As we took turns driving through the night in order to get my sons to work on time the next morning, they replayed favorite scenarios from the last four days of cousinhood. High on the enjoyment scale was the fun our 16-year-old David had playing tennis with his cousin, Bill. Those two were very much alike and enjoyed a similar sense of humor which made it fun for any of us who were around them.

It had been a very happy time for me, with no reminder of sadness to mar the time we had together. For me it was good that Bill had not come. I had just basked in the love around me and hadn't had to worry about keeping him happy. What a good thing that I had stored up lots of happiness to give me strength during the next few months, when I would be tossed around as if in a whirlwind.

God's Tender Mercies

Back home again, thoughts were beginning to turn to the start of the school year, only a month away. August was in the process of dragging the summer to a halt as I climbed the stairs to our third floor prayer room to begin my usual quiet time with the Lord on the morning of the twenty-third. I was sitting at a desk before a window in the tiny room with only a bookcase full of books for company. After my usual time of intercession I entered into a time spent in adoration. A bit later, I felt a pang of longing that caused me to cry out, "Lord, I really want to hear from you today. Please speak to me, Lord!"

Swiftly, his response came piercing through my heart: "I will always be with you." It caught me off guard. I said, "I know that. You are always faithful to me. Why are you telling me that again?" And the Lord answered me, "Because you need to hear it." The same phrase kept coming over and over. "I will always be with you. I will always be with you." Finally it dawned on me. I understood that a hard time was coming and God wanted me to remember, then, what he was telling me now. He would be with me.

Whenever I receive a word from the Lord, I always sense that there's a much deeper meaning than I can understand or convey with mere words. And as I meditated on those words, I was not reassured. I felt scared.

After dinner that night, I shared this episode with the whole household during our prayer time together. Bill wondered if it meant that we would soon be under some kind of attack, because no matter whatever he had opened to in the Bible lately, he keep reading about how God delivers us from our enemies. He said it had puzzled him, because he wasn't conscious of anybody out to get him. So we just prayed that I would remain peaceful, and eventually, I really didn't have any anxiety about the whole thing; I just filed it away somewhere in the back of my mind and forgot about it. Our four youngest children were still home all of September because of a teachers' strike, so my days remained very busy, with no time for anxious thoughts about the future.

On a Thursday, the 4th of October, David and I drove to an appointment with Dr. Lanny Johnson, an orthopaedic physician in East Lansing. I had taken him to our family physician, Dr. McElmurray when he first complained of his knee hurting in June, and Dr. McElmurray thought it was probably tendinitis, aggravated by daily tennis playing. He had mentioned that we could x-ray it, but he expected the pain would go away if David just gave it a rest for a couple of weeks. Then, of course, he still had a high school tennis tournament to play in, so he kept on playing until we got back from the reunion.

It wasn't any better by mid-August, though, so I called Dr. McElmurray back and he said we probably should have an orthopaedic doctor look at it. I decided to take David to Dr. Johnson because he had a national reputation for excellence, and, also, I knew that he was a devout Christian. I was a little concerned when the soonest his office could give us an appointment was six weeks away, but not unduly concerned.

Meanwhile, because of the teachers' strike, David wasn't in school so he was able to lead a fairly quiet life with his only regularly scheduled activity being his work at the neighborhood dime store. He found he was more comfortable when he tightly bound his leg with an ace bandage, so he took to wearing one constantly. We had been praying over him at our household prayer time every once in a while but we didn't have the sense that anything was drastically wrong. Our friend, Maria, mentioned that she had once had to have an operation for torn cartilage in her knee, so I had that possibility in mind as we drove to see Dr. Johnson.

After he examined David, they went off down the hall for an x-ray. While they were gone I was thinking how good it would be to know what was wrong and get it taken care of. David came back and had just sat down beside me, when a nurse popped her head in the door and said that the doctor wanted another x-ray, so he left the room again. As I waited, I felt irritated about the casual attitude doctors seem to have about x-rays, knowing there was another school of thought that said they could be dangerous, but still no sense of apprehension had touched me.

However, I reacted like I'd been hit with a ton of bricks when David came back to the examining room and told me they had x-rayed his chest. "Mom why would they x-ray my chest when it's my knee that hurts?" Why indeed!

Then Dr. Johnson arrived with the x-rays, and putting one of them in a viewer so we could see it, he said, "This is your left femur, David. You thought there was something the matter with your knee, but it isn't your knee that's injured; it's your femur. Do you see this hole here?" We got up and peered at the screen. I raised my finger and tentatively pointed at a white area near the knee end of his femur.

"Do you mean that this spot here, is a hole in his bone?" He nodded, and said,

"Yes, and here and here and here," as he moved his finger up the bone toward the hip, indicating numerous smaller areas.

I tried to see what he was talking about, but all I could really see was a spot the size of a golf ball at the end of David's femur. I was beginning to feel sick at heart, but I tried to stay calm, glancing from time to time at David, wondering what he was thinking.

"What do you think might be causing the holes?"

"It has to be either a tumor or a raging infection." Not wanting to stop and think, I poured out my next question,

"How do we find out what it is?"

"I'm going to order some blood tests. I'll be in a conference all day tomorrow, but I'll call when I get back to my office and see the results, around 5:00.

Subdued, David and I got into our car and headed for the laboratory where the blood tests were to be done. "You're probably going to have to think in terms of being off your feet for awhile," I said, and then I told him about the bone disease which had necessitated me being on crutches for three months and having my leg in a cast, when I was twelve.

All the time I was talking to him, I was trying to push to the back of my mind, the memory of a friend who had a leg amputated because of cancer when we were in high school, but, then, died when we were Seniors. I also was remembering another friend who had died of bone cancer recently. I had helped care for her during the final months of her life as she suffered terrible pain. I think I managed to stay pretty calm on the outside while he had the blood tests and we came on home. Then I phoned next door to Maria and asked her to call the whole prayer community through our phone chain, so that people could start interceding for David to be healed.

Once that was in motion, I went on up to the third floor prayer room and sat down to pray. I remembered sensing back in August when God told me he would always be with me, that a hard time was coming, and I knew that the hard time was here. I cried out, "Lord, I can't even pray! I'm too upset! My mind is shooting off in sixty directions! You've got to help me, Lord!" For want of something tangible to do, I randomly opened up my Bible to Luke 9:37 and started to read.

Then I felt the shock of recognition and a surge of hope. This was the same passage I had read when David was ten and hospitalized with severe stomach pain! The passage which told of a man's son being attacked by Satan and thrown into convulsions! The story of Jesus rebuking a spirit and healing the boy!

Remembering, that on that occasion, we had rebuked Satan and told him to leave David alone, I felt that God was saying to pray rebuking the Evil One, and

David would be healed just like he was before. I had to hang on to this. I needed to listen to what God was telling me and not worry about the circumstances that looked so scary. Bill had been sleeping, but when he awoke I told him all that had happened and we clung to each other, with panic and hope vying for first place in my emotions. Distraught, Bill went off to pray.

I scarcely slept Thursday night—waves of panic kept rolling over me. I'd concentrate on the fact that the Lord was helping us to understand that he was with us in a special way, and feel peace for a few minutes. Then another wave of panic would come. I knew that God could heal David miraculously but I also knew that might not happen. I'd had lots of experience with people who claimed that God healed them miraculously, when they weren't healed at all. I didn't want to misinterpret what God was saying to us. In spite of God's word to us, I was afraid to presume that David would be healed.

Friday was a long day. Our emotions were very strained as we all struggled to absorb what was happening, and pleaded with God to intervene on David's behalf. He was an unusually neat kid with a joyous sense of humor and a keen mind. He was much loved. Playing the drums in our prayer group music ministry and also with the Christian music group, "The Light," he was well known in our area, so as news of his illness spread, we kept getting phone calls from people who said they were praying for him. Everybody was trying to encourage each other by reminding them of what God was saying, rather than what the circumstances looked like.

Mike Ellis came from his home across the street to tell us that his wife had just phoned him from New York, where she was attending a conference. She said that as she was praying for us, she experienced a mental picture of me crying and the Lord telling me to go back to the scripture he gave me six years ago. She did not understand what that meant when she received it, but I was lifted up with renewed hope.

I thought surely God would not be telling me to pray commanding Satan to leave, if David wasn't going to be okay. I saw that God had given me something concrete to hold on to Thursday and now again on Friday, just as he had promised me in August. He would always be with me. The doctor had not yet called Friday evening as we prayed over David again during our household prayer time, and so eventually we went to bed without hearing from him.

Saturday morning, the adults in our prayer community gathered at our house as previously planned, to paint the house next door, which belonged to other community members. Dr. Johnson called around 10:00, and apologized for not getting back sooner. He said he was sorry to inform us that David's white count was normal, indicating no infection, and all of his blood tests were normal except the one showing a high rate of bone destruction, so his opinion was that David had a tumor. "Frankly," he said, "when I first saw the x-ray of his femur, it looked so bad I had expected it had already spread to other parts of his body. That's why I ordered the x-ray of David's chest. Now, that x-ray looks okay but I want you to bring him the to hospital Monday for a CAT scan of his lungs and then we'll do a full-body scan on Tuesday."

When I could bring myself to speak, I asked him, "What comes next?" He said the tumor might be benign, but there was so much damage to the femur he would rather not tamper with a biopsy here. "What would you do if he were your son, Dr. Johnson?" "If it were my son, I would take him to one of the major cancer treatment centers such as the M.D. Anderson Tumor Institute in Houston, the Mayo Clinic in Rochester or the National Institute of Health in Washington, D.C."

As he said that, I couldn't imagine how we could possibly make a decision about where to go. I told Dr. Johnson how God had been speaking to us about this whole thing, and how I was concerned that we go where the Lord wanted us to go. "I know a bone specialist in Cleveland who is also a Christian, he said. I'll call him to see where he would recommend you to take David." Dr. Johnson called back a few minutes later, saying that the doctor in Cleveland usually sent his patients to Washington or Houston.

Meanwhile, I had talked to my sister, Nancy, who is a nurse. She wanted us to bring David to Sloan-Kettering in New York so we could stay with her family there and receive support from them through whatever lay ahead. My parents were at their condo in Arkansas so I had left a message for them. They got through to us on Saturday, assuring me that they would be on their knees praying, as they had so many times through the years of raising a big family.

It seemed like we were on the telephone all day. In the midst of all the chaos, a new household member, David Connelly, arrived with his parents, and something akin to a fleeting foreboding, crossed my mind as I prepared to welcome another David into my home and my heart.

Bill and I kept bumping into one another, clinging for a minute and wandering on. We were both exhausted. At one point, he said, "Maybe we should go to Washington. I might be able to get a job at the Smithsonian again, and move the rest of the family there too." It upset me to hear him voice long-term, practical scenarios. Neither of us was thinking very clearly. It's crazy, the thoughts that go around in your mind when you're upset. Before we let our fears escalate into a fight, we recognized that Satan would love getting us upset with one another, so we talked about that danger and were alert for it from then on. The anger he had displayed toward me from time to time was no where evident now.

One of the phone calls I made Saturday morning after we heard from the doctor, was to the priests of our cathedral parish. They knew us well and David served there as an altar boy. I got hold of Father Murray, who said they would pray, and would also start asking for prayers at all the Masses. We learned that people who had signed up for the round-the-clock, phone prayer chain, were praying in half hour increments and would then call the next person on the list to tell them what they had gleaned from their time of intercession. These prayer warriors would continue their intense prayer effort as long as needed, and they kept us informed as to what they were hearing from the Lord.

Sandy Lee was reading from Jay Adam's book, *Competent to Counsel*, when a scripture passage he quoted leaped out at her, Heb. 12:12-13: *So strengthen your drooping hands and your weak knees. Make straight the paths you walk on, that your halting limb may not be dislocated but healed.* The thing that especially blew her mind, was what appeared to be a misprint; every version of that scripture we've ever seen, reads "halting *limbs*," not "halting *limb*."

When she told us about this, we accepted it as encouragement from the Lord, so Bill suggested to David that he go to receive the Sacrament of Reconciliation (Confession) as part of "making straight the paths." We had made arrangements for Fr. Murray to anoint David with oil for healing after noon Mass on Sunday, so The Sacrament of Reconciliation would be good preparation for that. I joined David after Bill left for work that afternoon, and we walked the three blocks to the cathedral to meet with Fr. Murray for confession.

While David was in the confessional with him, I opened my Bible to read at a place where I was systematically reading through the Old Testament, II Samuel 2:1*: After this David inquired of the Lord, "Shall we go up into one of the cities of Judah?" The Lord replied to him, "Yes." Then David asked, "Where shall I go?" He replied, "To Hebron."*

My spirit quickened as I read this, since I had wondered how we would ever figure out where God wanted us to take David for treatment. I felt the Lord was saying, "Here I am again, right here with you as I promised. You are going to another city as part of my plan for you, and I will tell you where to go."

As David and I left the cathedral, I shared with him how the Lord had spoken to us again, so we hurried home to get out the Bible commentary to see what "Hebron" meant. It meant "friend of God," so we figured, since it didn't fit any of the cities suggested to us, maybe there would be a Dr. Hebron somewhere that could help him. And so we waited and prayed for more direction.

I had a terrible time emotionally at noon Mass that Sunday, as David went limping up the aisle in procession to serve at the altar. He seemed so vulnerable. The whole church prayed for him during that Mass, and after receiving the Sacrament of the Anointing of the Sick, he quietly retired to his room. The whole household was very subdued that afternoon.

Margaret Shaver was there as the Lord's Delight Community gathered for our weekly prayer meeting in our living room Sunday night. She was one of Gerry and Dick's children whom we'd known since she was a little girl. As we were praying over David this time, she spoke out in prophecy, "This illness will not end in death but will give glory to God." How I wanted to believe that her prophecy was true! Because we are human we sometimes think we are hearing words from God which are only our wishful thinking, and although I knew Margaret to be a very solid Christian, I was almost afraid to believe those words, for fear I would later be disappointed.

The school strike was now over, so the rest of the household went off to jobs and school as David and I headed for Ingham Medical Hospital for a lung scan to see if there was any sign of cancer there. Dr. Johnson came looking for me in the waiting room to see how things were going for us. He said that he and his wife were praying together every morning for David, and he expected that we would know where to go for treatment when the time came to make the decision. After the lung scan, I took David to Sexton High School. There, chaos reigned in the gym, as 600 kids were all trying to register for classes at the same time. I found his counselor, and when I explained David's situation to her, her face crumpled in sorrow. She said she'd go to bat for David to get him registered quickly so I left him in capable hands and went home.

I had been thinking about the "friend of God" translation of "Hebron" and what it might mean. Bill still had contact with a few entomologists at the Smithsonian Institute in Washington, D.C., but we had no real friends there. We knew no one near the Mayo Clinic. But I had visited a community at the Church of the Redeemer in Houston in 1972, and remembered that they were a strong body of believers, so I decided to call them.

I talked to their guest-master, explaining David's situation and our dilemma about knowing where to go for treatment. I told him that we had a support system waiting for us in New York, but we wondered if there might be any similar help for us in Houston. "You have many brothers and sisters in the Lord here who will help you if you decide to come here," he assured me. "You can stay with a family in the community, they can provide transportation back and forth to the hospital and they will pray with you."

Monday night Nancy called from New York. "Go to Houston," she said. After she had checked with medical personnel she knew there, it was recommended that we go to M.D. Anderson Tumor Institute in Houston. God's direction was mercifully clear. It was a relief to have the decision made with such a definite sense of God leading us. We would go to Houston to whatever purpose God had for us there.

We tried to keep the focus of our minds on what God was saying to us and the excitement he was generating with his direction, but the panicky feelings were still overwhelming at times. Sometimes I felt literally physically supported by the prayers of all the people I knew were praying for us. I couldn't do much for myself; I really needed the prayers of other Christians who cared about us. Sometimes I would stop and picture one of them on their knees, especially some of them whom I knew were real prayer warriors, and that would comfort me.

Another source of comfort was a scripture passage that Faye had put to music in three-part harmony a couple of weeks before this problem with David came to light. *Trust in the Lord with all your heart and lean not on your own understanding. In all your ways acknowledge him and he will make your paths straight." (Prov. 3: 5-6)*

We had been singing it constantly, since it just would not leave our minds and hearts. I had been asking the Lord how to pray, since I couldn't just keep rebuking Satan all day. And I remembered how effective our prayer is when we pray with the gift of tongues. Then Mary Jo came over from next door, bringing a scripture from the Lord for us. It was from Romans 8:26-27, and confirmed that we should pray in tongues for David.

On Tuesday, Dr. Johnson talked with a doctor in Houston to arrange for David's appointment there the following Monday. Anxiety reared its ugly head again when we went to the hospital for a bone scan, but then a breakthrough finally came. Dr. Johnson kept popping in and out of the room where David was being scanned, saying first, "His head is clear!" Then, "His shoulders are clear!" When he could report to me with elation that there was no other hot spots on David's body except that femur, my spirits rose. He also said that David's femur was not as hot as they expected it to be from seeing the blood test results. "Keep up the prayers!" he said, "and remember that often tumors are benign."

Tuesday morning, Sandy Lee had read Jonah 2:3-11, during her quiet time, and then Fr. Murray read the same scripture at noon Mass. She heard him explain that the point of the passage was not that Jonah was swallowed by a whale but that God restored him to where he was in the beginning. Sandy Lee felt that God was telling her David would be restored.

Our son, Paul, called from work in the afternoon, all excited, saying that God spoke to him through Zephaniah 3:17-20, telling him David would be healed, especially verse 19, where God talked about the restoration he would give before our very eyes.

After the bone scan was clear, I felt peaceful. I never again succumbed to panic or tears regarding David's condition. I really felt that whatever happened would be all right. I started looking for what God would do through this experience. With Sandy Lee's and Paul's readings about restoration in mind, I looked at what we were all losing, what David was losing that needed restoring. On top of the primary concern—David's health, he would not be able to take driver's training this term at school so that he could have a driver's license, and he was losing a tennis scholarship at a local tennis club that was to have started. He had to resign from his job that had provided his spending money. He would be leaving his friends behind and most of his family when we left for Texas not knowing how long we would be gone. The trip and expenses involved, including the interruption of Bill's salary from his job, would be a loss to us. Michael took a leave from his construction job in order to go with us as part of the support team for David, so he, too, would lose the income he would have earned.

Wednesday morning Dr. Johnson's wife phoned us to tell us that as they were praying for David that morning, the Lord told them to give us $500 to take on the trip. "Even though you have health insurance," she said, "because you are from out of state, you will be required to pay $500 up front which will eventually be repaid to you. Also, a check for that amount will be waiting for you at Dr. Johnson's office when you pick up David's x-rays and blood test results later today."

I was so grateful for their kindness and their interest in our plight. What an unexpected gift showing God's provision! We never did receive a bill from Dr. Johnson. Other gifts of money started coming in and offers of more money if needed. Spirit of Christ Church made arrangements to receive money on our behalf and we were humbled by the generosity of so many people. As we prepared to leave on Friday, Mike and Karon Ellis offered us their van for the trip to Texas so David could travel comfortably.

His Mysterious Ways

God continued to provide encouragement through many scripture passages that I came across during my daily quiet time or received from other people who were praying for David. The 24-hour prayer chain was producing much fruit in comfort to us, and in fostering the sense of community in the participants. Several people spoke to us of their deep awareness of being part of something special as they labored on our behalf. Some of those we had helped in the past, shared how thankful they were to be able to do something for us in return.

And so on Friday, the twelfth of October, we left for Texas in a borrowed van, with peace in our hearts for whatever was to come, Bill, David, Michael and I. We stayed with Bill's mother and sister in St. Louis, the first night of the trip. All of his family there, nourished us with their love and concern.

Sunday night we arrived in Houston, at the home of Mac and Edie McNeill, who were most gracious and loving. We went to The Church of the Redeemer with them, where prayers were offered on David's behalf. Mac and Edie had raised three daughters who were adults living elsewhere now, so, they offered hospitality to others and currently had a young woman living with them who was mentally disturbed. Of course that was not an unusual thing for us, so we were quite comfortable there, sharing extended-household living experiences with each other. Our Michael was glad to lend his carpentry skills to the McNeills, by working with some members of the church who were helping Mac build a new deck at the back of their house.

Our son, Joe, arrived from Austin early on Monday morning, the fifteenth, in time to accompany us to the big hospital complex that is M.D. Anderson Tumor Institute. We were surrounded by caring people who confirmed the fact that the Lord was with us in these unfamiliar surroundings. There were many hours of waiting and filling out papers, more blood tests and x-rays, culminating in a team of five doctors examining David. We were told to come back the next day at 5:00 p.m. for a consultation.

The MacNeills owned a beach cottage on Galveston Island. Since we weren't due back to the hospital until late the next day, they thoughtfully gave us a key and directions to their cottage, where we soaked up the sun and had a lazy time with each other. After enjoying a beautiful night at the beach, keeping the anxiety of the coming consultation at bay for awhile, we were lulled to sleep by the sound of the waves at our door. It was Bill's fifty-third birthday the next day, as we headed back to Houston late in the afternoon to meet with the doctors.

One of them said to us, "We see thousands of tumors every year, and maybe two or three times a year we run into something strange like David's situation, that we can't explain." In spite of scientific tests to the contrary, they had a hunch that his leg problem was not caused by a tumor but by a massive infection—osteomylitis. This usually occurs when there has been an injury to the bone, but sometimes is found where there has been no injury. They had scheduled a biopsy to be done, but it would have to wait until the following Monday, and then they would meet with us the next day with the results of that procedure.

It felt like Bill had received a precious birthday present with that encouraging news, so we left the hospital in a near state of euphoria with thankfulness flooding our hearts. We joyfully called home with the news and, then, with almost a week ahead of us, we left Houston for Austin to stay at Joe's. After the trauma of the past two weeks, this was a blessed oasis of rest and recreation, and catching up on what was happening in Joe's life. The brothers enjoyed being together again adding a sense of normalcy to our days.

Joe came back to Houston with us and we took David to the hospital for the biopsy on Oct. 22nd with light hearts. It was the beginning of a more painful time for David though. He started to run a fever and appear noticeably ill afterwards. When we met with the doctors for the last time they had some interesting things to say. The biopsy did yield white blood cells but they could not get the culture from David's leg to grow anything. They were just referring to his infection as an unknown staph infection. They had done a razor-thin layer by layer scan of his femur so they had a clear picture of what was wrong, but they hadn't gotten all the way to the center so, they told us, they couldn't rule out a tumor under the infection.

They recommended that surgery be done to remove all the infection but it would need to be done in a different hospital nearby. Six weeks of hospitalization would be expected while the wound was left open with antibiotics bathing it continuously as it healed. If a tumor was found during the surgery he would be transferred back to M.D. Anderson.

They said we could consider the possibility of having the surgery done in Lansing but we would need to realize that if they found a tumor under the infection, we would have to airlift him back to Houston under more difficult circumstances than our current trip.

They also told us that the growth plate at the lower end of David's femur had been totally destroyed. so his leg would eventually be shorter than the other, necessitating the need for a built-up shoe on that foot. The damage was considered to be great enough that we should not expect the bone to be completely restored so he would always have to favor that leg. We heard what they said, but I kept remembering the scripture passages that Sandy Lee and Paul had gotten about him being restored.

We opted to go home to Lansing. Although the prediction of difficulties ahead for David might have seemed cause for sorrow, for us, under the circumstances, anything was better than him losing his leg or his life. With love and gratitude we bade farewell to the MacNeills, put Joe on a plane for Austin and drove home.

David had surgery October 30th at Ingham Medical Hospital performed by Dr. Michael Austin, one of Dr. Johnson's associates, since Dr. Johnson was out of the country for awhile. When Dr. Austin finished the surgery and came to talk to us, the most amazing thing he said was, he didn't find any holes in David's bone or infection inside the bone. "I drilled four holes into the center of the bone looking for infection or a tumor, but found none of either. On the other hand, the infection on the outside of the bone was so bad it soon would have burst through the skin."

As in Houston, they were unable to get the specimen of the infectious material removed from David's leg to grow, so it remained an unidentified staph. David endured three painful weeks in the hospital with his wound left open so it would heal from the inside out. The antibiotic IVs were tolerable, but the pouring of Betadine into the wound twice a day was agony for him. One time the nurse who was assisting with the procedure fainted. Although I practically lived at the hospital those three weeks, I never once heard David complain.

He had brought with him, his mascot, a huge stuffed pink panther that he put on the window sill where it was visible from the outside of the hospital, clearly identifying the location of his room. He was in isolation because of the danger of infection, but he was inundated with friends who donned the required sterile garments in order to visit him and cheer him up.

We were thrilled when the healing process was speeded up so he could be home on crutches for a Thanksgiving celebration that included a bunch of relatives from St. Louis and Dayton, who wanted to see for themselves that he was going to be fine again. Through a visiting teacher, he kept up with his studies and looked forward to the new year, when the wound would be healed enough to stand the jostling of crowded school corridors and he could return to a normal life. However, that was not yet to be.

My parents had come from Iowa for two weeks at Christmas time to rejoice with us that our David was going to be all right. But the New Year had barely been celebrated when he came to me worried because the old pain was back in his leg and it seemed to be swollen again. I called Dr. Austin, who said, "No! It just couldn't be a recurrence of the infection!" but he agreed to meet us at the hospital for a look. And after he examined David he reluctantly admitted that there was something to be concerned about.

By February there was nothing to do but for David to again submit to surgery and another three weeks of hospitalization. And typical of his generous spirit, when he woke up in his bed after surgery and saw me sitting on a chair there, the first thing he said was, "Poor Mom, you've got to go though it all over again." As in the first surgery, the infection refused to grow in any medium and remained an unidentified staph. But David endured again and kept his sense of humor through it all. He even managed to get out of the hospital for a few hours toward the end of his stay, long enough to attend the wedding of Dick and Jody on March 1, 1980 and to join the musical ensemble there, playing his drums to celebrate with them.

The Lord restored David to full health and restored all the things that had been lost. He had been a good student and kept his school work at that level throughout the ordeal in spite of missing most of his junior year. He rigged up his bicycle in the garage so he could work his legs to strengthen them again and he continued to grow sturdily. He was able to take driver training during the spring term and his tennis scholarship was reinstated when he was able to play again in the summer. He's over six feet tall with both legs perfectly even. As I update this twenty-four years later, he remains healthy and strong with only a scar to testify to his ordeal. He went through a dark valley he but came out with a strong body and a beautiful spirit.

Times of suffering usually come to all of us at one time or another. Whether the pain we experience is physical, spiritual or emotional, the Lord is there to help us get through it if we'll let him. We are prone to view suffering as evil and useless and a sign that God doesn't love us or care for us. But it is the difficulties we go through which form strong character and provide opportunities for tremendous inner growth in not only us but those who love us enough to suffer with us.

So many people told us how their faith was nurtured through David's battle. They talked of really experiencing "God with us." Perhaps one of the most quietly dramatic results of this episode began when I ran to my friend, Gerry, for prayer as soon as we knew that David was in serious trouble. Her oldest son, James, was a successful businessman who had once considered the priesthood but was now even drifting away from his religious upbringing as a Catholic. Since Gerry and I had raised our large families more or less together she asked all of her children to pray for David. James said that he didn't really believe that prayer worked, but because he was concerned about David he said he would pray. "I don't believe in miracles," he said, "but if God does heal David, I guess I'll have to re-examine some things." Re-examine he did and was ordained a Catholic priest a few years later.

Over and over people who were involved in the prayer effort for David spoke of the sense of oneness with us as we battled through the initial attack and battled again through the recurrence. We experienced what it is like to do battle in the heavens against the Evil One. Feeling the victory of overcoming bred new faith that would overcome future obstacles in our lives. I began to really understand what the scripture means when it says that the man who has much faith will have more, and the one who has little will lose what little he has. Faith acted on is the only real faith there is!

Several years later, when David took Bill and me out for dinner, he talked about his traumatic junior high school year. "I always thought the whole thing was something God was doing in you, Mom," he explained. Without a doubt, it was a time of growing in faith for all of us. But as I looked at this sturdy son of mine, I knew his unusual maturity, compassion, and faith in God, was some of the good fruit from that time of suffering he had endured.

During those months of the struggle for his return to health, I had lots of questions for God. "Why were you so messy about healing him?" I asked. "If you could make the holes in his femur disappear, why didn't you just do a thorough job?" I mulled that over for a while and then came up with my own answer. God is the Creator, right? And everybody knows creative people are messy, so why not give God room to be messy if he so chooses!

Of course I can't really understand what he's orchestrating. I just have to trust that he knows what he's doing. So I put my questions to rest, continued to thank God that David was healthy now, and waited to see what would grab my attention next. I felt so faith-filled from the events of the past year, that I felt pleasantly expectant as we approached another summer. I didn't know it but we were approaching mega-changes during the coming months.

Blessed by the Vietnamese

On the night of April 11, 1980 a prophecy came to me at the community gathering with Spirit of Christ:

"I do not muzzle the ox that treads the grain. Those of you who seek me and try to do my will, will not fail to receive from me the good fruit of my spirit. I will feed you with my love and my joy. I will nourish you abundantly as I promised. You most assuredly will feed at my rich table. It cannot be otherwise!"

As I meditated on that word, the "It cannot be otherwise" phrase, it made me take another look at why my relationship with Bill kept banging me around in my emotions, in spite of the joy I felt otherwise. I thought, "Since I know I'm trying to do God's will, I must continue to believe he'll do what he says he'll do. I will keep focused on him, not my problems, and he will fulfill his promises to me. It cannot be otherwise!"

The whole Lord's Delight Community decided to go camping during the Memorial Day weekend, staying overnight in Newago and canoeing down the Marquette River the next day. We were a caravan of one, many-peopled bus, plus a parade of vans and cars with more people, food, tents and camping equipment. We had a great time together despite having a couple of canoes flipping over during the trip.

I was one of those people blessed with an upside down view of the river. With me in my canoe were two young people, new to the art of canoeing. We drifted too close to the bank at one point, and too late, I spotted an overhanging branch all set to clip us if we didn't paddle quickly back toward the middle of the current. My shout of impending danger only panicked the youngsters, and we rolled over with the canoe. During the cold dousing I lost my glasses somewhere in the swiftly flowing current; nevermore to be found. There was plenty of help righting the canoe and finding some dry shirts to throw on until we could draw up onto a beach to dry out in the sun.

On the trip home, I got to thinking about how I would have to get new glasses, but I also was distracted by the recognition that I was ready for a change in more ways than one. I have always hated wearing glasses. I hated them so much, it was as if a sign saying "ugly" was placed in front of my face each time I looked in the mirror, barring me from seeing anything else. I had noticed that other people looked great in glasses, my sister, Carolyn is one of those, but I didn't.

So each time my glasses needed a prescription change I would lobby to get contact lenses and Bill always told me that I couldn't because I would get an infection in my eyes. He would not accept any of my arguments no matter what safety statistics I gave him. But this time when I went to get fitted with new glasses I decided to get contact lenses instead, in spite of knowing Bill would be unhappy with me. I took a bold step that June, seeing an opportunity, grabbing it and—damn the consequences!

That decision was a very freeing thing for me. Though Bill was not happy with my decision to disregard his wishes, he couldn't yank them out of my eyes so he had to put up with it. And I was so happy to be rid of the glasses! I could look in a mirror at a more agreeable image of myself and I liked, too, the fact that I had disobeyed Bill and still lived. Now, it makes me mad that I waited so long before asserting myself, but it was a big step for me then. It could have been construed as my first step toward either maturity or anarchy, depending on your point of view!

In August of 1980, we were all delighted to welcome Barry and Kim Lee back into the household with not only their daughter Bethany, but their son, Josh, who was eleven months old. They had quickly sold their house after their six-weeks' stay with us in 1979, but had been house-sitting for the Moncrief's for a year. Barry was recovering from surgery on a foot that had gotten badly infected when he stepped on a nail, so he had to be carried into the house right along with their belongings!

Simultaneously, another move was taking place that was of major proportion. A few months previously, at a joint meeting of the Spirit of Christ and the Lord's Delight, we had prayed about serving the poor together in some ministry, and what evolved from that prayer was an agreement to sponsor a Vietnamese family. There were thousands of Vietnamese refugees stranded in Thailand, and the United States was attempting to provide a home for some of these refugees through church organizations. After contacting Catholic Social Services, which was the coordinating agency for refugee services in the Lansing area, they asked us to sponsor a large, therefore hard-to-place family, and we agreed to do that.

Thai and Minh Cao had escaped from Vietnam on Thai's fishing boat with their eight children, Huong, Thi, Quoc, XugenThi, Hao, Hue, Dang and Lien Van, and had spent a year in a refugee camp in Thailand before they finally arrived at Capital City Airport on August 27, 1980. We moved them into the side of the house across the driveway from us, where the Broadbents had resided. With Dave and Maria Post and their children living on the other side of their house, it worked out beautifully for the Vietnamese family to move there where they would have assistance under the same roof. We had been informed by the refugee services staff to expect them to be very aloof, but our relationship with the them was a love affair from the start. And with the littlest child being only two and the oldest son eighteen, our kids had a wonderful time playing with them, sharing with them and teaching them how to be Americans.

The Caos had farmed and fished in South Vietnam so they were not used to city life and modern conveniences. Thai had been a deacon in the Catholic Church near his home. He had helped another fifty people escape with his family when they left. Both of the parents had a quiet dignity about them that was very appealing. As for getting them settled—everybody wanted to help!

Many hands made light work as we acquired furniture and clothing for them. The single women and my daughters did most of the shopping, taking the Caos to a number of stores until everyone in the family was outfitted properly. As they walked briskly and joyfully in front of us, on our way to Mass that first Sunday they were here, I noticed a number of price tags flapping conspicuously from their clothing. Obviously none of us had thought to explain to them that it was customary for us to remove price tags before wearing newly bought clothing. This simple lack on our part brought home to me that there could be other ways in which we might fail to adequately prepare them for living in our country, so I sent up a prayer that God would help us to do better in our attempts to serve them.

A crisis occurred shortly after they arrived, when Minh came rushing to Maria and Dave's side of the house one night because Thai appeared to be experiencing terrible abdominal pain. Their way of dealing with it was to rub hot oil on his abdomen, but we finally convinced them to let us take him to the hospital, where he had surgery to remove kidney stones. Watching him holding court as he sat crossed-legged on his hospital bed, I saw him giving it the dignity of a judge's bench, as he met with the many Vietnamese men who came to visit him. It was apparent that he was honored as a leader back in his home area.

He and Minh were intelligent people in their early forties, and they had a childlike simplicity that we dearly loved. Knowing that the whole family had been through terrible suffering on their journey to us, we couldn't help but be impressed by the grace with which they purposed to begin life anew by joyfully living each day. A less serious side of Thai caused us much merriment when he started teasing and joking with us. And when someone gave their children hula hoops, Thai joined in on the fun. He had a wonderful time gyrating his hips to keep the hoop spinning fast around his waist, doing a better job than I had been able to when I first tried it. With the first snow of the year, the whole family dashed outside, holding up their faces to feel the cool, tender touch of winter. They continually were a reminder for us to appreciate our blessings.

As soon as we got the family settled, they began to tell us about other relatives that had escaped with them on their boat, but were still stuck in Thailand. So, that December, we welcomed Vinh and Hue Cao and their sons, two-year-old Hao, and five-month-old Hien. Vinh and Hue were a sweet young couple and, like the elder Caos, a joy to know. We still chuckle over an incident that occurred the second day they were here.

I was sitting in the senior Cao's living room with Maria and some of the other Caos, attempting to get a bit more acquainted with Hue, who was holding Hien. At one point Hue left us to go into a nearby bedroom to change the baby. We continued to visit until we were interrupted by piercing cries from Hien. Maria stopped talking to me, her eyes widened with comprehension, and she darted away from me toward the bathroom crying, "Not the baby! Not the baby!" As Maria had feared, she found Hue dunking Hien up and down in the cold water of the toilet bowl! Earlier, Maria had instructed Hue and Vinh on the use of the bathroom toilet, but Hue had obviously misunderstood her when she had recommended dunking a soiled cloth diaper in the toilet before putting it in the diaper pail. There was more than ample room for confusion, when we didn't speak Vietnamese and they didn't speak English. Although a number of Vietnamese refugees in Lansing came to help the Caos get settled, they weren't always around to translate, and body language can be tricky!

We were very impressed by the industry of these people. Although they needed to go to English classes and get acclimated to our culture, it wasn't long before Thai and his older sons got paper routes with the Lansing State Journal in order to earn some money. We realized they could be too innovative, when we discovered they had rigged some extra electrical wiring in their apartment, leaving bare wires exposed that could have injured someone or burned down the building. But they put the men in our household to shame in the matter of taking out the trash.

Lansing residents had to buy orange trash bags to put on the curb each week on their designated day for pickup. There was a latticed storage area in back of the house across the driveway, where all of us from both our houses stacked the orange bags throughout the week. Then, every Monday night after our household meeting, the men in our household took the trash out to the curb. There was always great scurrying back and forth up and down our driveway as they did the chore.

When Thia first noticed this activity, he announced that from now on, his family would take out the trash on Monday nights. Of course, we were amenable to that, and we had to chuckle when we discovered that instead of having several guys running back and forth from the back of the house to the curb, they laid a long ladder on the ground, placed all the bags on the length of the ladder and then hoisted it up and made one trip. So much for Yankee ingenuity!

Thia and Minh frequently invited us to eat at their table, exposing us to lavish Vietnamese cooking. The Vietnamese egg-rolls were my favorite of all of their food, so I prevailed on Minh to teach me how to make them. She and Hue came across the driveway to our kitchen one day with big bowls and sat right down on the kitchen floor where they began to put the ingredients together. Although I was distracted watching the speed and accuracy shown as they wielded their knives cutting up vegetables and chicken, I still managed to write down everything they did and how much of each ingredient to use, and I still prepare that delicious food from those well-worn recipes on 3x5 cards today. Soon I was shopping with them at the House of Ing, buying nook maum, mien, ginger root, Spring Roll egg-roll wraps and the like, right along with the rest of them. There were a few recipes they made which were definitely an acquired taste, so I refrained from asking them to teach me about those. One sight I saw frequently in their kitchen was a big pot on the stove with a fish head sticking out of it, one eye seeming to look stoically back at me.

When the following Memorial Day weekend arrived, the Caos were with us at our second annual camping/canoeing overnight trip down the Marquette River, and they were a sight to behold! While we gingerly climbed in and out of canoes and sat down heavily to center our weight properly, they went scooting down the river standing up in theirs. Although we had known they were fishermen, we hadn't had a chance to see what that looked like until then.

They weren't invincible in the wild though. When Paul caught a huge blue racer, and held it up for all to see, we discovered they were all terrified of snakes. Typical of camping trips, this was a discovery trip and memory maker, but more special because of the evident delight the Vietnamese experienced being out in the midst of nature again.

Our Amy was eleven when they arrived, and though she was not always happy to receive some of the troublesome people who lived with us, she came alive with excitement when you asked her about the Caos.

> "I loved them! I loved being able to help them and I used to spend all of my time with them. I wanted to help them cook and teach them English. I just loved them, and Xuyen Thi was my best friend for a while. If I can have control of a situation and help someone, I love that. I used to say to them, 'You don't dress like that. You're supposed to dress like this.! And I'd show them."

She admitted that there were times when she told other kids at her school that she was Vietnamese.

Kim Long Tran and his sons, Hai and Son, were the next group that came to us. He was another "cousin" who had escaped on a different boat with his family but had not fared as well as the Vietnamese with us. His boat was attacked and his wife and two younger children were taken back to Vietnam, even though he and his older sons avoided capture.

Kim Long was a sweet man who had the simplicity of a child because he was mentally impaired. We heard stories from other Vietnamese, regarding his disability, that included a version where the impairment occurred after he was shot in the head when he was in Intelligence in the South Vietnamese Army, and another version that he was hung and left for dead, so his brain was deprived of oxygen before he was rescued. But the Post family merged him and his sons into their family, with the Vietnamese community lending a helping hand.

What an incredible privilege it is, to know people who have really suffered so much and yet retained such inner peace and dignity. They became an integral part of the community on Sycamore Street, sharing their lives with us as much as any of our extended family. We bought Vietnamese Bibles for them, and they participated happily with all the activities of the Lord's Delight and the Spirit of Christ. My Bible has Vietnamese scribbled all through it as we shared back and forth during prayer meetings. I loved it when Cao would decide to stand up and read from scripture in his own language.

Sy Kim was another dear member of our household. He had been studying for the priesthood when he was arrested and put in jail for eight months before he escaped from Vietnam. He moved in with us and struggled very hard to learn the language so he could resume his studies for the priesthood in our Diocese of Lansing. He would pour over the newspaper every day, trying to understand the crazy ways of Americans, and then get up with a section and come to Bill, saying, "Mr. Bill, what you think of this?" And Bill would sometimes have trouble himself trying to explain things that were considered news in our country.

We were happy for Sy when his younger brother, Chao Kim, was able to join us later. Sy was eventually ordained at the Cathedral, and serves in parish ministry in the Lansing area. He's visited us in Grand Rapids and I see him sometimes when I am in Lansing. We sponsored two more families before the flood of refugees slowed down, and I will always be thankful for their presence in our lives.

Patrick and Mark

On September 5, 1980, someone made a fancy cake to celebrate our 25th wedding anniversary. Looking at a picture of us admiring the cake, sitting with our arms around each other, we look like we're a twosome. Bill had been treating me pretty well for awhile, but we were living the life of married singles, with him doing his thing and me doing mine. Even when we were together, the togetherness was purely a case of us both being in the same vicinity at the same time. He still rarely shared his thoughts or feelings with me, and whenever I asked him what he was thinking he seemed suspicious of my reasons for asking. On the other hand, when I asked him one time, why he never asked me how my day had gone, he answered simply, "You always tell me everything anyway, so I don't need to ask you."

One evening we were sitting on a sofa in the dining room, and he had his arm along the back of the sofa behind my shoulders, when Faye leaned through the pass-through from the kitchen and grinned, saying, "Now I really like that! I like to see you two sitting there like that! It makes me feel secure!" I could only marvel that God could use the mere appearance of something healthy to help someone feel secure!

In November I needed to go to Cedar Rapids for a few days in order to visit my parents, and also to speak at two meetings of Aglow International, an organization of Christian women, and I was very happy when Anne-Marie decided to go with me. She had been spending so much time with her friend, Emily, during her high school years, that it seemed like she was only home when she had to be. She mentioned to me one time, that she wished we lived in a normal house and a normal neighborhood like Emily's. I kind of felt that she wished she had a more normal mother too, so I hoped that our time together would draw us closer to each other.

She accompanied me to the first talk I gave and also when I gave a talk about the household to a Sociology class at Mount Mercy College there. That was an impromptu event sparked by the enthusiasm of one of the Mercy nuns who had heard me speak at one of the Aglow meetings. The students asked Anne-Marie a few questions too, and she handled it all very well. I hoped that by hearing me talk of the household living experience and its beginnings, she might have a better appreciation of me. She continued to be present at all the familial, household and community gatherings, but I knew she was looking forward to living in a college dorm next year.

That winter of 1980-1981, one of the young men living with us was Patrick, a seventeen-year-old, who appeared to be only about twelve because he was suffering arrested growth development attributed to Failure to Thrive Syndrome. Before encountering him, I had thought that syndrome occurred only in infants who were left untouched except for basic feeding and cleanliness needs. A woman had asked us to take him in after she discovered him sleeping in their camper at the back of their lot during cold weather. She knew a bit of his background because his family went to their church.

She told me Patrick had a twin brother who was of normal height for his age and was totally accepted by his family, but Patrick had been ostracized by his parents and siblings since birth, living in the same house, but eating separately and being deprived of the normal companionship of the rest of the family. The woman said his clothes were often dirty and badly worn, although the rest of the family was nicely dressed. Both of us were puzzled that nothing had ever been done for him through the school system or social services system all these years. It was hard to believe.

We were about to leave with our younger children to go to Cedar Point Amusement Park in Ohio, when Patrick arrived, so we took him with us. Our children weren't enthused about taking a strange kid with us, but when they learned he had never been included in a family vacation before, they tried to accept him graciously. We had no trouble getting him to go back into school and he seemed to like participating in the household activities.

Some of the men living with us took him under their wing, and spent time doing things with him. But after being with us for a few months, he developed a relationship with a young girl he met at school and began drifting away from us. Although she came home after school with him sometimes, he spent most of his free time alone with her at her home when her parents weren't there. And when we cautioned him about that not being a good idea, he decided to move out.

The last time I saw him, he had shot up in stature and was working as a checkout person in a supermarket, presenting a cheery face to me as I went through his line. I hope he experienced enough caring concern from us to know that God loved him.

Mark was one of the young men in the household who had a servant heart and a willingness to pay personal attention to Patrick. He was a kind and generous person, attractive on the inside as well as on the outside. He eventually became a great help in the household, filling in holes left as some of our children moved out. The following is an account he wrote of his sojourn with us at Sycamore Fellowship:

"I was first exposed to the household by Paul Downes. Paul and I were acquaintances from high school. Although we talked some at school and seemed to get along, we lost touch after high school until about a year and a half later. As I recall, it was just a "chance" encounter on the street. We decided to get together to go bowling some night and get re-acquainted. Little did I know how little had been left up to chance!

"As Paul and I spent more time together, we talked about our problems and our dreams. We would argue about the best solutions to each other's problems: I would "logically" conclude some selfish reason for taking one course of action, and Paul would disagree, giving some obscure reason about how God had the solution to our problems. Paul would encourage me to pray about my problems and ask God for an answer. Well, we pretty near drove each other nuts! I would run circles around Paul with my mistaken premises and conclusions, yet he would steadfastly maintain his trust in God.

"The most peculiar thing happened as time went by. Paul's problems always seemed to get better, while mine became a morass from which I could see no escape. I clung to our relationship like a piece of timber from a wreck at sea, all the while trying to appear self-confident. Looking back, I can see how stubbornly human nature holds on to an imagined control to dictate life's path.

"Paul invited me to his house on several occasions. At first it would be to pick up something, or see if someone wanted to join us. Before long, I would come for dinner or an evening of cards. From the first time I stepped into that house, I experienced a sense of comfort, ease and peace that I will always remember. I knew the household and the people comprising it were different.

"As Paul and I continued to get together, we spent less time doing things, and more time just sitting and talking or arguing. He told me in a casual way, about the "Life in the Spirit" seminar and asked me if I might be interested in it. In my desire to appear open-minded, I politely said, "sure."

"Since God is the preeminent opportunist, he made certain that my friends and cronies were all occupied the night Paul called on the phone and casually said, "Hey, we're going to start the seminar tonight. Are you interested at all?" I had called every phone number I knew, to get out of my apartment that night and was bored stiff, so I said, "sure. I'll walk on over." That walk was the most important one of my life.

"The seminar had the answers I had been running from for years. The seminar presenter explained the working of the Holy Spirit. I learned of God's great desire for me to be reconciled with him; I also learned of my own great need for emotional healing and spiritual therapy. I decided to stop talking so much and start listening more.

"I started coming to the prayer meetings every week after the seminar, and experienced a peacefulness and a hunger for a deeper understanding of God. I would still have doubts about the reality of what I was experiencing, but Bill Downes dealt the final blow to my skepticism. He presented teachings at the prayer meetings that directly addressed my doubts and fears. So many times he would quote the same scripture that I had read in my private prayer time. I hope to pass on the message of the overwhelming desire of God for us to hear his voice. He is not limited by our poor hearing or understanding. "For the one who asks always receives; the one who searches always finds; the one who knocks will always have the door opened to him." (Mt. 7:8)

"A couple of months after the seminar, I asked to move into the household. It was the heavenly hospital that provided a place for God to repair the damage to my soul. The security and love that was there provided an environment where I could let down my defenses and still accept the advice and teaching that would help me die to myself. One example of this love occurred ten days after I moved in. On my birthday I received gifts and cards from people in the household I had barely become acquainted with. I was deeply moved by this gesture of acceptance and affection.

"The daily praise, prayers and petitions after the evening meal was an incalculable source of encouragement and grace. The abundance of scripture to address problems and abundance of answers to prayers was amazing. I learned to expect an answer to prayer. I had first-hand experience that God is faithful to his people. As we shared our trials and triumphs, we all developed a deeper appreciation for the supreme sacrifice Christ made for our salvation. We saw the terrible darkness of our sin in the wonderfully bright illumination of the loving sacrifice Jesus made for us on Good Friday.

"The household also served as a training ground for evangelization and conversion. After being there for about a year, two of my brothers started coming over, and within another year or so they were both baptized in the Spirit! Other relationships within my family were healed. I developed a relationship with my parents that I never dreamed possible.

"The roommates I had over the seven years I was at Sycamore Fellowship were many and varied. Through many of these relationships I was blessed with new perspectives on Christian thinking and ethics. Other roommates were more in need of my help, and I was grateful to have the opportunity to share my experiences and understanding with them.

"The household was also a very entertaining place to live. We always had birthday celebrations, and in addition to those, we would have skit nights that were absolutely hilarious! It was a fun place to be. But the most valuable things I learned there were about marriage and family life. The Lees were a living demonstration of what a Christian family should be. I learned what real love is and isn't. I have no use for what passes for dating and romance today. I learned not to build my life around getting married, and after pretty much giving up the idea, my wife-to-be moved into the house next door!

"More than anything else, I think the unity among such a diversity of individuals that comprised the household, is a testimony to the activity of the Holy Spirit and personal sacrifice of Bill and Laurie and their family. I know the living situation was a strain on their own family life in some ways, but the reward in heaven for their generosity will be great. Only then will the immense impact of the household be truly known. The impact of the Downeses and all the other saints I met there, on my life, is already immeasurable."

Mark spoke of the "Agape" love he experienced in the household; the brotherly love which occurs as God changes our hearts to be more like his. Jody and Dick's wedding had been our first celebration of "Eros" love, and romance was in the air again in 1980. This time it involved Tom, our first child to get married. I was becoming a mother-in-law.

Our Children

It was easy for me to see why Tom was bowled over by her, when I first met his future wife, Diana. She was an attractive statuesque red-head; exuding vitality from every pore. He was supremely happy, as we joyfully celebrated their wedding at St. Mary Cathedral before they left for Tampa, Florida, where he began work with the Tampa Police Department and Diana continued her career as a cardiac intensive care nurse.

Our Michael once said that when Joe went off to college he only came swooping through every so often, like a comet. And now, Tom became another comet, with a period as long and erratic as the Joe comet. So after hurling the second child out of the nest for good I plowed back into the life on Sycamore Street with all it's bumps and blessings.

There was a lot of physical activity on the block that summer as one of our community members added a room to her house and tore down her old garage to make way for a storage shed. Also, a number of us painted the outside of an elderly man's house as a community service project. There's something about working together that creates an environment conducive to getting acquainted with one another on another level. A shared pride of accomplishment, perhaps, and an uncovering of abilities in each other that aren't apparent in the usual social setting.

Early in January, 1982, two new women moved in and one was just fifteen, an adopted daughter whose parents were ready to give up on her. If my brain had been where it was supposed to be, we would surely not have agreed to take her. And if we had heard correctly when we prayed about it, I think I would have heard God saying: "No way!"

In fact that's exactly what our twelve-year-old Amy said when I asked her how she felt about sharing her room temporarily with Helen. Later, after Helen left, Amy told me, "I hated having her here. One time she was sitting in the bedroom with me, and she was screaming and yelling because she was in trouble for something she had done. She was awful!" Helen barely lasted a month and didn't seem to gain anything while with us. In spite of the many blessings for our children through household living, there were times when it was difficult for them too, especially for Amy, since she was the youngest.

Our children had known Sharon and Lucy even before they moved into our house but when we moved into the big house, they were not only faced with assimilating into our family people they didn't know, but they were also becoming outnumbered by adults and uprooted from their familiar house and neighborhood. If they were distressed by all of this, they hid it very well. At the time we moved to Sycamore Street, we were all too caught up in the excitement of what the Lord seemed to be doing with us, to worry about what might be going on under the surface of our consciousness. I now realize now, how substantially their lives changed when we entered that new phase.

Although some of our children had a hard time relating to a few of the really troubled people we took in, they also handled some rather bizarre situations with surprising maturity. Most of them had developed their own relationship with God by this time and had been aware of God leading us thus far, so the bottom line for all of us was our shared conviction that God was leading us to the new life in the big house.

The most frustrating things they ran into were the familiar vices we all struggle with, selfishness, laziness and irresponsibility, things that are pretty normal in any family. The one thing that caught me off guard, was how upset any of our children would get when they found out a household member had treated Bill or me unkindly or disrespectfully. On the other hand, we all grew to love some of our extended family, and we still keep in close touch with a number of these people. They shared skills, talents and even personal belongings with us, and many of them had significant impact for good in the lives of our children.

Although Joe was off to MSU before we moved to Sycamore Street, Tom stuck around home most of the time until he married at twenty-four. He was especially appreciated for the entertainment he provided for the kids and adults alike. His tales of undercover work as a narc for the Eaton County Sheriff's Department, and his ability to break boards with only his hands (a skill acquired with his Black Belt status in Tae Kwon Do), always kept the kids rapt with attention. He was kind and calm, a good diffusing agent to have around. He reflected on his teen and young adult years of household living this way:

"I guess any situation, no matter how unusual, becomes normal with time: even living with people who differed from apple-pie normal. I remember being proud of the fact that my parents were the emotional rock whom so many people depended on. We were never left out of the process, however. Even the youngest of us had some basic idea that we were helping.

"Some of the people who entered our lives were welcomed additions. Dick's dry sense of humor, Susan's quiet sweetness, David Connelly's enthusiasm, and the Lees' joyful family, were all bright, warm parts of the household. Sandy was a tiny lady with a big heart, who shared her vehicle with whomever needed one. Other people were hurting and trying to struggle through various difficulties. There were times when a crisis hit someone in the household. A problem at the job, a difficulty relating to a parent, a test coming up at school, an illness would occur, and we would have a need before us. The support we gave each other was one of the best parts of living in this type of situation. There was a sensitivity to other people's problems.

"If I was worried about a test, for instance, I knew that Martin, an unrelated person living with us, would listen with his ears and his heart. He would give advice if he thought he could help, he would tell me he would pray for me and I knew he would. The overwhelming majority of the people who lived with us responded in the same way. It was like having extra brothers and sisters, and it really taught me the value of mutual support.

"This mutual support had a very practical side to it. Jody backed down the icy driveway one morning, and one of her car's wheels slid over the edge of a concrete drop-off. If she had been living 'normally,' insulated from fellow apartment dwellers, she would have been looking at an irritating inconvenience and a hefty tow-truck bill. As it was, she came inside, and a half dozen men in the house went out, lifted the car up bodily and deposited it back onto the driveway.

"I never felt resentment toward my parents or any of our 'temporary family,' and I never felt deprived of a normal family life. We knew we were loved by our parents and the enrichment that comes from in-depth involvement with other lives, far outweighed any inconveniences."

As confident as Tommy has always felt, our son, Michael, never realized the fact that his sense of humor and quiet personality endeared him to household members in a very special way. He pointed out to me one thing about our living structure that was problematic for him sometimes:

"My father instituted family prayers after dinner every night. Always at the end of our time together we joined hands and recited the *Our Father*; and then everyone gave everyone else a hug. The big thing about having family prayers after dinner, at least at first, was we were delayed another fifteen to twenty minutes from going out to resume the ball game with the other neighborhood kids that had been interrupted by dinner. Or even bigger, come to think of it, was learning how to deal with guests invited to dinner.

"If you invited a school friend over, did you try to warn them beforehand? 'Look, you know, after dinner we always have family prayers, so if you want to join us, fine, but also you can just, umm...er...go outside and play ball, and I'll be out later.' If the friend did join the family prayers, look out when it came time for the hugs! Would they be monumentally embarrassed? Would they step back from all the hugging, and be totally stunned? Mom and Dad would most likely go over and give them a hug anyway, if they didn't literally run away.

"And of course, the invited guest need not be a friend of mine; they might be an adult, a complete stranger to all of us, just someone that Dad brought home one night for dinner, or worse, maybe the guest was an attractive girlfriend of one of my sisters. In cases where actual hugging seemed risky or definitely embarrassing, I would sort of drift around the living room, trying to keep away from the non-huggable guest. Hugging everyone in the family was de rigueur, and sometimes it required real ingenuity to make the circuit without running into the guest."

Our son, Paul, thinks he is more compassionate and more eager to share God with others than if he had grown up in a normal nuclear family setting. He had apologetic and ethical debates with many of the people who lived with us, and by defending his faith he became stronger in it. But he was aware of some of the drawbacks of household living too:

"Household living makes people more flexible. You become more patient and forgiving, ready to change your plans on short notice. You have to plan your life around more people. But I wish we had worked more at preserving the individuality of our family. Maybe that is a selfish attitude, but I think our extended family took important time away from our family, just by other people being present when we were doing things. I think we lost our family identity and became just the 'Downes Household' Our family got knocked around a bit, but I have a generally positive regard for Christian household living based on my experience."

Our daughter, Julie was a wonderful asset in the household, living with us through all the hassles and joys until she moved to Chicago in 1986. The following comments are her reflections of home:

"I've been trying to think back on how I felt about living with all those people! I don't recall ever thinking that it was that weird of a situation. Of course, there were some good things and some bad things about it, but I never wanted to dump everyone and revert back to ma and pa and the kids. Living in the household gave me a family closeness to so many people that I probably wouldn't have even met otherwise.

"There's a bond there from having to plow through difficulties together, and from eating popcorn at 3:00 a.m. in the kitchen together. I do notice that I am impatient with the social requirements and superficialness, and just the length of time it takes to make real friends now. I had a good taste of the way things could be and I feel the absence.

"I have such a special love for Paul and Amy, but I wonder what Lansing would feel like to me if Sandy Lee, Faye, Lydia, the Lees, Mark and Carrie etc. weren't there also. There's some confusion here at my work site, about who's related to me and who's not, when I talk about the folks back home. I kind of like that.

"Plus just the fact that I was exposed to so many different talents, perspectives, backgrounds, and levels of emotional and spiritual health, has given me a much more wide-open way of looking at things now, than I think most people have.

"Sure there were many irritants, like having a roommate who folded her dirty clothes, or having one who wore them. All those meetings, though necessary, got a little old at times. But I did have a bigger house than anyone at school, and lots of help shoveling the driveway. Besides, who can say that irritations are bad for you? You learn to deal with them. It takes an awful lot to really bug me now. That might be one of the best things I picked up from household living. If taken back and given a choice, yes, I would do it all over again, no contest, no doubt, no hesitation, absolutely!"

David was an integral part of the household, being present during all of the busy years, except two—when he lived in a dorm for nine months and when he lived in Japan for a year. He was always quick to jump in and help fix a leaky faucet or diffuse a hot household situation:

"Let's just say that the extended household approach (although we extended it to the brink of insanity) seemed to be a healthy and enriching way to grow up. I feel like I was immune to (or ignorant of) many of the 'problems' that came with the various people who lived with us.

"I don't doubt that the Lord had his hand in the move to Sycamore Street, and consequently, feel confident that both good and bad fit his plans one way or another. In hindsight, I think our 'Catholicity' was 'Protestantized' by our proximity to our non-Catholic brethren. Certainly the interdenominational aspects were valuable for all parties, and my urge to delve further into the realms of Catholic teaching now, may very well be a result of the differences that were learned in the household.

"The household provided (for the most part) decent peers for people to associate with. I notice how hard it is to find respectable friends these days. The only bad thing was that with all the people, it was easy to hide from some of the 'familial' connections. But maybe, as parents, mine knew more about the 'goings on' via the grapevine than if we'd lived in a small house with a closer, more solid family arrangement."

Anne-Marie was always a quiet person, not volunteering her thoughts unless asked. I think she and Amy, our two youngest children, yearned for a more normal home life at times:

"I think that living in the household was very good for me. I know some people didn't think it was wise of my parents to raise our family in that situation, but I disagree with them. Some things were difficult but there was a lot that I enjoyed. I learned so much from the Lees and I loved having them live with us. Barry and Kim were such great fun, and I enjoyed their children so very much. I am beginning to see how greatly they have influenced me, as I raise my children. I find myself remembering moments when I observed how they handled things with their children. Having them with us, gave me a wonderful opportunity to see at close range, motherhood and family life with little children, and they set me a good example to learn from.

"I also learned a lot from the many single people who shared our home. When I was younger, it meant a lot to me to have some of the older women take an interest in me. I have many good memories of time spent with them, doing fun things or just talking. It was good for me to be around them, learning from them as they shared their experiences, their lives.

"I have to admit that the thought of living that way again scares me. It was not easy. You give up some privacy and having things your own way. Hopefully, the sacrifices we made by opening our home, helped someone to feel loved, to heal, to draw close to the Lord, to grow. So we gave of ourselves but we also received so much. We experienced a lot of love, affirmation and encouragement. There were lots of people to play with and to pray with. Living like we did helped prepare me for college and family life."

Amy was only three when the first woman moved in with us, so her only remembrance of family life is extended-family life. She had the roughest time of all the kids, partly because of having too many moms. There was always someone telling her what to do or checking to see if she had permission to be doing what she was doing. It drove her nuts! She was still in her early teens when she wrote the following comments about her life in our household:

"I used to get mad when people in the household told me to do things. I thought they were taking advantage of the fact that I had to talk to them in a respectful way, even though they weren't respecting me.

"I got caught with everything I did because so many people lived with us. I'm serious! I remember I'd go down on Ionia Street, which I had been told not to do, and people would tell my mom, 'Oh yes, I saw Amy down on Ionia Street.' And she'd say to me later, 'What were you doing down on Ionia Street?' And I would go, 'What are you talking about?' And she'd say, 'Don't give me that. You know you were down there.'

"Kids at school would ask me all the time, if our house was an orphanage. I didn't like that. It was like we were too different from everybody. I tried to think of how, in a tactful way, I could explain to school friends why our house was like it was, without them thinking it was weird, because I wanted to be accepted so bad. I remember how I had to think about it in my mind, how I would say it. I cared about the fact that we were different, but not about the fact that all the people were there.

"One night when we were at the dinner table, Dad went to answer the door and there were two little black kids. They said, 'Is this a mansion?' And Dad said, 'No.' And they said, 'Can we come inside?' And Dad said, 'No.' I loved all the attention I got because we lived in that house. When I was in high school, the other kids thought we were filthy rich because we lived in such a big house.

"I loved to sit in front of the fireplace in the winter time with Mom and eat popcorn. Mom would be reading a book, and I would get a book and a pillow and sit beside her. It was cozy and fun! I loved that skinny long attic on third floor and I played house in there. I also used to go into the darkroom and sing. I would shut the door and sing at the top of my lungs. I liked to sing, but not at prayer meetings. The songs were too wishy for me.

"I used to ask people in the house if I could go places with them, and Mom would ask me, 'Did you ask them, or did they invite you?' 'Oh no, I invited her!' they'd reply, and I'd be relieved. I think sometimes they might have lied to save me from getting into trouble."

"I miss the house and all the attention now, but I don't miss all the meetings, after-dinner prayers and family nights. But now I see the really different environment was an advantage, not a disadvantage. I'm an open-minded person from living with so many different people."

So in spite of the difficulties, our children had a rich environment as they were growing up albeit an unusual one. They are all decent people now raising their own families and still enjoying the friendship of some of those who lived with us. I think Julie summed it up in her earlier comments when she mentioned that her love for many of the people who lived with our family is hard to distinguish from her love for her nuclear family siblings.

Emerging as Grandmother

It was in the middle of a very busy day when Tom phoned from Florida to tell us that our first grandchild had been born. I mentally tried on my grandmother hat and it felt good, very good. Six weeks later, in Tampa for Katheryne Leah Downes's Baptism, holding her for the first time, I deeply felt that scripture which says, *This one is bone of my bones and flesh of my flesh. (Gen. 2:23*)

I hadn't known those words when I first held each of my children. When I returned to Michigan I was thrust happily back into my busy daily life. We still had an absolutely full house, but in spite of the numbers, the blessings far outnumbered the inconveniences. One evening as I left the kitchen where people were eating popcorn and visiting around the table, I moved past another bunch hovered over a project at the dining room table. On into the living room more people were talking and laughing, some before the fire in the fireplace and others engaged in earnest conversation in another corner of the room. And I was struck momentarily by the deep sense of peace in our midst, and moved by my awareness of the work God was accomplishing in these people.

No one would know that this aura of peace clothed a woman struggling to overcome years of being sexually molested by her father, and a young single woman who had just released her baby for adoption. They might not immediately notice the marginally retarded man, who was beginning to feel acceptance from peers as he conversed with a man with emotional scars left by the father who had physically and verbally abused him all his life. How blest I felt to be moving about in the midst of the Lord's healing presence.

The household and community teaching and counseling were my usual venues for sharing the goodness of God but I also received invitations to speak further afield. I loved talking to women about the Lord, and I discovered that I was at ease speaking to church groups and women's groups about our household and the wonderful things I had seen God do in the lives of the people who lived with us.

One day when one of the women in the Lord's Delight Community saw me leaving to give a talk to a group of women at Faith United Methodist Church in Lansing, she questioned me about it. "Are you sure you're supposed to be doing this?" Although taken aback a bit, I listened as she admonished me, "You might get puffed up and get a big head from all these speaking engagements." So I thought about it, and asked God to show me if I was getting a big head.

Since I still struggled so hard to feel like I had any worth at all I didn't really think I was in any danger of doing that, but I stopped on the way to the Methodist Church engagement, to pray about it some more, asking God to tell me if I should be speaking to these women today. I grabbed my Bible, opened randomly to Romans 10:14, and began reading: *How beautiful are the feet of those who announce good news,* so I was comforted and encouraged to keep sharing that good news with everyone I could, including the women at the church that morning. I not only *preached* Christ there that day, I had taken some of my photo albums for the women to peruse so they could *see* Christ in photos of some of the household members and their activities.

So my life seemed good and full that spring of 1982, until a big financial concern reared its ugly head. The bakery where Bill had worked for almost ten years was shutting down. Knowing that God had taken care of our finances when Bill lost his job before, saved me from worrying about it and raised a sort of curious expectation about how God would provide for our financial needs this time. Bill began receiving income from unemployment checks, but he was fifty-seven now which made it even tougher to find work than it had been ten years previously. I had admired his humility then when he patiently went to work at the bakery in spite of his Ph.D., and I now saw that same humility when he started delivering newspapers every morning throughout the downtown business area to earn $100 per week. We didn't have a car at the time, so he delivered the papers by riding his bicycle. Since he rarely showed emotion, if he was unhappy with his lot, he never spoke of it and I admired the steadfast way that he did what he could to provide for us.

When fall rolled around, it was Anne-Marie's turn to begin her university career at Michigan State University. I was thankful this seventh child followed her siblings in being able to cover her college expenses by using grants and working part time. She moved into a dorm at MSU which was practically adjacent to the field where the MSU marching band practiced every day, so one of our favorite fall activities was taking little Josh and Bethany Lee out there to watch them.

One Friday night when I picked Anne-Marie up from the MSU campus to bring her home for the weekend, she was all excited. "Mother, I met the most wonderful boy! I've looked and looked, and I can't find a thing wrong with him!" When her excited monologue slowed down long enough for me to get a word in edgewise, I asked her how long she'd known him. "Two weeks!" she beamed, not seeming to catch the fact that I might not be impressed with her quick observational skills. I was amazed though, to hear all of this, since she was a girl who hadn't been interested in dating during high school, except for her school prom.

So Matthew Yanoschik entered our lives to stay, and has been a tremendous blessing to our whole family. As soon as Anne-Marie told him about our Friday night prayer meetings, he came with her, and they rarely missed a prayer meeting from then on. I had formed the habit of praying for the spouses our children would have someday, so I saw Matt as an answer to that prayer.

That December Rebekah Lee was born, the first baby born into our household. Kim had been sick a lot during the pregnancy, so we were relieved that her ordeal was over. Then early in the spring of 1983, our den doubled as a temporary bedroom for our fifth Vietnamese family, a single mother whose two children had an American father she was trying to locate. Not long after they left to move into an apartment next door, the den again became a bedroom, this time for a young couple who awaited the birth of their first child. Our Julie met them while working at their pizza business around the corner from us during the summer. Their little boy became the second baby born into the household.

I had enjoyed a few beautiful months of peace but in the summer of 1983, my peace was interrupted by major conflict with Bill again. He didn't want me to go to the wedding of my brother, Scott, in Billings, Montana, and I wanted to be there with the rest of my siblings and my parents. We would all be together for the first time since our 1979 family reunion, but Bill said I couldn't go. He pointed out that my brother wasn't being married in the Catholic Church, and besides, we didn't have the money.

When my sister, Nancy, learned I didn't have the money to make the trip, she told me her family could pick me up and bring me back since they were driving from New Jersey to Montana and camping along the way. When I told Bill that, he then said I couldn't go because Amy needed me. That statement made me very upset and angry because, of course, at fourteen, Amy did not need me to take care of her. She had her father, siblings and a whole household of people to keep her company while I was gone.

I was still this person who was taught to please her husband and keep everybody happy, but the thought of just accepting his decision and meekly staying home was intolerable to me. I mulled it over and even went to talk to Father Osborn about it before I went back to Bill and told him I had decided to go to the wedding in spite of his objections. His response to that was to retreat to his place of angry silence.

The whole household had to pay for my transgression. After a few days of staying in his bug room most of the time, Bill had that look of one under siege. I was sitting alone at the dining room table one afternoon, when Kim Lee sat down by me and said sweetly, "I really think you should be obedient to your husband, Laurie. That's what the Bible tells us to do. Maybe God is using him to stop you from going because God has a reason for you not to go. Maybe you'll be killed in an accident on the way there or something." Then our daughter, Julie, joined us. "For some reason, Mom, Dad seems to really need you to stay home this time. I know it doesn't make any sense, but he really needs you to stay home."

So I bowed to the pressure and told Bill I would not go to the wedding. How I loathed myself when I said that! That inner self-hatred came back to life in me with a vengeance. My intellect succumbed to the emotion and my inner joy was obliterated. A few days later, when Bill magnanimously told me he had decided to get a substitute for his paper route and take me to Montana for the wedding, I was barely able to rouse myself from the depression I felt. Enthusiastically he went on, "Sandy Lee said she would lend us her car, so we can take Julie and Amy with us.

I felt no joy in his reversed decision, but I talked myself into moving on with the business of being outwardly nice and happy as we left for Billings with a tent and sleeping bags to provide our nightly accommodations. Being with my Hogan family for a couple of days, I joined in the spirit of celebrating my brother's happiness, but when Bill then drove the four us on over to Montana State University at Bozeman, to spend a day at the University's Entomology Department there, my mind was still roiling with anger at the way he psychologically jerked me around. That night we drove up to the snow line at Fairy Lake Campground north of Bozeman, traversing a perilous muddy narrow road for seven miles to reach there. My spirit was traveling a perilous, muddy road also except instead of going up it was going in the opposite direction, down.

We arrived after dark and had just settled into our sleeping bags when the sweetest thing happened! We heard a guitar playing and people singing, "Sing Hallelujah to the Lord," one of our favorite praise songs. Julie and I sat up and looked at each other, grinning. "Hey, this is too cool!" we both thought. Of course, we quickly got up and followed the sound to a mini prayer meeting of two families of campers who loved to worship the Lord in the same way we did. That time of fellowship was balm to my soul, and I thanked God for lifting me up as we finally settled back down to sleep later that night.

I did enjoy the beautiful scenery in the Rockies, but camping the next night on a mountain top, we were hit by a violent, electrical storm that was terrifying.

As bolts of lightning seemed to ricochet around us, followed by almost instantaneous claps of thunder, I did some serious praying for our physical safety. At the same time, I was swinging my sword through a stormy battle occurring within me. My refreshment from the impromptu time of worship on the mountain top of the previous night had been only temporary. Deep inside I had fallen again down into that familiar pit of dark deadness in my heart. I would have to strive diligently to get back to some modicum of serenity.

It was God's mercy that kept me so busy that summer. In addition to our trip to Montana, six Blue Lake musical groups came for a few days each at regular intervals, and with household members also continually moving in and out there were always interesting distractions for me. I found, as usual, that keeping my visible self occupied with endless tasks was a blessing. Each morning when the Lord met me in my prayer time I would bawl, half the time not sure if it was my inner sadness or my overwhelming sense of his love for me in the midst of it.

But afterwards, I would put that behind me and come out of my room to face whatever the day presented. I must have done a good job of putting on a happy face because in September, while Bill and I were out for awhile, members of the household plastered banners across the front of the house reading, "Happy 28th Anniversary, Bill and Laurie!" I felt embarrassed when I saw that, feeling like a hypocrite, feeling lonely inside. But our Joe had been home from Texas for a visit and Bill's mother came for awhile, so these were extra bright spots for me that year, and I continued to function adequately in spite of the unhappiness in my marriage.

One dark, rainy Sunday evening in April of 1984, though, just before Bill's weekly meeting with the men in the community, we were up in our bedroom where he was giving me a talking to with barely controlled fury, "You're just nice to people to get them to like you!" he raved. Stabbing his index finger at me to punctuate his words, his tirade continued. "I know you better than you know yourself and I know your motives!" I had learned there wasn't any point in trying to defend myself so I kept my mouth shut. That only increased his agitation, and when he left to go downstairs to the meeting he angrily hurled these words at me as he closed the door, "I know you won't divorce me because you don't want to be known as a bad girl!"

I sat there for a while, trembling. Then I got up and walked downstairs, continuing out the front door into the pouring rain. I walked for hours through Lansing's west side and out into the country, eventually arriving around 11:30 at Sue and John's Bethel Farm near Grand Ledge. I was a cold sodden mess. Struggling to say anything, I told them, "I just have to get to God about something."

While Sue got me a hot cup of tea and some dry clothes to put on, I phoned the house and left a message as to where I was, and that I would be staying for awhile. Then I went out to the A-shaped chapel at the back of their orchard to be quiet before the Lord. There was a galley kitchen and a bathroom so I could make a cup of tea when I needed it, otherwise I needed to fast and pray.

Knowing nothing could touch me there, I just knelt or sat there for hours. I was too exhausted emotionally, physically and mentally to try to do or be anything. Sue checked on me a time or two but she understood how sometimes one just has to be alone with God. I knew God was there with me even though I didn't sense his presence. I just needed to be there for him to restore me to some semblance of function, knowing I was an empty clay pot needing to be filled up and planted with some grace and strength.

I nodded off at times, weak and messy like a wet dishrag. I just couldn't imagine how I could go on living my life the way it was. But Tuesday night, Sandy Lee and our David came to the chapel, urging me to come home. They spoke of Bill looking haggard and just staying in his room and they were worried about me too. I was not ready to go home yet but I went back with them anyway. I didn't know what else to do. I just let God carry me for awhile as I went about my business, let him continue to work his magic inside of me and one day I recognized that I was finally in a better place as I wrote in my journal: "I know I was trained to be a dutiful Martha. I have viewed my quiet time each morning as a responsibility, in that I must pray for all the people I promised to pray for, and listen for the wisdom I need from God to meet the day, before I can let myself go and just worship him.

"But I am getting bolder, letting myself be more of a Mary. Not the nice proper Mary I imagine the Mother of God to be, but a rather messy Mary. Again I can see God all around me so vividly that I'm beginning to grin at him throughout the day, and frequently stop in awe when I recognize him in all his loveliness. I feel an interior wantonness, a desire to launch myself into somewhere or something that I sense is almost in my grasp!"

I was aware of and identifying with a poem by Elizabeth Rooney that accurately depicted my inner joy:

I haven't cleaned the cellar,
I forgot to sweep the stair
There's a button off my jacket,
Jonny's blue jeans have a tear,
There's an old arthritic lady

Whom I should uphold in prayer,
And I'm sitting in the moonlight,
The moonlight, the moonlight,
Adoring you by moonlight,
As if I had no care!"

Early one morning later that spring, I received a desperate phone call from my father. I had known that my mother was ill with some type of pneumonia, but she was responding well to the medication the last I had heard. Now my father was sobbing that my mother was dying. I tried to comfort him, telling him I was on my way. Bill drove me to Chicago to catch a flight to Cedar Rapids, where my shaken father met my plane at noon that day.

There were nurses fussing over Mother when we arrived at the hospital, but when she saw me she smiled. In a few days, she rallied, and I saw to it that she was safely settled back at home before I returned to Michigan. She was more fragile than usual though so it would take a number of weeks for her to gain back all her strength. In the meantime, her children had been planning a big reunion to be held in Cedar Rapids that summer to celebrate their fifty years of marriage.

We all had been sewing for months on a huge quilt. Each child and grandchild stitched a square of cloth with a design or saying of some familial significance. The surviving aunts and uncles did the same and then we had the squares professionally quilted to present it to Mother and Daddy when we all gathered in Cedar Rapids for our celebration. Our time together reinforced the ideal of a long and loving marriage surrounded by children and grandchildren in your old age. What a rare blessing! I was filled up with the familial love present there, knowing it survived despite the fact that we all had our problems.

Another celebration that summer was Michael's graduation from Michigan State University. Safely past that awful time of depression, after first building houses and then working at the regional Post Office, he had gone back to MSU and finished a degree in Russian.

That fall I went to work for Right to Life of Michigan as the Executive Secretary of their legislative office a few blocks from our house. Bill's unemployment had run out and I had wondered if I should consider working as a secretary. I must have been wondering out loud, because one of our parish staff members phoned me with news of this job opportunity and urged me to apply for it.

Our kids were putting some money into the household kitty every month now and some household members started putting in more, assuring us that as we had supported a number of them until they were financially sound, so now they could reciprocate. But we hadn't had health insurance since Bill lost his job at the bakery and that coverage would be one of the perks of this job. So I went for an interview, was offered the position, and decided to go with the flow.

All of the household members at that time except the moms and children, were out and about during the day so I thought I could be spared then without compromising their care. I didn't realize at the time that it would mean more stress for me. I was fine once I was at the office but I regularly felt a reluctance to get out there and get going in the morning. A few years later I would understand what was going on inside of me, but in the meantime I just kept on keeping on.

Bicycling Adventures

In the spring of 1985, we celebrated the marriages of two of the women who had lived with us the longest (around ten years each). After all the things we had been through together, I had grown to love Sandy Lee and Faye as if they were my own daughters so it was with great happiness that we attended their respective Nuptial Masses just six weeks apart. Faye even wore my wedding dress as she began her new life with her husband, the brother of one of our household members.

A new experience began for me too, in April when Bill and I went for a bicycle ride one Sunday afternoon to Scott Woods in south Lansing. The woods were damp and had that pungent springtime odor of half-decaying, half-blooming plants that brought back memories of trips to Sisily Grove with my father. As we were meandering around I was also thinking of a book I had just read, *Miles from Nowhere,* about a couple who rode their bicycles around the world.

Mentioning the book to Bill, I related to him some of the interesting adventures recounted by the author. "I wish we could ride our bikes to somewhere sometime instead of just going for a short ride," I commented, thinking that DeWitt, five miles north of us as a would be a good target. "Why don't we go see my mother?" Bill suggested. I nearly fell off my bike! She lived in St. Louis, Missouri! "How could we do that!" I exclaimed. "Well, we start riding like we did today and just keep on riding," Bill calmly replied.

He spoke from experience since he had ridden his bicycle between Ames, Iowa and St. Louis, Missouri when he was a student at Iowa State. I was used to riding my bicycle around the neighborhood and even sometimes rode it to my monthly Community Mental Health Board meetings. But I had never before pictured myself doing what he proposed. I certainly hadn't imagined us old fogies roaming around like the young couple I had read about in that book! But I was intrigued with the idea.

Later that week, when I said something to our son, Paul, about possibly cycling to St. Louis, he reacted with astonishment. "For one thing, Ma," he said. "You've only got a 3-speed bike and Dad's is an antique no-speed, and then there's the matter of training to ride long distances. You don't just up and ride a long way like that." He seemed to dismiss the idea.

I didn't dismiss the idea though. This willingness to be a bit adventuresome was one of the things I appreciated about Bill. The more I thought about it the more I liked the idea of a long cross-country trip. As he and I talked it over, we decided to go riding after lunch the next Sunday just as we had the week before, but this time we headed east through East Lansing, Okemos and Haslett until we reached the home of friends out in the country. By the time we got back to our house it was 11:30 that evening. Lights were blazing from the downstairs windows and fretful voices reproached us when we rode in. "Where *were* you? We were so worried about you!" they cried.

We apologized for not thinking to report our whereabouts sooner, but were secretly quite pleased with ourselves. We had only covered about thirty miles but it was a start. Flushed with that accomplishment, we started riding thirty or forty miles each weekend. We started making plans as if we really would be riding our bicycles all the way to St. Louis that summer.

Bill was the detail person of this duo though, not me, so he made lists of stuff we would need. We bought panniers for our bikes, sleeping bags and self-inflating mats to go under our sleeping bags, and a tent. Then Bill added spare tires, bike tools and Band Aids to his entomology collecting gear and decided we would be ready for anything.

When the kids saw that we were serious, Paul said he'd lend his 15-speed touring bike to Bill, and Anne-Marie insisted I ride her 10-speed. We both had to adjust to riding this type of bicycle because we had to bend forward instead of sitting upright. And that took quite a bit of getting used to.

Bill's assurance that we could do this was encouraging, but I still wondered if his memory served him well. He had accumulated almost thirty years and double that in pounds since his last trip of this length, and I was no spring chicken either. The Sunday before we left home for St. Louis, we rode farther than we ever had—sixty miles—and we were really pooped by the time we got back home. I had gotten permission to be off work for three weeks and hoped that would be enough time to get there and back.

We were such novices, neither one of us wore helmets and I shod myself in sandals instead of a more protective type of footwear. The day we left I came home from work early, we finished loading our bikes, and by 4:30 we were on our way amid bon voyage wishes. Maria and Dave Post presented us with bright orange T-shirts. One said, "Lansing" on the back and the other said, "Michigan."

We rode for thirty-five miles that evening, encountering a few hassles right away. My water bottle kept slipping sideways until Bill reinforced the holder with a wadded Kleenex, and one road designated on our county map as paved, wasn't, but we had the pleasure of enjoying an unexpected Bluegrass Festival in Bennett Park before we ended up at Pine Lake south of Olivet, camping there for the night.

On a back road around noon the next day, a snarling dog took off after me as we cycled by his turf. I tried spraying it with my can of Mace but that didn't seem to dissuade the critter at all. Thankfully, he gave up the chase before I gave out, but it was good to be able to slow down and catch my breath after that encounter. Our slow-down turned into a stop as we realized that all along that road were tons of ripe, wild raspberries. We enjoyed an unexpected feast as we rested in the sweet tall grass there. Riding for one hundred eight miles through seven small towns before we quit that day, we were thankful to find a campground and collapse.

Weather-wise, it had been a perfect day. Otherwise the day was painful as I struggled with sore, bruised hands in spite of the padded gloves I wore and the sponge rubber handlebar covers. My upper thighs were sore also, and my saddle-sore posterior motivated me to keep adjusting my seat, trying to ease the discomfort. Then there was a stinging rash forming on my inner thighs from the abrasive way they rubbed the seat as I peddled. This was no piece of cake!

When we awoke the next morning our tent was very wet because of heavy dew. We took our time getting away and adjusted our watches back an hour to Indiana time. After we attended Mass in South Bend, the day was best described as continuing pain. With the aforementioned physical problems still afflicting me, plus the temperature hovering at 89 degrees and sun blazing much of the day, I wondered what in the world I had gotten myself into. To fuel my concern, those Indiana county roads were bad, jarring us to bits.

We only did sixty-five miles that day, quitting when we reached Tippecanoe State Park. Once we had our tent up we had to wait for it to dry out before we could sleep in it, and I wondered if I could function at all the next day, but I had been comforted by the kindness and courtesy of people we encountered along the way. A group of bicyclists in South Bend had led us through a maze of downtown traffic, and a cyclist camping next to us that night gave us helpful advice about roads in the area. Guardian angels seemed to be riding with us.

The next day we didn't leave Tippecanoe until afternoon because Bill climbed up in a fire tower that morning to collect flies. It sprinkled on us the whole time but the cloud cover was nicer than the hot sun. We cycled only fifty-nine miles and then put up our tent in a bunch of weeds behind a transmitting tower in the middle of nowhere. Before settling down to sleep that night, with no restroom available, I found it challenging removing my contact lenses in the dark while trying to hold a flashlight and a small mirror at the same time.

The next morning we biked eight miles to Watseka, Illinois, where we stopped to buy some food at a supermarket. As we exited the market, a lady hailed us, introduced herself, and invited us to eat our brunch at a picnic table in her backyard nearby. We had a nice visit with her and thanked her for her kindness.

As we continued south, Bill had a flat tire just south of Cissna Park. If we hadn't had to stop and fix it, we probably would have been out in the open during a violent thunderstorm that rapidly caught up with us. Before we reached Rankin, the next town down the road, we noticed the storm bearing down on us, but we were able to roll under the canopy of what used to be a filling station in Rankin, just as the torrential rain let loose. We heard the fire sirens go off, either calling the volunteer fire department or sounding a tornado warning. We didn't know which.

Copious amounts of lightning and thunder flashed and crashed on top of us. I was feeling very vulnerable being out in it, even with the canopy. Then a guy inside the building invited us to come inside and we were quite cozy there. When the din of the storm abated enough that we could hear ourselves talk, we visited a bit with our host, an engineer who was occupied designing transformers.

Friends in Urbana, Illinois, Wally and Betty LaBerge, were expecting us to spend the night with them so once the rain eased up, I stopped at a little restaurant to phone and tell them we would be delayed. The place was full of farmers in from the fields and the hum of conversation hesitated as I entered the place. I must have looked a bit ratty, feeling very conspicuous as I made my call. Explaining to Betty that we would just camp somewhere tonight and see them for lunch the next day, she made noises about being worried about us being out in the rain, but I assured her we'd be fine, declining her generous offer for them to come and get us.

We started out again, but three miles out of Rankin another storm system came up behind us. Seeing a young girl out in a farmyard near a barn with a wide open door, I rode up to her and asked permission to take cover in the barn. Then her mother came out. "Come on into the house," she beckoned. "We've just returned from our vacation and I'm whipping up a meal. You can surely share it with us." We were glad to be embraced by the safety of her kindness and her house, and when her husband returned, it appeared that we had sung for our supper.

He had just come from the restaurant in town. "You provided quite a bit of entertainment for us as you came through a while ago,' he said, grinning. "Everybody had a different opinion as to your state of sanity, riding bikes in this weather. I'll have quite a spot of fun filling them in later. You know there's a tornado warning out until 11:00, so you'd best put your sleeping bags down in our living room tonight." We had only gone fifty-six miles that day, but visiting with them throughout that stormy evening was an experience that gave us another memory.

On the way again the next morning, we stopped in St. Joseph, where we had time to visit with some friends there before riding the rest of our thirty-nine miles for the day. By noon we arrived at Betty and Wally's home in Urbana, and I was astounded to learn they were very upset with themselves for letting us be out in the storm. "What you must think of us!" cried Betty. "I knew the weather was bad when I talked to you, but I didn't know at the time that there was a tornado warning! When we heard that, we called the sheriff's department and they looked for you out along the highway but couldn't find you. We were so worried!" So after many assurances from us, that we hadn't felt neglected, and our apologies for causing them worry, we settled down to enjoy a good time of sharing with them.

The next day was the Fourth of July, so I expected to see fire works before the day was over. We didn't leave Urbana until 9:00 and it started raining on us a half hour after we left. We struggled against terrible winds through several small towns, finally stopping late in the afternoon for some pizza at a place in Stoneyville called The Watering Hole. We checked to see if there was anybody in the town who rented rooms for the night but were told that there wasn't, so we frantically peddled another eight miles in rain and wind with tornado sirens blowing around us.

I made note of a ditch between the road and a railroad track on our right, thinking I might dive into it in case a funnel cloud came spinning toward me. I mostly kept my eyes on the road directly in front of me, but whenever I did look up and around, I was surprised that even through the rain we could see fireworks in the sky in a couple of directions. It finally got so dark we took to the weeds whenever a car came up behind us, fearing the driver might not see us at the side of the road despite our tail lights.

I remember telling the Lord at one point during that segment of the trip, "I know you're taking care of us but I don't feel like I'm being taken care of!" So when I spotted a place called Ryan's Inn up ahead, I told Bill that's where I was headed. He objected, saying we couldn't afford it, but my desire to be under cover was too great to heed him. I paid $34 for the room and was thankful that it was available. When I rolled my bike into our unit, I noticed Bill was right behind me, but he remained angry all night, refusing to speak to me. We had ridden ninety-two miles and I was too tired to care.

We were back on the road about 6:00 on July 5th with a freshly washed world awaiting us. It was good for all of five—maybe seven minutes and then we settled into battling headwinds and heat. Near the little town of Staunton, Illinois, my derailleur broke so I could no longer shift gears. I stopped at a little store and asked the cashier if she knew anywhere that I could get a bicycle part. She told me there just happened to be a senior citizen about four blocks away who fooled around with bikes and might be able to help me.

Sure enough, there was Remo Messalino, right where the cashier said he'd be! And with him was his wife, Virginia, who offered us a soda and lawn chairs, and then sat herself down, ready to visit. Remo told us he had bought out a Schwinn bike shop and stuffed it into his garage, and he felt quite sure that somewhere in there he could find the part I needed. So while Virginia and I chatted, Bill visited with Remo as he removed my broken derailleur and replaced it with a new one, charging us only $5.00 for the part and the two hours it took to complete our business. Did I feel the Lord was taking care of me then? I surely did!

The day wasn't over yet though, and we still had to struggle up and around the hills, wind and heat that had been there all day for us. We finally reached the Mississippi River and the McKinley Bridge over it just before 9:00 p.m., so you might imagine our dismay when we pulled up beside a toll booth at the bridge and were informed that we couldn't ride our bikes across the bridge. In consternation we were trying to digest the implications of that information, when a pickup truck pulled up and the toll booth guy asked the driver to take us across. He obligingly help us load our bikes into the bed of his truck and then beckoned us into the cab with him. As we crossed the river we could see fireworks going off down river near the St. Louis Arch, where the Fourth of July activities had obviously been extended at least another day. We disembarked from the truck with many thanks to our modern day St. Christopher, and then started peddling up still another hill.

It took 2½ more hours for us to reach the home of Bill's sister, Alice Jean, in Rock Hill, a western suburb of St. Louis. Within only two blocks of the end our 106-mile day, we nearly experienced disaster. We were just too exhausted. First, my front wheel got caught in a rut along the edge of a busy street and I fell with my bike into the path of a car coming up behind me. Luckily the driver was able to stop before hitting me, and the fall itself hadn't injured me or the bike. Then, when we were right in front of Alice Jean's house, Bill tried to stop, but he and his bike went down in the street. What an ignominious finale for both of us! I was very glad nobody saw us. His bike's front light was broken by the fall, and both of the glass killing tubes he had in his hip pockets were shattered, but like me, he wasn't injured. It was a bit tricky separating all of the pulverized glass from the pockets of his jeans though. We had ridden five hundred fifty-six miles total so far, in one week's time.

After four days of resting and visiting with lots of relatives in the St. Louis area, we figured we were prepared for the return trip. We left at 5:00 a.m. in order to get through most of St. Louis before the rush hour traffic got too bad. We were able to ride our bikes across the Mississippi River north of there at Alton, Illinois. The bridge was so narrow that the cars didn't try to pass us, so we were leading a long parade by the time we got to the other side.

Then we decided to follow the Mississippi for awhile, peddling on a bike path which paralleled the Great River Road on the Illinois side of the river. It was wonderful to be able to ride on a bike trail, relaxing from the vigilance needed when you're sharing space with semitrailers. I enjoyed exploring some of the little towns along the way and eventually we headed east, camping at Beaver Dam State Park, after cycling seventy-seven miles that day.

It rained during the night and early morning the next day, so we got a late start. At one point I was riding behind Bill and was inattentive enough that my front tire bumped his back tire. Although neither of us fell, perhaps the incident scared him, because he turned around and really let me have it! He was very angry with me! Whenever he acted like that I just wanted to get as far away from him as possible, so I lagged far behind him for several hours. We traveled 94 miles that day, a lot of it after dark on remote back roads. At one point we really didn't know where we were or even what direction we were traveling, but we finally made it to Eagle Creek State Park, a primitive campsite.

I was never thrilled when we had to camp somewhere without a shower facility. The dirt of the road assaults you all day and the stench of road kills you pass seems to cling to your clothes. You get so grungy that a sponge bath just isn't adequate, so we were longing for showers as we headed out the next day. You might say our longing was satisfied when it started raining on us in earnest by the time we'd reached Bement, and we were thoroughly soaked way before we reached Wally and Betty's Urbana home around 8:00 that evening after riding seventy-eight miles. Needless to say, we looked like something the cat dragged in so their more conventional showers were greatly appreciated.

After Bill spent the morning getting his rear wheel repaired, we began a marathon of visiting with old friends in the Champaign/Urbana area. Then, our friend, Wes Duncan, made me smile when he insisted on coming for us his pickup truck, saying it was too hot for us to cycle the eight miles to St. Joseph where a number of old friends had assembled to visit with us. I had a wonderful time! We slept at the Duncan's and continued visiting for another day before leaving early in the morning on July 15th under cloudy skies. We made good time that day—107 miles to Little Creek Campground near Monon, Indiana.

It had helped that the headwinds we had struggled against on the trip west were now our friends, pushing us along. Also, we were in much better physical shape than we had been when we left Lansing. We had stopped at a McDonald's around noon that day and observed a line of around twenty teenage cyclists come into the parking lot with much moaning and groaning about how exhausted they were, despite the fact that they had a vehicle to carry their camping gear and baggage.

After we'd finished our meal and ridden about an hour down the road through fields of corn and beans, we came across a brick Catholic church and school, standing like an ship in the middle of the ocean of fields around them. The buildings were swarming with parishioners who were bustling about with brooms and buckets, paint and pots. As we stopped to visit a bit, one of them exclaimed, "Oh, you're cycling cross country too! We just had a group of teenagers from Massachusetts camp here last night! It must be very interesting!" It amused us to think that the teenagers seemed to be exhausted after riding only one hour. They were evidently in much worse shape than we were. I have to admit that we felt a bit smug as we started off on down the road, figuratively patting ourselves on the back a little.

The next morning, Bill collected flies again, so we didn't leave until afternoon, riding only forty-two miles because our tail wind had turned around and betrayed us for some diabolical reason. We returned to Tippecanoe State Park, where the next morning Bill made another trip back up the fire tower. I was glad to spend the morning visiting with other campers and reading.

I always carry a book with me as a lifeline to sanity when I go anywhere with Bill. Then it's easier for me to be patient with his penchant for roaming around with his insect net for hours at a time. Bill also had to work on his rear tire again which was bent crooked. We rode eighteen miles into Bass Lake to eat supper and then rode around the park some. It was a peaceful time. We called home and learned that all was well there.

Riding through the flat countryside amid fields and fields and fields of corn and beans had a pleasantness about it. A lady sitting at her vegetable stand along the road in front of her house, waved to us, inviting us to have lunch with her. A man and his son working from tractors in their field, stopped long enough when they saw us riding by, to rise in their seats, clap their hands above their heads, and cheer us on. For several hours, we rode through Amish country where people would wave to us and want to visit with us for a bit. Being on a bicycle makes one very approachable. And the soft clopping sound of a horse and buggy trotting by us at a good clip, was soothing after cringing before the roar of semis.

Bill had a mirror on his handlebar. When he was riding behind me he would sometimes call out to me, "car coming!" or "truck coming!" One time I heard, "house coming!" I stopped and spun around. Sure enough, a house was on the move behind us, towed by a big truck with cars fore and aft flashing their caution lights.

The convoy was approaching at fifteen miles per hour. We prolonged our stop to watch it go by, admiring the engineering that makes such a thing possible and ruminating a bit about the house's history. We actually saw quite a bit of history as we peddled through the countryside. It was a usual thing for us to stop to rest or to picnic in a cemetery along the way. We often napped under a tree for a while, joining the quiet spirits there and sometimes perusing the tombstones, speculating about the lives of those resting there with us.

On the 18th of July, Bill did some early collecting again so we didn't get started until after mid-morning, but in spite of that we rode 95 miles through northern Indiana. Although the temperature was in the high 80's, the humidity was low so it was not bad. We camped at Shipshewana near the Michigan border. This camp was strictly utilitarian, and located in the middle of the town which was noted for its huge flea market where many Amish goods were available. I wasn't tempted to look at the goods, though. By now I was just looking forward to getting home and back into my own bed.

Just after crossing into Michigan, on July 19th, we encountered the only discourteous experience of the entire trip. As we peddled over a narrow bridge, a woman driver became impatient with us, honking repeatedly and practically sideswiping us as she finally pushed her way past us, even though there was no place for us to get out of her way if we had gotten off our bikes. We were only seventeen miles from home at 8:30 that night when Bill had another flat tire which delayed us awhile. But at 10:00 p.m. we rode into our driveway after one hundred seventeen miles of cycling that day. It was very satisfying to know we had ridden one thousand, two-hundred and forty miles without a serious mishap, no doubt because our guardian angels worked overtime.

Our children had always treated us with respect, but they told us that their respect got boosted up a few notches after this undertaking. And I felt stronger not just physically, but emotionally. Bill had experienced problems with an arthritic knee, but by the time we got back he was feeling great and had lost some weight. So we did a lot of bicycling that summer and fall, discovering rails-to-trails biking paths and getting to know well, all the country roads in the Lansing area. I really enjoyed the beauty around me, the healthy exercise and the fact that we were doing something together. It made possible the illusion that we were growing closer together as a couple because of this shared activity, if I didn't look too closely at the fact that our private life remained unchanged.

I appreciated what I thought of as ordinary married life during the periods when Bill related peacefully to me. The wonderful, magical part of my life still came from the Lord, my family and my friends. And surely my greatest blessing was my children even as I knew that most of them would soon be disappearing from my daily life.

Romance

The romance of the spring weddings of Sandy and Faye was still in the air at the end of the summer. Our son, Paul and our daughter, Anne-Marie were both planning weddings for the following spring and their future spouses, Paul's Karen and Anne-Marie's Matt, were living with us until then, so both the physical and the spiritual preparation for those weddings was a regular presence in our midst.

We were thrilled just before Christmas when one of the Vietnamese refugee families we had sponsored, Kim Long Tran and his sons, Son and Hai, were reunited with the rest of their family. It had been six years since they were separated from his wife Ru and the two younger children when the boat they were using to escape Vietnam was attacked, so this was an incredibly poignant occasion.

There was a huge crowd of us at the airport to greet them when Ru, Kim Long's daughter Kim Linh and his son, Ngoc Anh walked off the plane. For years we had sent packages of goods and medicine to Ru, through a complicated network of European and Vietnamese refugees and friends. She sold most of the goods she received, hoping that she could eventually save enough money to make her way here. It seemed almost unreal that they were all finally together. Our hearts were full of thankfulness that Christmas.

In early January, on one of the coldest days of the year, our old beast of a furnace finally collapsed. Mr. Simmons, the elderly man who had for years used his considerable wisdom and expertise to keep it running, announced that even all the kings men could not put it together again. He installed a new efficient boiler that took up only a fraction of the space the old one had inhabited. This was the first household expense that we did not have the money for, so we were forced to resort to a $5,000 loan from the bank to cover the cost.

As the boiler was being installed, a package arrived from our son Joe, who now lived in Boston. It contained enough black or white tee-shirts for the whole family, with the name of his band, *Beat Surrender* emblazoned across the front of each. How appropriate was the timing! We all donned the shirts with other pieces of black clothing and draped ourselves around the new boiler for a silly family picture. The phrase, "beat surrender" aptly fit the situation as we watched piece after piece of the old boiler carted up the stairs and out of the house.

A large contingent of us traveled five hundred miles north to Paul and Karen's wedding in April, and then celebrated Anne-Marie and Matt's nuptials at St. Mary Cathedral the end of May of 1986. I was very thankful for the spouses my children had chosen. Living with them in the household had enabled me to know them and love them even before they were officially family, so there was a sense of gaining a daughter and a son instead of losing a daughter and a son.

But the fact of the matter was that my children were on the move big-time. That August, David left with another household member, to live in Osaka, Japan where they would be teaching English and learning Japanese for a year. And Julie's work for the Catholic Newman Center attached to Lansing Community College was a nowhere job for her so she moved to Chicago to try to get work as a graphic illustrator there. She would live with the mother of my friend, Maria.

That would leave Amy as our only child at home. Of course, we still had eleven other household members in August. Then eight more came in September, one in October and four more in November. Loaves and Fishes, a local shelter, sent Kayla and Sean to us with their ten-month old son. A Michigan State University student from Indonesia moved in, a woman who was rethinking the three abortions she had chosen to have, joined us, and then a family with three children came to rest up after a stint of working at Bethel Farm. Another woman who came at that time had just given her baby up for adoption and was still going through the grieving process. These were just some of the people who joined us that fall.

Since I was now working, Kim Lee was the constant caring presence in the house during the day. Some of the other people like Kim, were an absolute joy but we also had some really hard situations to deal with. One woman stole some of my clothes and some of Julie's belongings which we had stored for her in our basement. Another person was a man who was recovering from severe burns and head trauma incurred when he smashed his car into a tree at high speed. Every night when I came in the door he was waiting for me, wanting something. And I was tired by then and found it difficult to give.

The romance bug was still alive and well though. Michael came home from Providence at Thanksgiving, bringing his fiance, Debbie and we also knew that Joe would be marrying his Marcia in Boston in February. Kayla and Sean were married in our living room with Fr. Peter Dougherty officiating. And Mark, who had lived with us for years, had found the love of his life next door. My parents were with us for Thanksgiving too, so the holiday season that year was a happy one.

I might legitimately say the year 1987 was one of upheaval. In early February my routine physical examination revealed that I had tumors on my cervix and ovaries, so surgery was needed to remove them, and there was concern that they might be cancerous. A couple of days after that news, Bill and I flew to Boston to attend Joe and Marcia's wedding and then we came back to Michigan in time to welcome Anne-Marie and Matt's firstborn son, David. Then a battery of medical tests and lots of prayers preceded the surgery I had in early March. Thankfully all the tumors were benign.

I spent the season of Lent relegated to either my bedroom or the second floor living room as I was treated like the princess of the place. Bill guarded me like a hawk and treated me with much kindness and concern. He had been scared enough the night before the surgery to tell me that he wouldn't want to live if something happened to me. That was the first time he ever indicated in a way that I could understand, that he did care about me. Although I was tempted to think he would miss me just because of the services I provided him, I still realized that this was a good thing that had come out of all the bother.

Anne-Marie and Matt decided to come back to the house to stay during my convalescence so I could be distracted by my new grandson and she could help with my care. It was a time of joy and reflection for me, probably the first Lenten season in my adult life that I hadn't been practicing some form of penance in preparation for Easter. The week before Easter I was allowed downstairs and then received a call asking me to serve at Holy Thursday Mass by being one of the people to have their feet washed by the Bishop. I had to chuckle at the irony of it all.

Unbeknownst to me, a lot of chit chat was going on between my children about their concern for my health if I continued to work at Right to Life and also try to keep the household going. They approached us with their concern and suggested that we consider giving up the household. We prayed for guidance and looked at the situation. My physician exhorted me to pay attention to my body and what it was trying to tell me. I had to admit that I felt tired and pressured most of the time.

Two of the men in the household would be getting married during the summer and most of the people presently in the household were planning to leave by the end of summer and could do so without duress. Paul and Anne-Marie had talked with their spouses and suggested to us that we put the house up for sale in June for three months. If it didn't sell by the end of August, they would move back into the house with us to help us meet the financial expense of keeping it going until we could sell it. So, after much thought and prayer we stopped taking in new people and concentrated on winding things down.

Winding Down

During the active years of the household it had seemed like it would go on forever because there was such a need for it. I don't think I ever speculated on what might occur that would cause us to close it down. The rich diversity of the spiritual state and cultural background of the people living with us made each day pregnant with the unexpected. It was never dull at our house!

My faith grew tremendously through those years as God's generosity was displayed in our midst with such abandon. I had been trained to be responsible for so many things, but God had shown me a way to let him carry my burdens and just do the tasks that were before me each day. This gave me an enormous sense of freedom and peace.

Although I knew I would miss the excitement of the ministry in the household, I think we were both ready for a big change in our life. Bill suggested we might go to live in Costa Rica for the winter months. There he could do volunteer work, collecting and identifying insects for the University of Costa Rica Department of Insects and for the National Parks of Costa Rica. Staff from those two institutions were regularly sending him insects to identify but he would really enjoy getting out in the field there. He convinced me that the country was a stable and safe place to live, and, furthermore, there was a large Catholic Charismatic Community of people there who would welcome us into their midst.

He figured that with his retirement money augmented by interest off the money from the sale of the house we would have enough to live on there. In the meantime we could live on the bus and visit our kids when we were back in the states. Bill had talked about us living on the bus full-time before this but I'd always told him I'd have to have a real kitchen and a bathroom on it before I'd be willing to try living that way. With that in mind he said he might try to find a newer bus to fix up into a more permanent habitation for us.

As my strength returned we resumed our practice of bicycling on the weekends, often riding on old railroad bed trails as far as Laingsburg, twenty miles northeast of us where there was a pizza place we could refuel at before heading back home. We were riding on a country road east of Perry, Michigan one Sunday in early May, when I noticed a school bus for sale in someone's yard. I stopped in my tracks. Bill was ahead of me but he hadn't seen it. I hailed him and we decided to take a look.

A young couple greeted us when we knocked on the door of the house, and they filled us in on the history of the bus as they unlocked it for us to appraise. They had fixed it up when they were first married but now they had been able to buy a real motor home so they didn't need it anymore. I got a pleasurable feeling of recognition as we explored it since it was the same make and model as our old bus. But it was longer, four years newer and it had a real kitchen and a real bathroom. We didn't have the $3,000 they were asking for it but we told them we'd stay in touch and see if we could find a way to buy it.

As news got around about the bus we had found, Sandy Darga and her husband offered to lend us the money until we could sell our house and pay her back. If we bought it right away, Bill would have the time to get it adapted to our needs before we left to go south for the winter so we accepted her offer and bought it. As you might expect, there were problems with it immediately as Bill attempted to drive it to our house, but he got those handled in time for us to drive it to Michael's wedding toward the end of May.

We took Anne-Marie, Matt, their little David, Paul, Karen, Julie and Amy with us. It was a bit crowded for sleeping so we set up a tent for more room at night as we camped along the way and we had a grand time. It was a pleasure for my kids, too, to have a table, a kitchen and a bathroom after all those years of roughing it on the old bus without those amenities.

When we returned from the festivities in the east, we listed the house for sale and Bill immediately got busy restructuring the inside of the new bus, banishing the living room area first by donating the couch and a fancy hanging lamp to Paul and Karen. Then up went a counter with tons of insect drawers underneath. In went two file cabinets and a computer table where the couch had been. There was no help for it. The man had to have his work space.

The bedroom area at the back of the bus was actually empty space where the previous owners had put up portable cots. So Bill built bunks with drawers under them and I had foam mattresses cut to size, upholstered them, and made curtains for the windows. The bus felt light and airy inside after I painted all the dark paneled woodwork white. I was happy feathering my new nest.

We reached the end of August with no buyer for the house but I had to chuckle, when the very next day, a buyer appeared at our door and put down his earnest money. I wasn't surprised at the cliff-hanger aspect of the deal because I'd experienced the Lord working that way before. So we trusted that the deal would go through and started planning on driving the bus to Tampa, where we'd put it in storage and then live in Costa Rica through the winter months.

Late in September I finished my work with Right to Life of Michigan and turned to devoting my time to the onerous task of reassigning all our furniture and most of our other belongings to either our children or friends, while belongings too personal to part with we boxed up to be stored at Anne-Marie and Matt's home in Grand Rapids.

We would have liked Amy to go with us to Costa Rica but she wanted to remain and start her college courses at Lansing Community College in September. Like most of our other children she had received a Pell grant, and with her part-time job she felt she could manage. She moved into an apartment around the corner with another young woman who was a student. Shortly before we left for Costa Rica, however, we learned that Amy had resumed a relationship with a young man we had felt was not good for her and was pregnant with his child.

Heartsick about that turn of events, we again urged her to go with us to Costa Rica but she didn't want to go and would be eighteen on the day we left, so there was nothing we could do. It was some comfort to us that she had siblings and extended family members close by for support but my heart was still aching for her. I could only pray for her and promise to be back in plenty of time for the child's birth in June. We said a lot of good-byes to family and friends during the month of October, closed the deal for the sale of our house on the thirty-first, and then began our new life as we left for Tampa.

I had always loved the feeling of rolling down the open road. One night we were the only ones camping at Indian Springs State Park in Indiana. It was beautiful and warm but we went to bed about 6:00 p.m. because it was dark and we were tired. We got up at 2:00 in the morning and saw that the full moon had bathed the park in light so bright that the trees cast shadows for us to walk in.

After enjoying nice hot showers, orange juice and morning prayers, we left at 3:30 a.m. The winding country road was eerie as we went in and out of patches of ground fog. Once, I thought I saw a vast lake off to the right of us but it was only fog lying over a field. At 6:30.a.m., we stopped at a rest stop and slept a couple of hours, waking up to rain, needing then to wipe up water where we'd left the roof vent open.

One night when we pulled into the last available slot at a rest stop near Clarksville, Tennessee, we were surrounded by so many giant rigs that our bus was practically invisible. About 1:00 a.m., I awoke and walked the short distance to the restroom, and when I returned, Bill left to do the same thing. I got back into my sleeping bag and lay on my side, looking out the window beside me, speculating about the interior arrangement of the huge truck parked so close I thought I could almost reach out and touch it. Suddenly a man with black hair and moustache walked jauntily into my line of vision and his eyes widened in surprise as they met mine.

He kept right on going, but a moment later he swept past my window again going the opposite direction, making a few outrageous comments to me as he flew by. I yanked my curtains shut without a word, but I giggled too, knowing the guy was just trying to get a rise out of me. It never is dull out on the road!

Driving through the Cumberland Mountains the scenery was breathtaking, the trees so many hues of gold, orange, red, green and brown. And over our speaker system the music was playing a hymn from Isaiah 55:12: *You shall go out with joy and be led back with peace. The mountains and the hills will break forth before you. And all the trees of the field shall clap their hands with joy.*

A truck loaded with live chickens; crates and crates of live chickens, passed us drifting white feathers in its wake. I felt like one of those snowmen inside a glass globe that you shake to simulate a snowstorm. Instead of leaving feathers behind, I liked to think I was leaving heavy burdens behind me. We had a few days to visit with my sister and her family in Orlando and with Tom and his family in Tampa and then we were off to Costa Rica on November 11, 1987, off to a whole new way of living.

Costa Rica

Aboard the *Sansa* Airline flight to Costa Rica from Miami, our fellow passengers were joyfully boisterous, eating, drinking wine, and constantly visiting up and down the aisles as if they were in their own living room. I fell in love with Costa Rica! As we roamed their country for the next few months, the *Ticos* (Costa Ricans) were unfailingly gentle and kind to us.

Once we landed in San Jose, the first people we encountered were from *Agape*, a Catholic Charismatic Community that welcomed us into their midst. Several of the community families housed and fed us for ten days, until we found a small house we were able to rent from one of the women in the community.

So on a Sunday morning we were dropped off at the house (named la Casa Café) in downtown San Pedro, to begin life more or less on our own again. As I unlocked the front door so that Bill could bring in our suitcases, I felt my feet and lower legs burning. I had stepped into a nest of fire ants! I stripped off my hose and got rid of them and Bill sprayed the doorstep with insecticide, but it was several days before the burning discomfort of the stings subsided.

As we entered the house I felt discouraged because it was obvious that the landlady's promise to have it cleaned and to have sheets and another bed brought over, had not been realized. We dashed up the street to a supermarket and bought sheets and pillowcases. Then we walked over to the Church of San Pedro to 11:00 Mass which didn't get started until 11:15. This phenomenon of lateness (known as *Tico* Time) was widespread in Costa Rica.

After Mass we tried to do a little cleaning. I started with the ceiling, trying to sweep down spiders and dead flies while Bill killed fifteen of the spiders. I managed to kill three of them, which was pretty good for me since I'm terrified of spiders. After taking down the filthy, rotting, kitchen curtains so I could wash the windows, the landlady finally showed up with the promised sheets and pillow cases but only the box springs for another bed. "My grandson was born today," she explained, "and my daughter had to have a C-section so I wasn't able to get here sooner."

Apology given and accepted, she took the two dirty bedspreads to wash and left us with one dubious blanket between us. We were already in bed at 9:00

when we thought we heard someone trying to open our kitchen window. Bill grabbed two insect nets and charged down the stairs to confront the culprit but we had locked everything up tight and he didn't find anyone who had breached our defense system.

The night was an eternity with my legs still burning, new sounds all around, visions of spiders, and a cold wind blowing. Bill had the only blanket on his bed because I am usually too warm at night anyway, but I finally got cold enough to get up and put on a jogging suit and eventually my robe over that. I had noted in my journal: "We went to sleep with 1½ beds and lots of critters. May God help me!"

Bill was kept busy killing spiders as long as we lived there. I told him he should notch his belt for every spider he killed, but his pants would have fallen down if he had. After a couple of days there, we weren't able to get more than a trickle of water out of either sink or shower. Then I got sick with chills, fever and diarrhea to the point where I fainted every time I tried to stand up. Once I had fainted in the bathroom and when Bill leaned on the sink to pick me up off the floor, the sink came off the wall. He went to a *farmacia* and bought some Kaopectate, which helped me to get better, and then we bought a *Tico Times* newspaper and started looking through the advertising section for another place to live.

I phoned in response to an ad which offered a bungalow for rent to an elderly Christian couple, checking to see if we qualified. It sounded good and the bus ride to see the house revealed lush beautiful vegetation and views as we climbed the mountain to San Ramon de Tres Rios. The owners, Mary and Dolf Jonker, retired from the Dutch Foreign Service, seemed as happy to find us as we were happy to find them. The furnished bungalow behind their house was like a box-car of two rooms with a proper bathroom in between. It was only $200 a month, was clean as a whistle, and Mary even said I could use her washing machine.

I was so relieved to move there! Our new address was *La Casa Pequena Detras de la Casa Grande Contigua Este de la Iglesia de San Ramon de Tres Rios, San Jose, Costa Rica.* Which translated, meant—the small house behind the big house just east of the Church of San Ramon of Three Rivers near San Jose. There weren't street addresses at that time, so all addresses were descriptions of the geography around the location of your house, unless you had a post office box.

So in San Ramon we settled down to a routine of sorts. Usually we left with backpacks early on Monday mornings to get the 5:00 a.m. bus into San Jose, where we'd get another bus to take us to whatever area we were expecting to explore that week. A few times we stayed at scientific research stations belonging to the National Parks of Costa Rica, but most of the time we'd be camping out somewhere in the wild until Friday, with Bill collecting insects and me enjoying the surrounding beauty while enduring life in the raw. As always, I took a couple of books along to comfort me when I ran out of things to do. I don't know how I could have survived if I hadn't found Casey's Book Exchange in downtown San Jose. This was run by a character who set up the business after retiring from piloting boats through the Panama Canal.

On Fridays, we came back to our bungalow and cleaned up, so as to be fit to socialize with the community members of *Agape* or other friends on the weekend. Mary Jonker introduced me to women from the Christian Women's Club in San Jose, and before long I was asked to be the speaker at one of the monthly meetings of that organization, and another, similar organization, Women Aglow International. So sometimes I stayed home during the week to fulfill those obligations and attend the weekly Bible study. But most of the time I was with Bill out in the boonies.

For the first time in over thirty years we didn't have to be responsible for anyone but ourselves. There was a tremendous freedom in that and we felt like kids being let out of school. I also couldn't help but think that this might be an opportunity for us to form a more solid relationship since we would be in a totally foreign environment together and in a position to learn new things together. Although Bill would still be absorbed in collecting and identifying insects he could no longer be glued to a computer.

I felt safe everywhere we went but the accommodations were so filthy that Bill decided to have a tent made for us. From then on he carried it in addition to his back pack whenever we left the San Jose area. Everywhere, my senses were assaulted by vivid color, incredible views, delightful people and wonderful adventures. But there were many difficulties and downright calamities to cope with also, and our little sojourn at la Casa Café was merely a drop in that bucket.

Returning from a trip to Cerro de la Muerte, high above the clouds in the Chirripo Mountains, we discovered that our bungalow had been broken into and several things were stolen. Dolf and Mary told us they had investigated, when their guard dogs had barked frantically one night, but an external check of their property had shown nothing amiss. We discovered that our small bathroom window had been broken, despite there being nothing but a deep ravine directly under it. So the day after Christmas, Dolf had the window repaired and bars put on it, while we went to the American Express office to get our travelers checks reimbursed.

Four days later, I set out walking a short distance down the hill from our house to the *pulperia* (little store) nearby. Blissfully unaware of the danger as I carried my straw bag of empty Pepsi bottles, I was attacked by two pit bull guard dogs and bitten on the back of my left leg. Fortunately I didn't fall down, but swung my bag of bottles around at the dogs while men who had been hanging around the pulperia came running and succeeded in keeping the dogs from doing me in any further. They told me that the same dogs had attacked a teenager, once, and a four-year-old, another time, so when I got back to Jonker's, Mary called the Rural Guards to come and collect the dogs.

This occurred a couple of hours before Bill and I left to go to Barra de Colorado with a retired missionary nurse, Evangeline (Vangie) Payne, a staff member of the Pastoral Center in San Ramon. She kept treating my wound during the week we were gone, and I had no permanent physical repercussions from that experience. But I still feel uneasy when I encounter unaccompanied dogs.

The first leg of the Barra de Colorado trip was made by car as Vangie drove a dark section of road through the Chirripo Mountains to Limon, a Caribbean port city. The darkness of the night was so penetrating, it was difficult for her to miss the many potholes lurking in the road so we were royally shaken up on the journey.

After staying the night in a seedy hotel, we went to Port Moin to catch the *Tico* supply boat that travels up and down a coastal canal along the Caribbean. It was supposed to leave at 6:00 that morning, but we stood in drizzling rain for almost two hours before we were jammed with fifty or sixty *Ticos* onto the boat which then headed north up the canal. The boat got stuck on a sand bar half way to Barro de Colorado so the men hauled a small boat down off the roof of the boat and ferried about thirty of us adults over to another sand bar. Then a dozen men stripped down and jumped into the canal to help push the boat into deeper water.

I thoroughly enjoyed the trip. We saw rich jungle foliage, lots of exotic birds, and monkeys swinging in the trees along the river, but other than a few single dwellings here and there we saw no sign of human habitation. The people traveling with us reflected the mostly black population of the Caribbean side of Costa Rica. It took us 12 hours to reach our destination.

It was dark when we arrived to stay for a week in a village of nine hundred Nicaraguan refugees on the northern border of Costa Rica across the Colorado River from Nicaragua. Vangie had brought us with her there to visit her friend, Myrtle, a Nicaraguan nurse who was the only one in the village with medical knowledge of any kind.

Myrtle met us as we docked and her friend, Julio, took our backpacks to her house in a home-made wheelbarrow, the only vehicle in the village. There were paths around the houses but no roads. We had rice and beans and a cup of tea as we met Myrtle's children and her pastor husband. Vangie was to sleep there with the family while Bill and I were sheltered three doors from them in a one-room shack that, I'm sure, was made available to us by temporarily evicting the present owners.

Most of the homes were constructed of rough, ill-fitting boards with thatched or corrugated iron roofs. They were all on stilts and there were always chickens, dogs, cats and children under them. The windows and door of our shack had no screens or glass in them. The walls didn't go all the way up so we had air flowing through all the time. Once it was dark, mosquitoes also flowed through the house so we smeared ourselves with repellant as we tried to go to sleep in the double bed provided for us.

That first night, torrential rain came down. Bill had diarrhea and had to go out in the darkness and driving rain to try to find the outhouse down the path. I could feel cows bumping up against our house and I could hear and smell their wheezing breath at the window by our bed as they chomped on some of the greenery around us. Bill slopped around in the mud and water and finally made it back. It was one of those very long nights.

The next day someone butchered a pig and gave the liver to Myrtle in payment for services she had rendered so we had it for dinner. Fresh meat was a great luxury since there was no refrigeration in the camp. I later saw children under the shack across the path, playing with the remains of the head of the pig, dragging it around and poking at various orifices in what was left of it. All the food we ate tasted good but I kept reminding the Lord of his word which said: *They will be able to drink deadly poison without harm,* (Mark 16:18b) because we were violating all the rules about not eating local uncooked food or drinking untreated water.

Because it kept raining off and on day and night, our feet were always wet and muddy—most people didn't attempt to wear shoes. Everywhere we looked there were clothes hanging on clotheslines, fences, bushes and porches, in hopes they would dry in the sunshine, and I was soon putting our clothing out, too, in an attempt to have something dry and clean to put on. The regular rain showers were our only source of water.

One day, Myrtle had Julio take us two hours up the Colorado River in an unstable boat that was so low in the water I constantly feared we would be swamped. However, we safely reached our destination, a peninsula where another refugee camp was being built. We spent several hours there, touring the house that had been built for a missionary family soon to arrive from the states, and watching men building a school for the refugee children. I couldn't help noticing one little boy among the swarm of children following us everywhere, who proudly wore a T-shirt which had Holland, Michigan emblazoned across the front. Everywhere we went we were met with welcoming smiles. On our way back to Barra de Colorado we ran out of gas twice but both times another boat eventually came along and lent us enough gasoline to get us back safely.

After a week there, Myrtle learned that a pilot would be dropping off some Japanese vacationers at a fishing lodge across the river and she arranged for him to take us with him on his return trip to San Jose. Bill had been catching insects the whole time we were there and he always had a trail of kids either leading him to a supposedly great spot for collecting, or following him out of curiosity. We chuckled as we took off, looking down at a number of children running around with white Styrofoam cups trying to catch insects. We had paid $1.30 for the 12 hour trip to Barra de Colorado and $10.00 for the twenty-minute plane ride back. We were so eager to get cleaned up and re-civilized that we would have gladly have paid the pilot much more!

These experiences were examples of the Costa Rica we came to know by traveling back and forth from coast to coast, up mountains and down rivers, looking into the craters of inactive volcanoes and staying at a respectful distance as we watched Arenal Volcano erupting. The cities were loud, dirty, polluted, crammed and fascinating. The little villages we visited in our roaming about, were hospitable oases where we enjoyed whatever the inhabitants could spare for our comfort. When trudging down remote roads, we were picked up by every manner of truck and jeep; almost always by a *Tico* driver who wanted to practice his English on us.

Our son, David had returned from Japan a couple of months before we left Lansing and decided to take winter term off from his studies at MSU in order to spend that time in Costa Rica with us. Mary and Dolf gave us a roll-away bed for him and enjoyed his presence in our midst as much as we did.

For David, it was a bit of a revelation to experience his parents as people instead of just parents. He later said that he was upset with Bill's behavior toward me, particularly when we were in Santa Rosa National Park on the northern Pacific, where I suffered a bout of pain in my left hip and leg so severe that it was agony for me to take a step. His comment surprised me because I had thought Bill was treating me better than usual. Maybe I had finally deadened myself to what I could not change.

We came home to the States at the end of March and what struck me immediately was how clean the streets were. After putting David on a plane to Michigan we visited with Tom for a few days and got the bus out of storage. Then we visited many relatives and friends in Florida, Missouri and Illinois as we made our way home to Michigan. I was anxious to get home though, especially to see for myself how Amy was faring.

1988

Amy's boyfriend, Donnell, had abandoned her when she refused to have an abortion so I could only imagine the heartache she felt as she planned for the baby's birth. Knowing that she was not equipped to take care of a baby, she planned to place him with Bethany Christian Services in order for him to be adopted into a stable home with two parents. Once her son, Raphael, was born, Donnell signed the adoption papers, but a week later, his parents objected to Raphael being adopted, so he notified the adoption agency that he was coming to get him. When the adoption agency notified Amy of Donnell's intent, she went to get him herself since she knew that Donnell used drugs. So as she settled down into her own home with her son, her future would be much more difficult than the pursuit of a university degree.

We visited family members around the Midwest early that summer and then experienced a bizarre incident as we were almost home. Bill was driving our bus north on I-131 south of Grand Rapids in the rain, when he began noticing an electrical problem so he pulled off on the side of the highway to check for the source of the problem. While he was tinkering around underneath it and I was sitting in the computer seat on the bus, reading, the motor started up all by itself and the bus began to move forward. Bill yelled and I flung myself into the driver's seat to try to stop it.

The motor kept roaring for a few more seconds even after I had my foot jammed onto the brake pedal. The smell of burning rubber was strong as I dashed off the bus in time to see my very white-faced husband pulling himself out from under it. He managed to lean against the right front wheel while I ran out onto the four lane highway, waving my arms and jumping up and down. The first car I saw coming, was being driven by a paramedic who stopped to help us. Bill said that the bus wheel had run over his left leg and he had obvious abrasions the length of the left side of his body but he seemed stable enough that the paramedic said he'd take us to the nearest hospital in his car.

But before we could get into his car, the bus started up again. I was able to board it and once more slam on the brakes and then Bill and the paramedic took the battery completely out of it before we went on to the hospital.

His entire leg was swelling up like a balloon but the medical personnel ascertained that no bones were broken. As he was being attended to, I talked to two police officers, who were checking to be sure that I hadn't deliberately tried to run my husband down, so I was glad to have the testimony of the paramedic to clear me from that suspicion. During the six weeks that it took for Bill to recuperate, we enjoyed some quiet peaceful camping trips together with various family members, in some of Michigan's most beautiful forests. Bill ventured about a bit with his still gimpy leg, content to swing his net around a little and just enjoy being surrounded by the beauty we encountered. I was still basking in the generally peaceful relationship with him and thankful for the present calm. I was also looking forward to the fall when we would go to my parent's condo in Fairfield Bay, Arkansas, for the winter.

The idea was for Bill to continue with his research and writing there and for me to write a book about our extended-family living experience. For years, whenever I had given a talk about what God had blessed us with on Sycamore Street, I had been asked if I had written an account of those fruitful years. I had thought I might try to do that while we were in Costa Rica but Costa Rica wouldn't let me. It was far too distracting, enticing me out and about every day. So in Arkansas, I planned to settle down to write the book while Bill kept busy with his own work. But after I had written the first few chapters Bill picked them up and starting changing everything all around, waving the papers at me saying:

"You say I, I, I. You shouldn't say I did this or I did that so much. And you need to stick to the facts more, You're digressing too much, etc."

"Wait a minute, Bill! You're wanting it to sound like a scientific paper! Whose book is this anyway?"

"We'll, we're writing it together, of course."

"Where did you get the idea we would be writing the book together? I can't possibly write a book with you! You view things too differently from me. I'm writing about my own experience of household living!"

"But we both lived in the household," he objected.

"Then write your own account of household living. Nobody's stopping you. There's no reason why you can't do that."

We went around and around with it and he was very frustrated with me, but he eventually settled back into his work and left me alone. I felt alone all right! I'd written a children's book when I was nineteen, but except for letters, a few term papers, grocery lists and my journal writings, I hadn't written anything in the past thirty-five years. I prayed earnestly for God to guide me and was taken back in time to the struggles and the wonder of those years, as I sketched an outline of the events and began filling in the stories contained there.

I realized a definable newness in my relationship with God as I revisited the incidents that stood out in my memory or were recorded in my journals. A joyous awareness of God's mercy and his love for me in the midst of all the pain of the past, co-mingled with my sorrow for my sins and brought me to tears. This fresh, grace-filled time was so precious that I approached my prayer times-merged-with-writing-times with a reverent eagerness, knowing I would meet God in the process. And ever since that time, tears of joy and/or sorrow still accompany me whenever I let myself be aware of his presence.

And there in that isolated area of Arkansas, God also provided fellowship with wonderful Christian women to enrich my life. I joined a weekly Bible study and then was asked to speak about the household at the March 1989 meeting of Women Aglow, an international organization of women who know they have been filled with the Holy Spirit. Bill decided, for the first time ever, to go with me to hear me speak. I was so caught up in telling the story of God's work in the household, I was thankfully oblivious of his presence and he made no negative comment to me afterward.

In the spring of 1989, grandchildren were being born and children were coming back to Michigan to visit during the summer, so we headed back there, also, where we usually parked our bus at Paul's or Anne-Marie's as we filled up our lives with our family and friends. I was deep into *The Journal of John Woolman* at that time, feasting on his words of wisdom during quiet moments which were few because of all the activity. It was an extremely busy summer.

In the midst of all the bustle I received a letter from an editor for Word Books in Waco, Texas, inviting me to send my manuscript to him for editing when it was finished. The grapevine had evidently put out a tendril which touched him.

But although a rough draft of the book was progressing, it needed a lot more work before I would be ready to send it to an editor. I also wanted to include input from a number of the people who had lived with us and had told me they were writing about their experience. I was still waiting for the rest of those accounts o I could weave them into the narrative. There would be no more book writing for awhile. We were headed back to Costa Rica.

Moving into the 90's

After months of visiting in the United States during the fall of 1989, we headed south again and flew back to Costa Rica the day after Thanksgiving. *Communidad Agape* had changed its name to *Communidad Arbol de Vida* by now but the people were still the same, so we entered back into the relationship of marvelous fellowship with them.

First we spent a month in the home of the Nelsons, who were part of the staff at the Pastoral Center in San Ramon de Tres Rios. Theirs was one of three homes on the grounds of the Pastoral Center, which was a ministry focused on providing a place of rest and learning for missionaries working in Central and South America. We kept their home occupied, paying the maid's wages and the utilities while they were on leave in the United States for a few weeks.

When they returned, we moved a couple of miles down the San Ramon Road to San Rafael to live in the home of a Costa Rican lady while she spent three months in the United States. It was while living at her house that we experienced a 6.5 earthquake which was quite spectacular for us. It hit early on a Sunday morning, waking me up as our whole house was rocking, accompanied by the sound of books and dishes falling from shelves.

After fleeing to the grassy back yard in our bare feet, we felt the trembling movement of the earth and watched the wrought-iron gate in the adobe wall surrounding the yard move up and down until the wall finally separated from where it was joined to the house. All of the creaking of the house and the sound of breaking glass was accompanied by a grand chorus of howling dogs. This was quite different from the small tremors we had felt the last time we were in Costa Rica!

Fortunately, only minor cleanup was needed in our house, and although most of central business section of San Jose was littered with broken glass, few people were injured because the earthquake occurred when most of them were still in their homes. Aftershocks were strong though and there were hundreds of them for months.

Our daughter, Julie, came to visit us during our time in San Rafael so we took her to some of our favorite wild places, and one of the Nicaraguan youths sent to

Communidad Arbol de Vida for safety from the Contras, came to live with us for a time. I continued to be busy with a number of friends and going on collecting trips with Bill but I cut back on the number of trips I took into the jungle with him this time.

After three months in the San Rafael house, we moved to the home of another couple at the Pastoral Center, the Remingtons, while they went on leave to the states. Our bedroom was on the second floor, where we could lie in bed and look through a huge window out over an idyllic pastoral mountain scene complete with sheep and cows. Inside our house, the scene was less than idyllic as I became more and more distressed with Bill's regular hammering again at my psyche.

He had recently read a psychological book which convinced him that I was what the book termed, "performance oriented," meaning that I work hard for the wrong reasons. He felt it vindicated his attempt to break me down to where I'd admit that my behavior was determined by only doing what I thought other people wanted me to do. He was back in the "you just do nice things so people will think you're nice" mode. It was incredibly frustrating to regularly be told that my motives were wrong. And he just wouldn't leave it alone.

Since I had so much joy in my life apart from my trouble with Bill, I had thought that I had kept my sadness hidden very well. But I was faced with the fallacy of that one day when my American missionary friend, Norma, told me she had always felt there was a deep sadness within me just below the surface of my life. Since I had not told her anything about the difficulties I struggled with in my marriage, her remark had been unexpected and made me wonder if her discernment was a gift, or if I had sadness leaking into a puddle around my feet in spite of trying to keep it hidden.

Norma was responsible for scheduling fun activities for the Work and Witness teams which came from various United States Nazarene churches, to spend a week or two at the Seminary of the Americas where her husband taught. This couple had been rather amazed to find out that we knew the Lord in spite of being Catholics! We got to be quite good friends with them and they liked to show us off (as if our knowing the Lord were a phenomenon), frequently asking us to fellowship with these visiting teams by joining some of the excursions Norma had planned to other parts of the country. I enjoyed those trips tremendously.

Our sojourn in Costa Rica came to a halt abruptly in June, just after we had moved into the home of our Costa Rican friends, the Monteros. When word reached us that Bill's mother was in a coma and not expected to live, Steve Montero had to go into the jungle to find Bill. We made plans to come home as quickly as possible, flying to St. Louis where Bill's brother met our plane and took us directly to the nursing home to see her. Although we expected her to be comatose, she said "Hello" when we spoke to her and remained somewhat responsive from time to time until she died ten days later.

We stayed with Bill's brother, Jack and his wife during this time. Jack took me to the nursing home each morning on his way to work. There I remained during the day, monitoring his mother's care while the rest of the family members were at their jobs. Bill declined to relate to his mother in a personal way after that first visit to her, staying away from the nursing home except to pick me up in the evening. I had a lot of time to ponder this behavior of his and to think back over what I knew of his relationship with her and with me.

Years ago Bill had told me that he resented his mother because when he was a teenager she had always wanted to know what he was doing. It had annoyed him so much that he had made a firm decision not to share anything with her. And it was only during one of our difficult conversations in San Ramon that he told me he realized he had been transferring his resentment of his mother onto me. I thought he needed to give up all the resentment and had told him so, but he didn't seem to be able to do that. I had a lot of time to ponder this problem but had no idea how to surmount it.

After Bill's mother's funeral he took a plane back to Tampa to get our bus, and I rode back to Lansing with David. He had just graduated from Michigan State University with a degree in Engineering and had been living with our son, Paul, and his wife since he returned from Japan the previous year. Staying with them, I enjoyed an interlude of peace with lots of interaction with family and friends. But once Bill returned I had to struggle to keep my equilibrium again.

One of the things that helped me to cope were some writings I came across which stated that pain can be a teacher, a rich source of grace which will bring growth in discipline and sensitivity if I let it work for me. Viewing my struggles as something God meant for ultimate good for me was comforting.

Meanwhile, back at Anne-Marie's, she had begun to talk about the idea of us living with them instead of going back to Costa Rica later in the year as we had planned. By now she had two sons and she said she hated that I wouldn't be near enough to enjoy them. The fact of the matter, though, was that their house was too small to accommodate all of us. David had just started a job in Grand Rapids and was living with them for awhile, sleeping on a cot in their basement.

We talked it over more thoroughly with them and then made a commitment to give them the down payment if they could find a house that would meet all of our needs for living together, before we left for Costa Rica again in the fall. As we traveled around the country that summer they kept house hunting without any success. But they persisted, and that fall they found a house that was perfect for our needs. We were able to move into it right after Thanksgiving along with David, Amy and her now two-year-old son, Raphael.

When I had first gotten back to Michigan that summer I had spent a lot of time with Amy, trying to talk her out of moving with her son to Orlando to join her present boyfriend, who had recently moved there. But she disregarded my advice and found a job there with Disney after moving into an apartment with her boyfriend's family. And by the time I was in Orlando in the fall, helping my sister, Carolyn, during her convalescence from surgery, Amys boyfriend had gotten drunk and beaten her so she decided to return to Michigan. She was also pregnant again, needing a place to stay until after the birth of her daughter, so Matt and Anne-Marie invited her to join us when we moved into the new house.

Therefore, the end of 1990 found us living with three of our children, three grandsons and a son-in-law in a circa 1839 homestead located in the middle of an acre of land in Grand Rapids. We began a three-generation, three-family challenge and although there were many joyful moments and events celebrated during the next few years, they turned out to be extremely difficult years for me and for Anne-Marie.

In our new home we furnished an upstairs bedroom for us and Bill built a basement room for his bug collection and computer. Then we settled into our new life as I got acquainted with a few women from our new church and focused on the joy of having three grandchildren to cuddle on a daily basis. There was plenty of housework to do and I enjoyed helping with painting and wallpapering as Anne-Marie gradually made the house her home.

The spacious house lent itself to entertaining so it got to be a favorite place for many of their friends. Our whole extended family (who regarded the house as the home place now that we were all settled there) were often popping in and out, too, so it sometimes seemed like Grand Central Station. Anne-Marie had been used to a quieter, more structured living environment so this became stressful for her.

Even more so, though, she experienced stress because of her differences with Amy. She was upset that Amy had gotten pregnant again and she also had to deal with discord between her oldest son and Amy's son, trouble she hadn't experienced with only her own two children. So both women were unhappy with the situation and I felt torn in the middle of it all. Although once Amy had her baby daughter, Andria, and moved to her own apartment, things calmed down a bit.

Other than frequent local bicycle jaunts and walking to daily Mass, Bill and I spent little time together. Plagued with feelings of loneliness, I had not yet developed a sense of belonging in this new environment. Intellectually I understood that because I had left my own home, my ministry, my friends and the city I knew so well, it was normal for me to feel lonely in my present situation so I tried to be patient as I waited for my inner peace to return, but it was not easy.

During the following year we spent a lot of time with people involved in the Catholic Charismatic Renewal in the Grand Rapids area. I made trips to both the East and the West coasts and also a number of trips with Bill. So the months flew by until early in 1992, when I sensed that Anne-Marie needed a break from having extra people in her house. As I talked to her about it, she said she really wished that she could live alone with just her own family again. I can now appreciate her need and not take it so personally, but at the time I felt devastated when she told me that, hating to be somewhere I felt I wasn't wanted. So Bill and I began to look at the possibility of taking another long bicycle trip in order to give her some space. This time our destination would be Europe and we would need to plan carefully for the three months duration we had in mind.

Europe in 1992

We planned to stay for three months because there were old friends to see in England, Belgium, Germany, Norway, and Denmark. Bill talked of us going to Spain, too, and I particularly wanted to visit Ireland. To train for the trip, we started riding more and longer distances whenever the snow was cleared from the roads and trails that spring. So by the 21st of May, when we left Grand Rapids to ride seventy-two miles to Paul's house in Lansing on the first leg of our journey, we thought we were ready.

But with panniers on the front wheels as well as the back ones, we were more heavily laden than any other trip we had taken. And only a couple of hours down the road, when Bill had to upend his bike to repair his rear wheel just after we had crossed a river, hoards of mosquitos swarmed out from the brush as soon as we stopped. They surrounded us and started using us as a full-course meal, graphically reminding me of the many perils of the road.

Although the day was beautiful, the strong headwind made me want to quit before we had gone thirty miles and also had me wondering if our plans had been too ambitious. But we kept on riding, past fields of fuzzy white dandelions where the wind blew the fluff in our faces; past fields of gaudy-gold rape which seemed to radiate their iridescent yellow against the rich green of the trees and the blue of the sky. "It will be worth the pain," I thought.

Our final preparations included putting each bike in a box designed for that purpose. Then Paul put all of our gear in the back of his pick-up and drove us to the Detroit airport. The security people there took both bikes completely out of their boxes so we had to re-pack them, and the garden trowel in my carry-on pannier was confiscated, but we finally passed muster and were allowed to board our flight to Boston. Our son, Joe, and his family met us at the airport there, visiting with us until our 8:00 flight to Europe was boarding. Then we settled into our seats for the overnight flight to London.

Although exhausted, I don't think I slept during the entire flight so I was really groggy when we landed at Gatwick at 2:30, our time. It took us a while to get our bikes un-boxed and put back together with all our gear in place, so it was 9:00, their time, when we rode out of the airport. It was a warm sunny day with terrible traffic and people out in droves. In East Grinstead we bought a loaf of bread and a couple of bananas that I put with the apples and peanut butter we'd brought with us for lunch. Bill had thought we would cycle all the way to Dover that first day, but because of our fatigue and the difficulties we encountered, we only went ten miles.

Bill fell with his bike once and a passing car stopped immediately. The driver asked if he could help but Bill was okay. The heavy traffic was really bothering us, though, in spite of being used to it in the states. It was very disconcerting to be riding on the opposite side of the road from U.S. traffic. I kept flinching when I saw cars coming toward us on the "wrong" side of the road.

My chain jammed as we were headed to the city center, and I had to remove one of my back panniers so Bill could get at it to fix it. Riding along an hour later, I realized that I had left the pannier sitting on the grassy bank where we had stopped. I couldn't believe I had done such a stupid thing and was especially dismayed when I realized that my address book was in it. In a panic, we went back, and when we finally found the place where I had left the pannier, there was no sign of it.

There had been some construction workers nearby who were still at work so I approached them. And before a word was out of my mouth, one of the workers said he had seen the pannier and put it in his truck for safe-keeping. Profoundly relieved, I couldn't thank him enough when he retrieved it from his truck for me. But I was really shaken by that incident, realizing how vulnerable we were in our extreme fatigue, knowing we needed somewhere to rest. There were no campgrounds around so I stopped at a bed & breakfast to check the cost but it was way over our budget.

We had stopped to look at a beautiful old Catholic Church (Our Lady and St. Peter) when we first rode into East Grinstead, so I suggested to Bill that we return there and pray for guidance. We parked our bikes inside a walled courtyard, and after a time of prayer I walked on a side path to the back of the church where I found Fr. Kevin Gaskin working in his flower bed. I told him who we were, how exhausted we were, and asked him if we could camp there tonight so we could attend Mass the next morning, which was Ascension Thursday.

He was very kind, saying that we could sleep in the parish hall, but apologizing because there were meetings scheduled to be held there until 10:00 p.m. He offered us food and the use of his livingroom and bath in the meantime, bringing me towels to use for our showers. After cleaning up and dozing through the evening until we could bed down in our sleeping bags, I fervently wished we had never set out on this venture. I seriously considered turning right around and heading back home. I knew we would eventually get rested up, but I was also worried about how much more expensive everything was, and beginning to think we couldn't afford to continue.

After a good night's sleep and the refreshment of Mass, though, my mood was more upbeat. Especially when I remembered how kind Fr. Gaskin had been, and also the kindness of the man who had offered to help Bill when he fell and the construction worker who had guarded my pannier.

Back on our bikes, the day's weather was again warm and sunny but we continued to struggle with narrow roads and lots of traffic. Bill wanted to try some back roads and they were much more pleasant to ride on. The trouble was we got lost, not once but twice, so, though we rode thirty-four miles that day we ended up only thirteen miles from where we had started.

There were no straight or level sections of road. We biked through Groombridge, Frant, and Bells Yew Green, and then stopped at Bayham Abbey to take pictures. Near Hythe, at 4:30 that afternoon, we came to a bed and breakfast place but the proprietress didn't want any guests because she had sick people in the house. I persuaded her to let us camp in a meadow near the house and by paying her six pounds for the privilege, she gave us the outside access to a bathroom where we could also get water. We got the tent up, washed up amidst honking geese milling around us, and went to bed when it started raining at 6:30, a rain that continued through the night.

The next morning it was a hassle taking down a sopping wet tent while trying to avoid piles of goose poop in the rain. We bought some rolls for breakfast in Lamberhurst and continued on to Goudhurt. There I had another setback when I tried to use the phone-card I had bought, because I put it in the slot for used cards by mistake. The rain stopped around 11:00 and we progressed more comfortably along narrow roads, some only one lane, through beautiful countryside, lots of sheep, flowers and lush greenery. I took pictures of a steam engine passenger train going by. We appreciated the fact that in all these little towns, there were signs pointing to free public restrooms which were always clean. We spent the night at Sunny Bank Bed and Breakfast in Hythe.

There we had our first real meal the next morning, cereal and ham & eggs with mushrooms, and toast. It was a good thing we had all that internal fuel because riding to Dover we had to climb those white cliffs, and in the rain no less. But by the time we had queued up for the Hovercraft to France it had stopped raining and by the time we had completed our twenty-five minute crossing of the English Channel, the sun had actually come out all the way.

We stayed at the municipal caravan park on the waterfront at Calais and our tent dried out nicely. We were surrounded by ships, hotels and people. The tents around us were gaily decorated as houses, some even had brightly painted windows complete with flower pots on the sills. It never seemed to get dark that night as I could still see well enough to read in the tent at 10:00. Although we wandered around Calais searching for a church for Sunday Mass the next day, it was to no avail, but we enjoyed the unusual sights along the way, especially the pastries, which we absolutely had to investigate intimately.

On Monday we headed south to Boulogne, taking secondary roads along the coast as we climbed tremendous hills. Bill had thought that the beach road would be flat and parts of it were, but we had to cycle over cliffs that jutted out into the sea. It was very tiring, but loads of red poppies growing wild along the roads and in the fields were a feast for our eyes. At one point we met an American bike tour group followed by their sag wagon. We couldn't help but reflect on how easy our trip would be if we didn't have to lug all our stuff, and had warm beds and prepared meals when we stopped.

The morning was merely hazy but rain really poured down again when we got to Boulogne. Two little boys helped me to figure out how to use a public restroom at an intersection in the city center. It was a concrete oval tube. I put forty cents in a slot and a metal door slid open. After I used it, washed my hands and left, water and cleanser shot out all over the inside to clean it and then warm air dried it for the next person's use. This was definitely superior to anything I had seen in the States.

After cycling only thirty-two miles that day, we again discussed getting a Seacat back to England and home. However, we hated to admit defeat so we turned into a huge caravan park in the little town of Le Portal, adjacent to Boulogne. It was full of little trailers that looked like people lived in them permanently, but beyond all of that, we camped on a site which backed onto a meadow where cows grazed, and five heavy concrete bunkers (fortifications) faced the sea from high above us where the meadow slopes upward. We learned that Boulogne was under siege in December of 1942 and was defended from there.

We walked all over Boulogne and Le Portel the next day, absorbing some history and admiring the architecture. I was determined to see Paris as long as we were this close to it, so we checked into a hotel for two nights and took the train to Paris the next morning. At first we didn't know what to do with our bikes but the hotel proprietor led us to a storage garage a few blocks away where he squeezed them in with a lot of hotel supplies and locked them up.

We met Sarah and her mother, Polly, staying at our hotel on a brief holiday from Essex. As we chatted a bit Sarah brightly asked me, "Are you having a good time?" "Yes, but it's been a bit rough with all the rain because we're cycling," I confessed. Imagine my surprise when she said, "What fun! My husband and I bicycled in northern France and Belgium last year!" She tried to encourage us to go on, and then pulled out a Michelene map to show us the route they had taken. We had been praying for guidance. Was this a coincidence or a God-incident?

Our day in Paris was a beautiful experience in every way. The train ride took us through countryside scenery familiar from the French impressionist painters. We took the Metro to Pont St. Michel and emerged into an exciting atmosphere of high energy and beauty. I was awestruck! It was sunny all day as we walked for miles near the Seine up one side and down the other. Taking in the Cathedral of Notre Dame down the Rue Rivoli and onto Des Champs Elysees almost to the Arc de Triomphe before we crossed the Seine to the Tour Eiffel where we took an elevator to the top.

I was intrigued that people lived on the long narrow boats in the Seine and amazed at all the gold trimming on so many of the buildings. We had supper in a little sidewalk café before we boarded our train back to Boulogne that evening. I had acted the part of a tourist all day long, taking far too many pictures, I'm sure.

We went from Technicolor back to black and white when we returned to rain again in Boulogne. We found Sarah and Polly in the hotel restaurant so we joined them for a glass of wine and visited until almost midnight. Sarah invited us to visit them in Essex and encouraged us to cycle around that area of England. We were definitely heading back to England the next morning so we would keep that in mind.

We awoke to a drizzle the next morning, thankful we weren't in our tent. When we asked for our bicycles, it was discovered that the manager was gone, with the key to the storage garage in his pocket. We spent an anxious hour while they tracked him down, retrieving our bikes barely in time to board our Seacat to England. We sailed through choppy seas to Folkstone, where we found a Laundromat and got all our clothes clean and dry. Then I was able to phone my friend, Wini Meikle, and it was so good to hear her familiar voice! She urged us to come to their house in Winchester and tour from there, so I was only too glad to tell her we'd head in her direction and see her in a few days. I felt encouraged to think we might yet experience a bit of that jolly old England that had eluded us thus far.

With that happy expectation, we splurged the $18 it cost for us to have Kentucky Fried Chicken for dinner and I swear it had never tasted better! Then we biked through blessedly flat terrain on our way down the coast during the late afternoon and evening. We rode alongside marshland on little one-lane roads through Newchurch, Ivychurch and Brookland. We stayed at Dean's Court Bed and Breakfast, an Elizabethan farmhouse located in the middle of nowhere. Our accommodations were luxurious and we were the only guests sharing the home of a young couple with a baby.

We delayed our leaving their warm kitchen as long as possible the next morning, hoping the rain would let up, but we finally had to go, accompanied all day by cold, drizzly weather through Rye, Icklesham, Guestling, Green, Ore and Hastings on the Sea. While Bill spent two hours in Hastings replacing a spoke in his rear wheel, I phoned home to let folks there know our immediate plans, and told them how we were too uncomfortable and poor to go on to Ireland, Belgium and Germany as planned. David couldn't believe it!. "You have to go to Ireland, Mom!" he insisted. "Then you come over here and ride my bike for me!" I retorted. "It's so bad I've found myself envying the backpackers because they don't have to push a heavy bike up these hills!"

My phone calling over, I enjoyed the carnival atmosphere at this southeast coastal town. There were lots of amusement park rides, junky booths and tons of people. The mackerel were running so fishermen stood all along the seawall for miles, flipping fish out of the sea and into their buckets. We only went thirty-five miles before finding a campsite in a meadow around 7:00 that night. Bill graciously insisted that I use both air mattresses under my sleeping bag because I'd been having back problems. I did sleep wonderfully better except for feeling a bit guilty.

We continued to ride in rain. At one point, I was trying to push my bike up this slippery, busy road, so steep a sign said "Trucks Use Low Gear," and I thought I couldn't go another step. My right shoulder ached fiercely from pushing the heavy bike. So by afternoon, when we met a couple of bicyclists who suggested we take a train to South Downs Way, which is a path just for pedestrians, equestrians and bicyclists, it sounded good to me. The sun came out and we decided to camp at Bucklers Campground near Eastbourne.

I took pictures of people all dressed in white, playing cricket in one field and in an adjacent field, more people were rolling balls across a lawn playing Boulet. That night some of the campers were staking out a course with rope where they would try to roll their water buckets blindfolded. Those types of recreation were certainly new to me!

June 10th we were up at 5:00 with everything wet, but the sun dried things out before we boarded the train to Twyford where Wini and her husband, Alan, lived. Our bikes were stored during the journey in what was called the guard van section of the train. Our friends met us and then we rode behind their car for about a mile to their home. We enjoyed a week with them, roaming local footpaths and visiting places of beauty and interest in the area. The day we had planned to go to Stonehenge, I had serious back pain which wouldn't allow me to ride in a car in comfort, but on another day we enjoyed a visit to Windsor Castle nearby.

Bill and I also made a day-trip by train to London during our stay in Twyford. While he spent a couple of hours at the British Museum, I walked from there to Harrod's Department Store and through the neighborhood of Hyde Park and Knightsbridge. We visited Trafalgar Square, Leichester Square, Parliament Square, and the National Art Museum. I took a picture of a woman on a houseboat on the Thames hanging out her laundry.

Around 4:00, we were in St. James Park on our way to Buckingham Palace when a tremendous thunderstorm hit and we were quickly soaked to the skin. Trains were held up by a lightning strike which damaged transformers that operated the train signals, so it was very late by the time we got back to Twyford, but Alan was faithfully waiting for us and bustled us quickly home. We were shaking with cold by then, but warm baths and warm food provided for us restored us and we recovered from our escapade with no ill effects.

The day we left their home to visit Gillian in Oxford as the next leg of our trip, we again opted to travel by train but when we got to the station the train was late. We were told the train was delayed because someone had committed suicide by throwing themselves in front of it, so we eventually had to go to Oxford by another route. This had us changing trains at Basingstoke and again at Reading instead of the direct train we had expected to take. Because of this, Bill had to wrestle the bikes up and down long flights of stairs to change platforms. There was no way I could have handled my unwieldy, heavy bike on stairs, especially with my tricky back.

But the supposedly cold English were very nice to us during that trip. At Reading a man shoved his briefcase at me and took my bike up two flights of stairs when we had another last minute change of platform. And a woman insisted I use her phone-card to call Gillian to tell her of the delay.

Gillian had visited us three times during the Sycamore Fellowship years, and had invited us to stay with her for a time in her council house which she had bought eighteen years ago. When she wasn't working at the university she rode her bicycle all over the area, so she lead us along many bike paths throughout the university campus, the beautiful streets of Oxford and along the River Thames.

We had lunch at the White Hart Pub in Wytham about five miles northeast of Oxford, and watched people punting on the River Thames. Gillian sang in the choir as we attended Evensong service at Christ Church.

Sunday morning we cycled to Blackfriars for 9:00 Mass. Run by Dominicans, it was like a hippy gathering with everyone in very casual dress, children in blue jeans making their First Holy Communion and music by Schubert provided by a violinist, a cellist, a bassoonist and a barefoot flautist. Afterwards we cycled to Gillian's thirteenth-century University Church of St. Mary the Virgin, where we had a simple bread and soup lunch in what used to be the first library ever created to be used by ordinary students. Then we climbed the bell tower for a spectacular view of Oxford.

When we left Gillian, we began cycling toward Aynho where Dolf and Mary Jonker, our former landlords in Costa Rica, now lived. We went through Woodeaton, Islip, Bettingdon, Kirlington and Heyford where we ate the lunch that Gillian had packed for us. We were touched to find that she had included two forty pound notes, with instructions on how to use the money for our train fare to Gatwick instead of cycling there. As we ate lunch we watched pilots from the nearby Royal Air Force base practicing flying in formation. We came across mysterious round circles of flattened areas, several yards in diameter, in the midst of fields with no hint of how they came to be there. Some of the locals talked about them showing up in other fields, speculating that the circles had been made by aliens.

At Somerton we decided to try cycling along a tow path of the Oxford Canal. Unfortunately, it gave out into a meadow of sheep, so we had to push our bikes about five miles through weeds and nettles. It was hot and flies buzzing around my head irritated me no end. At one point, we asked a guy in a long, narrow boat floating by in the canal, how much further it was to Aynho and he replied, "About two miles more." When we said we'd be meeting friends there, he laconically commented that we'd need them.

We finally arrived at a road by a big docking area and refreshed ourselves with popsicles at a refreshment stand there. Then we cycled past Aynho to our campground, Bo Peep Farm, finding it to be the nicest campground yet. We had time to set up our tent and have showers before the Jonkers picked us up and took us to their home for dinner. Their house was one of those several-hundred-year-old small cottages that could not possibly be lived in by a tall person, but it was charming and we enjoyed visiting with Dolf and Mary again.

We toured the picturesque Cotswolds with the them the next day. I was glad that I would be able to take home with me the memory of the thatched-roofed cottages and beautiful countryside. After supper at their home that day, I phoned Paul to tell him that we were coming home on the 19th of June, and he, like David, found it hard to believe we would forfeit the rest of our planned trip, especially our plans to visit Ireland, but he promised to be at the airport to pick us up.

Mary and Dolf kept insisting they would take us to Gatwick but we felt that was way too much trouble for them. Instead, the next day we cycled into Banbury where we found Flightlink, a bus which would take us and our bikes to Gatwick, and we made arrangements to use that transportation service the next day. At the city center we went to a library where I wrote letters to the people we were no longer planning to visit, and down by the Oxford Canal, Bill collected flies while I took pictures of boats coming through the locks. Later we had one more visit with the Jonkers in the evening before we went back to Bo Peep Farm.

The next morning we were able to get everything dried out before it had to be packed. Once we reached the Flightlink bus station, Bill had to prepare the bikes for transport by removing the pedals and turning the handlebars sideways. Then he tied and duct-taped ground-cloths over each of them to cover the oily chains. Once at Gatwick, Bill removed the ground-cloths and used them to make two bundles out of our rear panniers and the tent stuff. Then all we had to do was sit up all night in a busy airport. That was tough.

We had a miserable night but a safe trip home. There had been no place to put our bike helmets so we carried them onto the plane with us. Bill then put his helmet on because he didn't want to hold it and I had to laugh when, at one point, the stewardess coming down the aisle stopped by him and said seriously, "Sir, it's really safe to take your helmet off now." Paul was waiting for us in Detroit to take us to Lansing and I was so exhausted when we got to his house, I went to bed and slept around the clock.

Reviewing in my mind, our aborted extended trip, I realized that I had not been in good enough emotional shape at the time to handle the difficulties encountered in that type of travel. I carried with me the sense that Anne-Marie was regretting having us share her home, and I was worn out by constant emotional stress with Bill. I was the one who wanted to come back home, not him. In fact, he wanted us to ride down south to Spain. He didn't seem to comprehend how many weeks it would have taken us to do that.

Once safely back home, I didn't regret that we had undertaken the trip. And I was glad that I had been able to see even a little bit of Europe, appreciating even now that I had been able to touch base with a bit of history and see old friends. I expected, too, that we had probably made our last long bicycle trip unless we could afford a sag wagon and overnight accommodations someday. We had run up against the fact that we weren’t as young as we used to be.

The Gift of Mid-Life Crisis

We settled back into our life in Grand Rapids, busy with family, church and friends the rest of the summer but emotionally I was going downhill fast. One afternoon in July I was in the garage helping Anne-Marie paint some screens. I'd noticed her seeming angry a good deal of the time lately so I asked her if she was upset with me. She thought about it for awhile before answering me. "Well, I really just want to live with my immediate family. Because you're here the rest of our family want to come a lot and the big family gatherings are more work than I can cope with. And it's irritating finding Dad's crumbs on the table when he eats and doesn't clean up after himself. And I appreciate you doing the dishes, but sometimes you don't get them clean and when I hear you banging the dishes around in the kitchen it makes me cringe."

My heart stood still. Even though I had suspected as much, I still was crushed by her candor. As I tried to talk to her further about it she said, "It's just hard for me because I'm such a private person. I'm asking God to change my heart and I don't want you to feel like you have to always be worrying about whether you're in my way or not."

But, of course I'd already felt that way and it was bound to be worse now. I couldn't imagine going on this way. I wrote in my journal: "What is the Lord trying to do in me through this sadness? Where *do* I belong?"

Anne-Marie was concerned that she'd hurt me and asked for forgiveness which I readily gave to her. "I'll just have to be even more careful and quieter when I do the dishes," I thought. "I don't have a problem with that. It's the fact that she just doesn't want us here that's hard. Her irritation with us seems to be over such minor things that there must be resentment toward us underneath." After I'd had time to reflect on our life together there, I think it's reasonable to conclude that the tension between Bill and I was something that she must have sensed whether she realized it or not. And that tension was truly an intrusion into their happy home.

Sensing my old enemy, rejection, from her body language and her seeming avoidance of me throughout the rest of the summer, I was miserable. Later, when I talked to her again about our situation and how awful I felt, she reiterated that she loved me and would keep praying for God to change her attitude about us living together. I continued to keep as busy as possible and we took numerous trips on our bus to give Anne-Marie the privacy she desired, but I was keenly aware that I didn't belong anywhere and went through weeks of attempting to fend off the depression I felt.

We were staying in our bus parked at Paul's for awhile when my 57th birthday occurred on a Saturday that summer. Julie came from Chicago to share cake and ice-cream with us, and some of my children and grandchildren were around to wish me well. Julie left to go back on Sunday, and that evening when we went to the bus to go to bed, I felt the sadness I always felt on my birthday, Mothers Day or Christmas when Bill didn't get anything for me or even acknowledge the occasion. It made me kind of mad at myself that I still let it bother me even though I had long ago ceased expecting anything from him.

I went quietly to bed but Bill knew my sadness even though I didn't say anything and he became so furious with me that he told me if I didn't like living with him to get my things and get off the bus. I didn't acknowledge that I'd heard him but spent a miserable night trying to sleep with the weight of oppression dragging me down. Early the next morning I roused briefly when I heard him get up and leave, remembering that he was going to the university library for awhile, and then I fell back asleep.

Around 9:30, I awoke to the sound of someone pounding on the bus door and went to open it. My friend, Maria was there wanting a shoulder to cry on. I told her I needed one too, so I hurriedly dressed and left with her. We drove to a park and sat at a picnic table talking until noon. I tried to call Paul's house to let his wife, Karen, know where I was, but no one answered. So we went to a restaurant for lunch and then Maria dropped me off at around 2:00. The bus motor was running and Bill had packed my belongings in grocery bags and was about to set them off the bus and leave without me. He was upset and angry, saying, "I've been waiting four hours for you!" I hurriedly said goodbye to Karen and we left for Grand Rapids.

As we headed down the freeway Bill shoved a printed religious tract at me which said we should repent and reconcile. Then, as we pulled into the east side of Grand Rapids he stopped at Frank's Nursery, telling me to pick out some flowers and call it my birthday present from him. I told him I didn't know how to be reconciled and picking out flowers three days after my birthday didn't make me feel honored or cared for. But as a gesture to meet him halfway, I went into Frank's with him and chose a $2.00 ivy plant to go in the vase Julie had given me.

Then he offered to take me next door to a restaurant for a meal but I didn't feel like eating so we went on home.

There, since they hadn't been with me on my birthday, Anne-Marie had prepared a delicious birthday dinner for us. She seemed glad to see me and full of chit chat as we had our meal together when Matt and David got home from work. My life seemed to be a mass of confusion and mixed messages.

I was weary of everything and knew enough about mental illness to consider that I could be diagnosed as being clinically depressed. I felt I needed to get away for some significant quiet time. So the next day, after I had my annual physical and went to a dentist appointment, a friend picked me up and took me to her cottage an hour's drive away, leaving me there so I could have some privacy.

After spending a few days alone there, gazing out over the peaceful lake, walking in the woods, sleeping long hours, reading, praying and weeding the flower garden, I was still in a state of sorrow with no sense of direction except to get a prescription to combat the bad case of poison ivy I'd contracted. Maria came to take me to Lansing for a few days but I eventually went back to life in Grand Rapids and the familiar daily Mass, bike rides or walks with Bill, and the blessed comfort of the usual household tasks. But I knew something had to change. For years I had told myself I would stay in my marriage as long as I could stay healthy but I sure wasn't healthy anymore.

In October I went to Maggie Valley, North Carolina, to join my three sisters for our bi-annual week-long vacation together. Using Carolyn's summer home there as our base, we spent the lovely days talking, playing cards, shopping, horseback riding and walking through the beautiful mountains. I was not my usual jolly self so they prodded me to tell them what was wrong. When I told them about my present difficulties they started brainstorming for solutions. By the time our week together was over, Charlotte had a suggestion that I decided to take to heart.

She recommended, for a start, that I attend a two-day self-esteem workshop that her husband, Don would be facilitating in Dallas in November. I flew down there to stay with them for two weeks, and besides going through the workshop they used their considerable counseling skills to give me a thorough going-over. "You are feeling trapped," said Charlotte, "and you're not trapped." They opened up the world of possibilities for me again and at the end of that time with them I had a long-term plan in place.

In addition to Don's counseling business, the two of them had a national reputation for business counseling using the Performax DiSC Personal Profile as a management training tool. They proposed that I train under Don, who was a National Trainer for Performax, and become a Personal Profile consultant also:

"Your skills are in the counseling area," Don said. "You could have taught that self esteem seminar, yourself. You just went right through it because of your ability to click with people."

"There's a profile that's a biblical profile used with church people, and there are other profiles for children and family relationships," joined in Charlotte.

"You can work in that area. So you just need to come back here in January and I can train you," said Don.

"And you won't be trapped anymore!" chortled Charlotte.

While I was there, early one morning, around dawn, I had a vivid dream. I was in a living room with a bunch of people, when an old woman limped in as if she had a sprained ankle and sat down in a wing-back chair in a corner with her back to us. People were taking turns talking and when it came to her turn, she still had her back to us as she burst out in despair, loudly crying about how terribly lonely she was. All of us in the room were stunned because of this outburst. Then I got up and went to her as everybody else just sat there.

When I came around from the back of the chair I saw that it was like a beach chair in that the seat cushion was on the floor and she had slid down so far that she was lying flat with her head on the seat of the chair. By then she had tears silently coursing down her cheeks. I knelt beside her and began stroking her face and holding her hand. I told her I would visit her and spoke soothing words to her. I knew this was happening in St. Joseph and I asked her where she lived. Someone said she was visiting her sister on a street over near the grade school, but she lived a long way away across the country.

The next scene in the dream was again in a living room with other people around, but I recognized it was my son, Michael's living room. I watched this same woman limp out of the dining room and head for the door into the hall. At that point, when I had turned to the person next to me, I heard a sharp "crack" sound and looked back to see the woman sitting on the floor with a dazed look on her face. She reached down to her ankle and pulled out a piece of bone. I went to her and offered her pain medication and called to the others in the room to help me get her to a hospital.

When I awoke it was very clear to me that I was the woman in so much pain, screaming out my loneliness, limping along, very compromised in my ability to function. I realized that if I didn't do something to get relief I would snap, break completely. I also saw myself as the woman trying to nurture the woman in pain.

One morning, Charlotte came to me with that day's reading from her devotional book, saying she felt the reading was for me. It was speaking of how we sometimes wish that someone would just tell us what to do about a particular situation in our life, but we just need to listen to the still small voice of God speaking to our heart and mind. I needed to be reminded to trust that.

One minute I was filled with hope at the thought of being free and then I'd also think that with my new insights I could go back to my old situation modified and freer with new strength. Don and Charlotte had taken me through the Personal Profile in seven of the different environments in which I have functioned and the results were incredibly revealing to me. I was very impressed with the value of the tool and eager to learn more about using it.

Before I left to go back to Michigan I had decided I would come back to Dallas in January and begin to train as a consultant under Don. While they worked in the business realm I would work in the area where I was comfortable and experienced—with families and churches. And I could stay at their house until I got on my feet financially. It was a good plan, but I was frightened at the thought of such a big change, leaving my husband and family and moving there.

I had been talking to my parents by phone during my time in Dallas, and they had been very supportive of my doing whatever it took to get my life back. They offered to buy me a car in Dallas if I decided to live there. Another positive thing about being in Dallas was I had a promise of a job when I returned in January so I would be able to earn money while I was going through the training with Don.

The main thing I had to figure out in my mind, though, was if this was God's plan for me. More than anything I was afraid of offending God. It was very hard to work my way through all the teaching I had received that said I needed to obey my husband, to the place where I could feel that God was bringing me out of that unhealthy relationship to freedom. So this was a big step of faith for me. It felt safer to just obey than it was to trust that God was leading in a way that seemed contrary to what I had been taught. But, hey, being a Christian is risky living. That's what makes it so exciting!

Bill and I had already bought our tickets to go back to Costa Rica in January, so I was really nervous as to what Bill would do when I told him of my change of plans. I was so scared of going against him, that I phoned a Grand Rapids priest that I knew, Father James Chelich, making an appointment with him before I ever left Dallas. I respected Fr. Chelich from attending weeks of theology teachings he had presented during the past year. When I explained to him my anxiety, he made an appointment to see me the day after I got back. I was filled with excitement and dread on the trip home. Bill had ruled me for thirty-seven years so I knew he would not be pleased with my new decision.

Defection to Dallas

The only thing bumpy about my return flight to Michigan was the thudding of my heart. When I did get back home, I went through the usual motions of rejoining the family and the next morning I presented myself at Father Chelich's front door. I had wanted to talk to him instead of our regular confessor in order to have the possibility of bias out of the picture. And for the first time in my life, I told another person about the circumstances of my marriage from the beginning.

Painfully I plodded through the years until I had come to my present dilemma. "I feel like I am just barely holding on to my sanity, Father. I want so much to sense a purpose for my life again. I feel full of hope at the thought of going to Dallas and learning a new way to help people again, but my husband won't want me to go and won't want to go with me. This isn't his plan for us. What if I go without his permission?"

His counsel was very emphatic. "You have a moral obligation to do whatever it takes to get the help you need and you don't need permission from anyone in order to do it. You are in an unhealthy co-dependency relationship." I was shocked when he said that, because I just hadn't applied the term "co-dependency" to me before. He also told me he didn't think my marriage had been a sacramental marriage anyway, since we had never arrived at that place of oneness that establishes the sacrament in our lives.

Recognizing how pitiful I was, that I needed Father Chelich's encouragement in order to face my husband with my planned measure of independence, I was nonetheless grateful for that encouragement. After dinner that night, I talked to Bill, explaining to him what I was going to do, and he stayed fairly calm under the circumstances, turning to me, saying, "I'm not following *you* anywhere." "That's okay," I responded, "I didn't expect you to." But by the time he had spent the night rehashing our brief conversation, he was really angry. "I am going to Costa Rica without you. You should not go to Dallas to a worldly situation. You are a women's libber!"

I went to the travel agency and got a refund on my ticket to Costa Rica. A few days later, Bill and I talked to Anne-Marie's husband, Matt, about the situation and then Matt talked to Bill for a long time. As a result, Bill told me he would not go to Costa Rica but would join me in Dallas in the spring, so I felt relief that at least that hurdle was overcome. Then family members started arriving from all over to celebrate Thanksgiving Day and that hubbub took over our lives for the weekend.

Bill vacillated all over the place. A couple of weeks later he said that he had changed his mind about going to Dallas with me. "You are leaving the marriage, going to a cult, going against scripture, you're getting worldly." Then in the next breath, he said, "I'm going to talk to Father Antekeier and if Father tells me to go then I'll go with you."

When Father Antekeier told him to go with me, Bill said he'd go and would remain firm in that decision. But I didn't want him to come with me because someone told him to do that. I wanted him to come if he wanted to work on our relationship. His sister, Alice Jean, phoned and talked to me for a long time, encouraging me to make a life for myself. This was a very discombobulating time for me. My emotions were all over the place.

We spent most of the month of December in Rhode Island at Michael's, helping around the house and getting acquainted with their new daughter, Zoe, born December fourth. I spent a lot of time reading and pondering Lewis Smedes book, *Forgive and Forget.* With its excellent help, Bill and I talked through a lot of things.

He surprised me by saying he was afraid he had ruined our marriage and it was ended. And he asked me to give him a list of possible Christmas gifts I would like to receive so he could get me something. I did that, happy that he was willing to try to put forth some effort in that area, and he followed through, even showing some creativity by throwing in a bag of potato chips which had not been on my want list.

But on December 26th I had written in my journal: "I stopped in front of Bill at one point when he was standing in the dining room and I put my arms around him. As it usually happens when I initiate some personal intimacy, he let his arms hang at his side and did not return my embrace. Again I felt pain. Can I ever get to the point where I can be me and not feel pain relating to this man who can't or won't express love to me? I think I'd surely be happier living apart from him."

So David and Bill drove me to Chicago on January second and left me at Julie's, with Bill still ambivalent as to when or if he'd join me in Dallas. I had just come across the scripture from the twelfth chapter of Genesis, about the road of faith Abraham and Sara traveled on, not knowing where they were going, and it encouraged me that even in their old age God still had some marvelous surprises in store for them. After a few delicious days with Julie and experiencing a beautiful heavy snowfall, she put me on the train to Dallas. It was a "ready or not, here I come" thing!

During the train trip I had a lot of time to think. One of the passages in Smedes' book, talked about our need to respect ourselves enough to set limits on the amount of abuse that we will accept. This really hit home with me to the point where I was sure God was speaking through it. And as the soothing sound of the train wheels lulled me into a transition from my old life into the new, I wrote in my journal: "Last year's road has been a pit of despair in some places; a rubble of desolation with the sense of being unwanted in my home with Anne-Marie, the arduous European trip, and the continual conflict and lack of appreciation or love from Bill. But that life is a dead end road. I can't and won't go back to it.

The coming year looks like a road fraught with possible disaster, but it is so enticing as it bids me to follow it into the biggest adventure of my adult life. Parallel to this outer road, there is an inner road that I want to travel, and I know I have to let the Lord light my way because it's too dark for me to see the way by myself."

I had barely gotten settled in at Charlotte's when I had a letter from Bill, basically saying that he'd read a book about how women who had been raising children for years finally came to a point of crisis when the children were raised. Then they needed to take a class or branch into some other interest and needed their husband's encouragement to do so. So he had thought about that and decided it was all right for me to be in Texas. He said that he'd probably join me sometime in April when he could get our bus out of it's storage lot, where it was buried under twelve feet of snow. I thought, "Is this something to be happy about? Is God beginning to break through to a new Bill, or is his agreeing to everything, just his way to have the appearance of still being in charge, ergo, he gives his permission for what I'm doing so now it's okay?"

Setting all that aside, I plunged into making a life in Dallas, studying all the material from Performax via teaching videos and spending hours talking to Don and Charlotte regarding the information I needed. I also did the practical things—getting the license and insurance for a 1985 Chevy my parents bought me and checking into work possibilities.

When I had been in Dallas before, I had read a newspaper article about a woman, Giselle, who had an all-female painting business, and when I had called her about being a member of her crew she told me to call her when I returned. When I contacted her again, she told me she would take me on for her next project which would begin in a week.

The project was to paint the lobby of a prominent hotel on the other side of the city. A day or two after we got started, the working hours changed from days to nights because the management said we'd have to work when there was the least amount of lobby traffic. I'd never worked a night job before and it was a bit unsettling to turn my world upside down and drive back and forth through the nightlife of the city.

I'd done lots of painting but this job was like nothing I had ever experienced before. The other six women on the crew appeared to be rough and tough. They each drove a truck, smoked incessantly and frequently used words I wished I had never heard and hoped I wouldn't remember. Some of them were drunk on the job and they all went to the nearest bar when we got off work each morning.

Giselle fit the description of all of her crew, but she was also a slave driver in charge of her biggest project ever. The preparation work was taking much longer than she had anticipated, so she was getting antsy. And when she discovered that some of the paint was the wrong paint after we'd already applied two days of it, she was very upset.

I seemed to get along comfortably with all the women on a casual basis, and had even received an invitation to one of their homes to watch a ball game. Working one day close by one of the women, Sherry, she hesitantly asked me:

"Did you know that most of our crew are lesbians?"

"I thought that might be the case," I replied. "Why do you ask?"

"Um, you know—you aren't."

"Well, does that make you uncomfortable around me?"

"Um, no, you seem okay. Like, um, you don't act like you think we're weird or anything."

"Well, I'm not really spending any time thinking about your lesbian issues. Maybe I haven't talked much with you all because I've got a lot on my mind. There's a lot of stuff going on inside of me that I'm trying to deal with."

Meanwhile, Giselle was having big problems. Halfway through the project she was getting more upset every day, telling us her costs were going way over what she had bid. One night when we were almost done with the project, she came to inspect an area of trim I was painting and said, "That looks like shit! Do it over!" I was shocked as she berated me for the terrible job I was doing because I knew darn well I had done a good job all along! But I was bone-weary and therefore teary as I finished up that morning and drove home.

Sherry phoned me the next day to tell me they had all been called in to work one more day to finish the project and would then start a new job, but Giselle was not going to call me or pay me for the work I had already done. My only way to contact Giselle was a pager number, but Sherry gave me Giselle's home phone number so I kept calling her until I finally reached her.

"Remember how the newspaper article I saw about you in November told what a wonderful woman you were?" I said. "Remember all the work I did, how I was always there when you called me, how I stuck it out with your crew even when we had to work nights instead of days? You had better pay me, or I will go to the hotel people and the newspaper and tell them how you refused to pay me, and that it wasn't because I did inferior work, but because you had mismanaged the job."

After a moment of silence, she grudgingly agreed to pay me, "I'll mail you a check when I get my money," she replied. A month later I got a check that was $33 dollars short of what she owed me, but I was so glad to get it, I went immediately to her bank and cashed it, thankful to put that experience behind me.

Concurrently with this job I had been hired by the local parish to put on a weekend retreat for a group of thirty-three families and I was putting hours of work into getting it all together. And since I was still training to be a consultant for Performax, I was feeling pretty harried, still feeling very vulnerable in this new unproven life of mine. The many phone calls and letters that came to me from back home were like an anchor, keeping me from floating too far away to be reeled in.

Looking for fellowship with other people who loved the Lord, I contacted the Community of God's Delight, a Catholic Charismatic Community in Dallas, and began attending the weekly meetings. One of the couples in the community, Ellen Rossini and her husband, lived only a block from our house in Richardson. Ellen was a bit of a nut in a wonderful way so we kept each other laughing as well as sharing our faith with each other. She and some of the other women from the community opened up other social opportunities for me, so I began to acquire a circle of acquaintances.

Along with everything that was happening on the surface of my life, I constantly had reassurances from the Lord that I was exactly where I needed to be. Over and over in my quiet time I opened to scriptures that were so loving and so specific to my situation. I was reassured by a strong sense of God's love for me and his faithful presence by my side.

Bill sent me rather distant philosophical letters from time to time. In March I started looking at apartments in the area, because he had said he was coming in April, but when I told him about that he said, "We can't afford to live in an apartment, we will have to live on the bus." I just repeated to him that I was planning on living in an apartment and left it at that.

Charlotte kept pushing me to forget him and get on with my life. "Look, he's so much older than you, you need to dump him before he gets sick and you think you have to stay with him to take care of him!" That was too callous a way for me to look at things. I had to work this relationship through very prayerfully. Putting my needs ahead of someone else's was risky business. I had to find the balance in order to live with myself.

So I did go on with my life. I worked office jobs through a temporary services agency and I also got a job at a flower shop for Secretary's Week through Mothers Day. The parish retreat weekend I had been planning for weeks went okay, I guess, but I was disappointed that most of the participants didn't really seem interested in spiritual things. Perhaps it was my presentation that failed to move them. Perhaps I had been spoiled by years of working with people who were earnest about seeking God.

In March, I flew to Boston to babysit for two weeks with my granddaughter, Rachel, while Joe and Marcia were gone on business trips at the same time. Joe talked to me for quite a while about my situation and said he felt strongly, that I should not try to live with his dad again soon. Easter came and went and then Bill informed me that he was on his way to Dallas.

The Semblance of Reunion in Dallas

I rented an apartment and moved in with my meager belongings plus the new table and chairs I had bought. It was located near Charlotte and Don's home in part of a huge, upscale complex in North Dallas and I looked forward to moving into the peaceful setting. The last letter I got from Bill before he arrived was one in which he said he had received a scripture from God which talked about how difficult it is for a man to live with an evil wife. When I showed it to Don, he said, "Geeze! This guy is really shooting himself in the foot, isn't he!"

Bill stopped in St. Louis to visit his sister, Alice Jean and his brother on his way here. Alice Jean, phoned me. "Bill left around 4:00 yesterday afternoon, Laurie, and I have to tell you, I had a hard time talking with him. Jack came over and talked to him for three hours, but both of us felt he didn't listen to us, and both of us felt he is disturbed in his mind. I talked to Eileen (his other sister) about Bill, too and we all feel concerned that you would have a hard time with him if you try to live with him again."

Alice Jean also said that Bill had struck a car on the way to St. Louis. It was not a serious accident, but still significant in that he just wasn't careful enough anymore. I hadn't been looking forward to this reunion and Alice Jean's phone call seemed to justify my lack of enthusiasm.

When Bill arrived he looked so exhausted that I encouraged him to rest before doing anything else. But he insisted on unloading the bus and getting settled in, so we started doing that with Don and Charlotte's help. I was not happy to see him. I was working full-time at the florist shop then and left for work the first thing the next morning. When I walked in the door that night he started in on me again, listing my faults and rebelliousness. "I have to live in peace, Bill," I said, "so if you're not willing to do that then get right back on your bus and go!"

It felt so good to stick up for myself! The more I did it the better I felt. I had reached the point where I felt enough emotional distance from Bill that I could remain courteous to him and tell him how we might relate peacefully, but I also told him I was unwilling to live with conflict. The next morning as I left for work his words trailed after me, "I won't be here when you get home tonight."

But he was there when I got home and he stayed. We went back to the Midwest late in May, attending a wedding in St. Louis, visiting family in Michigan, Chicago and Iowa. I had been worried about returning to Anne-Marie's, where I held my new granddaughter, Claire, for the first time, but Anne-Marie greeted me cheerfully and I managed to be positive, shoving down the scary feelings still festering inside me. I had really missed my grandsons, David and Michael. It was so good to spend time with those little guys again!

Visiting my parents in Iowa, I saw that the father I loved so much was battling a recurrence of his cancer that had first been diagnosed in 1986, and he was weary. The blarney still rolled from his lips and his eyes still twinkled, but the series of radiation treatments he had just finished seemed harder on him than the surgery that he had in 1986. Mother twittered around so incessantly positive, that she seemed to be in denial regarding the seriousness of Daddy's condition. I guess that was her way of coping. I felt really bad for them as we traveled back to Dallas.

We got back into the pattern of going to daily Mass together, riding our bicycles in the area, attending Catholic Charismatic meetings, and the usual outward appearance of a modicum of congeniality, but I was very unhappy to be living with him again because his behavior toward me hadn't changed. I didn't insist that he leave, so I got lots of practice in taking care of myself in the midst of adversity. Although I didn't want the struggle of trying to live with Bill anymore, I still couldn't take the initiative to end our relationship. I hoped that my new business venture and other activities in Dallas would keep me going.

On July 6th that year, I went on a five-day, silent retreat at Montserrat Jesuit Retreat House. It was an incredibly profitable time for me spiritually! There I received so many riches related to this new thrust of my life, (using the Performax DiSC Personal Profile to counsel people) as well as riches for my own spiritual growth. The things the Lord showed me through prayer, readings and the personal counsel I received, equipped me with the knowledge I would need both for my benefit and to share with others.

I met with Fr. Joseph McGill the first morning I was there. He was a missionary who had served for years in Africa, but had been returned to Dallas because of his medical problems and was now assisting with retreats. I wrote in my journal that night: "I shared with him, my love for God, my groping with the futility of being able to return any measure of that love, my incredible joy in the midst of the terrible feelings of inadequacy, and a smattering of my current situation. The time flew, and when a knock at the door indicated that our time was up, he appeared disconcerted and I was taken aback when he said, 'I must see you again as soon as possible. You have that rare gift of a genuine relationship with God.' There was no time left on his schedule, so he told me to come back tomorrow at 2:00, during what was to have been his rest period.

"I left his office feeling a bit uneasy with his comment about my relationship with God being rare. Was having a relationship with God really rare? I thought he was making too much of it. But I also felt hopeful at the thought of meeting with him again. Maybe he could clarify some of the struggles I was having. He had told me that my problem was that there *was* no problem, and that I needed to give myself permission to just *be*. I guess the 'giving myself the permission to just be' was where I had trouble. It seemed a bit risky."

There were three things that stood out in my mind from my meeting with Father McGill the next day. First he told me I needed to let go of introspection. I hadn't realized I was introspecting. I wasn't even sure if I knew what introspecting was. Then he explained, "You've been going through years of purification, but by trying to analyze your behavior and figure everything out you are giving in to subtle temptations to focus on yourself." That was helpful. Secondly, in place of introspection I was to sit quietly before the Lord in my total emptiness, knowing that I am nothing. And thirdly, he commented that I was beginning to experience that gift of impoverishment of spirit. Well, maybe.

My efforts to concentrate on my spiritual life during those five days were distracted by my need to combat an army of insects in the room I was assigned to: first, I found spiders in my shower and bathroom, then I found one in my bed between the sheets! Fleas bit my legs as I sat at the desk in my room, and mosquitoes went after me when I went for an early morning walk. And I even had a woman sitting behind me during Mass one day, break silence to tell me there was a bug crawling on the back of my blouse.

As the retreat continued, a flood of inspirational reading began to excite me, as if God had just been waiting for me to pay attention seriously enough for him to fill me with stuff that I would soak up like a sponge. It was a time of such rich spiritual feasting. Writings from St. Augustine, John of the Cross, Julian of Norwich, and Thomas Merton were special to me during that time and continue to be. And I kept running into writings that emphasized the uniqueness of each individual from the moment we're born, and how we lose sight of that as we're growing up and being exposed to more and more of the world. These thoughts fit like a glove with what I was learning through my studies regarding the DiSC Personal Profile.

I met with Fr. McGill a few more times during the summer to help me keep things in perspective as I practiced "just being." I found it hard to give myself permission to do that at first; it seemed like an invitation to be selfish, but by persisting in my attempts for balance I became more comfortable. I finally passed the buck to God, telling him I knew he could yell loud enough to stop me if I was going off the deep end somewhere.

I spent the rest of the summer enlisting many of my friends and their families to sit down and let me take them through the DiSC counseling tool. It was a great time of learning the material and getting better acquainted with them. When I had episodes of emotional fencing with Bill, I would turn to my friend, Ellen, for comic relief.

One day I even worked with her as an extra on the set of a TV program I had never heard of, *Walker, Texas Ranger*. The shooting of that day's scenes was taking place in and around the Courthouse in Ft. Worth, where I spent part of the day being thrown to the ground by a fellow actor as Walker and his side-kick came bursting out the front doors of the courthouse with guns blazing. After several takes of that scene, I watched while they repeatedly blew up a Monte Carlo parked at the curb, and then I was involved in some scenes inside the Courthouse too. It was a very long day but very interesting and educational, and I earned $95 for my participation.

In July, Anne-Marie phoned, bringing up the subject of our relationship, apologizing again for what she said was immature behavior on her part the past year. She asked us to come back and live with them again, citing reasons why it would be good for all of us. I told her I didn't think I could possibly be comfortable there anymore. Even if I could be healed enough emotionally, I figured we'd both feel like we had to try so hard not to offend the other that it would only be added pressure. But I told her I would try to be open to that.

A friend of mine, Sue Young, who was a National Director for Mary Kay Cosmetics came to Dallas that summer, and when she saw what I was doing with the DiSC Personal Profile, she asked me to come to Michigan and do a seminar for her down-line managers on the 6th of November. The fact that my sphere of acquaintances was huge in Michigan compared to Dallas, made it good business sense to go back to Michigan to get something going.

So we decided that we'd move back to the area in the fall, but I told Anne-Marie we would be renting an apartment there. I still didn't see how I could live with them again. "Just come and stay with us for a few days, Mom, and see how you feel, just be willing to try it," she pleaded. I told her I'd pray about it. I had very mixed emotions as we headed back up north.

Return to Michigan

Returning to Michigan in September, I knew I wasn't the person who had left there a few months ago but I was still clearly a work in progress. We did try staying at Anne-Marie's, and I eventually grew less apprehensive about being there. Their home is run on an orderly basis with much practice of our Catholic faith in evidence, and the children were so darling that I let go of fussing about my emotions and tried to "just be" as Fr. McGill had advised.

The winter weather of 1994 was harsh at times and I was laid low twice by what is called "walking pneumonia" so I had a lot of quiet time. As I had suspected, I had changed enough that the troubles with Bill, although they continued, did not emotionally affect me as much as in the past. When I stuck up for myself instead of playing the victim role, I displaced part of the self-loathing beast that had haunted me for years.

My business venture into counseling people through use of the DiSC instrument was good for me. Starting off with individual sessions with many of Sue's Mary Kay consultants, I went on to work with families and individuals throughout the next couple of years. I loved the work and also the freedom I had to schedule clients at my convenience, which allowed me to travel out of the area when I wanted to. Most of my travels were with Bill to family sites or academic sites where he still did some identification work. But sometimes I went alone or with others. I'll never forget one trip in particular, when I lived with the people of the dump in Juarez, Mexico.

Our youth group at church needed chaperones and drivers to go with them on this mercy trip in June of 1995. Our group consisted of five girls, six boys, one young married couple and two men in their twenties. I helped to drive an old 12-passenger van, as we traveled for thirty-six hours until we crossed into Juarez. The motor kept heating up, so we had to drive with the heater on even though the temperature outside was already very hot. One of the men had driven his pickup truck, which hauled all of our sleeping bags, back packs and water.

We arrived mid-morning on a Sunday, at a tamped-down acre of garbage where our base was located. The modest, cement block, mission building housed the center and health clinic for the people who live in and around the dump. Our arrival was just in time to help set up for a weekly food distribution to the people, so I weighed and bagged potatoes, made a precarious pyramid of cans of Hunts tomato sauce, and piled numerous stacks of bags of flour and pasta into some semblance of order. All of us were hungry, but in spite of food all around us no food was available for us to eat. It brought home the fact that these people were hungry most of the time.

When we were done with the set up, I worked bare-handed with others, picking up loose garbage and throwing it into the present dumping area on the other side of a fence. We had brought work gloves, but weren't able to access them until later when they unloaded our van. Then we raked dirt over the harder, tamped-down part of the dump to enlarge the area where the combination center and clinic sat.

The men in our group and some of the girls, loaded cement blocks onto an old truck to take them nearby where we would work the next day building three simple homes to replace ones that had recently burned down. I was back to carrying Kleenex to use as toilet paper, as I had done when we were in Costa Rica,. It couldn't be put into the only toilet, which was plugged up, but must be put into an already overflowing basket beside the toilet. There was one other toilet facility—a decrepit outhouse which really looked scary. By the time we were able to spread out our sleeping bags on the floor of the all-purpose room, it was very late, so we cleaned ourselves up as best we could with some of our drinking water and I slept like a log.

Monday we split into small groups. Some repaired the roof of the mission, while I helped care for the children in the day-care center now operating in the space we had used for sleeping. Later I cleaned up debris and broken glass from the children's playground area, and also joined those raking up garbage between the street and a makeshift fence which extended for 150 feet in front of the mission building area. Others in our group were painting the fence, moving along behind us as we cleaned up enough debris for them to have room to paint.

Water was available from an old tank truck parked near the building. It delivered water throughout the neighborhoods in the dump, two or three days per week, but no showers were available. That night we cleaned up as best we could with baby wipes we had brought with us and Coke bottles of water. Then we went to Mass at a nearby church.

The next day was spent digging the foundation for the first of the three houses that had burned. The hundreds of people who live in the dump take wooden pallets discarded by factories and make a frame for a little house no bigger than a typical small den in our houses back home. Then they nail pieces of cardboard to the frame and put some plastic or tar paper over the top for a roof. An average of six people live in that room. As you can imagine, these homes burn easily, so the cement block homes we were building were highly prized.

We worked long, hard, hot days. Most of the time I raked the dump, throwing burnable trash into a pit where a fire was kept going, and sorting glass into different piles according to color, to be carted to the glass factories in Juarez. I experienced a "what a small world" moment when I returned home and my son, David, told me that one of those glass factories was where he goes regularly in his work of designing automobile mirrors and windows.

It was a subdued bunch that set out for the rigorous journey home after working there for a week. At one point when I was driving in the middle of the night, the sliding side door of the van came loose and would have been gone, but for the efforts of the guys who managed to hang onto it until I could pull over. The water pump broke completely in Oklahoma, but we were near a town so we were able to buy a new one without much difficulty.

These mission trips are never easy. Everyone was stinky and exhausted by the time we got home, but our church has such strong ties with the people of the dump, that twice a year we make trips like the one we had just finished. Besides the service it provided, it was always an experience to remember for our young people and worth all the hardship it entailed.

Although I had phoned Bill when we were an hour away from home, to give him our estimated time of arrival so he could pick me up, I waited another half hour after all the others were gone, before he arrived to collect me. He didn't even greet me, but just sat in the car while I lugged my sleeping bag and suitcase to the trunk by myself. The hours spent raking glass in the hot sun of the dump had provided lots of time to think, and I knew I had reached the point where I was not willing to live the life in Grand Rapids with Bill any longer. I would find a place of peace for me as soon as possible. Enough was enough.

Boggled Mind

Because I had spent so much time traveling since we sold our home and went to Costa Rica, my closest friends were still the ones who lived in the Lansing area. I visited them frequently even as I visited my children there, so several of them were well aware of the difficulty I was having with Bill and were concerned about how long I could cope with him without getting sick myself. Some of them encouraged me to go back to work in order to have health insurance and normal living space away from him. Several friends suggested that I get a job in Lansing and stay with them during the week, only making the sixty mile trip to Grand Rapids on the weekends.

Indeed, Bill was getting more difficult to cope with. After learning the particular traits connected with Alzheimer's Disease as part of my work as a Hospice volunteer, I couldn't help but notice that Bill showed many of the symptoms of that disease. His problem with balance continued to progress, he had stopped taking care of his personal hygiene, his speech seemed to be slurring quite a bit, he'd lost a lot of weight, and his behavior seemed to be getting more bizarre.

During our last visit to my parents in Iowa, he had stayed most of the time in the bedroom we were using, afraid to be out in the living room where the television was on most of the time, for fear that his mind would be polluted. And he was agitated because he thought our minds were being polluted too.

We had been meeting weekly with a group of couples involved in the Catholic Charismatic movement in Grand Rapids, and as he began behaving inappropriately in the meetings I became increasingly uneasy. During discussions he would frequently and abruptly say things that had absolutely no connection to the current topic of conversation, and when refreshment time arrived he remained seated with the women instead of joining the men in an adjoining room, as was the custom.

One Saturday morning, at a meeting of several small Charismatic groups in a local gymnasium, once the business part of the meeting was over, everyone mingled and enjoyed refreshments. During that time, I talked with several different people but Bill had just stood along a wall observing the activity, and by the time we left for home he was furious with me. "You just went off and left me!" he exclaimed. Everyone in the group was very kind, but Bill's behavior was a bit disconcerting for them too, so for the good of all we stopped going.

I was so constantly unhappy with Bill's agitation toward me that one night when he reached for me in bed I told him, "Bill, please don't touch me in bed if you can't be kind to me otherwise." With that he abruptly turned his back to me and didn't say another word. But late one night, a few days later when I came into our bedroom to go to sleep, I saw that he had brought a mattress up from the basement storage area and was placing it on the floor beside our queen-size bed.

Shocked, I asked him, "What's going on here?" He turned to me and angrily replied, "You are going to hell and the Bible says that in the last days, two will be sleeping in a bed and one will be taken and one will be left, so I'm not sleeping in the same bed with you anymore!"

"Bill Downes, you take that mattress right back down the basement!" I said indignantly. "I will not have your grandchildren popping in here like they do and wonder what the heck a mattress is doing on the floor! How would you explain that to them? Do you want to upset them?" Since he knew that the little kids were constantly climbing into bed with us for a story or to snuggle, he looked a bit disconcerted, so when he took his toothbrush and disappeared into the bathroom, I dragged the mattress back down the to basement. From then on, if I was in our bed, he just laid down on the floor and went to sleep.

During this time, we had frequently been going to noon Mass during the week at the Catholic Information Center in downtown Grand Rapids with Anne-Marie's family. The Paulist priests there gave really good homilies and one of them, Father Robert Sirico, was outstanding. I had been going to Fr. Sirico for confession for awhile, so the morning after the mattress episode I phoned him and told him of the consternation I felt with Bill's behavior. "Do you think you are safe," he asked me? I told him I thought I was, but Bill was getting so bizarre that it was a little scary. When he suggested I come to see him later that day I was relieved that I could do so.

I went to the laundry room and began ironing some jeans as I mulled over my dilemma. A bit later, Bill appeared in the doorway and started in on me again:

> "You need to go to confession. You're going to hell!"
>
> "Bill, I am going to see Fr. Sirico this afternoon so I'll tell him of your concern."
>
> "I'll go with you, and I'm going to tell him about you and you're not going to like what you're going to hear. You're going to have to listen to the truth!"

> "No, Bill, you are not going with me this afternoon because I am going to confession. But I have no problem hearing the truth and would welcome it, so if you want me to, I will make an appointment for both of us to go talk to him at another time."

That seemed to satisfy him and he nodded affirmatively as he left me in peace.

When I sat down with Father Sirico later that day, I told him about our marriage in the same manner that I had talked to Father Chelich in 1993. Father Sirico said the same thing that Father Chelich had said, that he didn't think we had a valid sacramental marriage. We talked about the possibility of Alzheimer's Disease being part of the problem and we made an appointment to meet with Bill.

As prearranged with Fr. Sirico, when we went to the appointment a few days later, we spoke to him only briefly before he suggested that I wait in another room while he got acquainted with Bill. When I rejoined them a little later, he turned to me and explained that he had recommended to Bill a good Catholic psychologist we could go to for some advice about our relationship. So we left it at that, silently driving home, each lost in our own thoughts. A few days later Bill informed me that he had called and made an appointment for us with Dr. Peter Birkeland, the clinical psychologist that Father Sirico had recommended.

When we entered Dr. Birkeland's office, we went through the ritual of introductions and sat down. Then Dr. Birkeland said:

"Well, what seems to be the trouble?"

Bill blurted out, "She won't have sex with me!"

A bit taken aback at this revelation and his bluntness, I turned to him:

"Don't you remember, Bill? I simply asked you not to touch me in bed unless you could treat me with kindness out of the bed."

He didn't respond to that so Dr. Birkeland asked: "Did you hear what she said, Bill?"

"Oh, I don't pay any attention to what she says."

"Well, did you notice her demeanor, the tone of her voice, her posture?"

"No, I didn't see anything."

And so the counseling session continued with nothing apparently accomplished. Dr. Birkeland told us he saw two people saying words to each other but neither of them understanding what the other said. He concluded that if Bill would like to come back and work on his communication skills, he would see if he could help him, but it was for him to decide. As we left there, I felt no hope that things would change for the better and since Bill had always refused to go to counseling in the past, I doubted that he would get back in touch with Dr. Birkeland.

But although he didn't talk to me about it, he did go back to Dr. Birkeland and went through an extensive psychological testing process. Then one day he came to me with a letter written by Dr. Birkeland, reiterating his conclusion of the counseling with Bill. "See," he said, brandishing a letter at me. "I'm *not* crazy!"

Basically, Dr. Birkeland had written that Bill's style of relating was one of detachment, disconnection, introversion and isolation and that he indicated he preferred to stay that way. He noted that we were quite mismatched, and since I needed connection in order to be happy, he didn't believe any marital counseling would be helpful. He also wrote that Bill had stated that he used to pretend to be connected though he desired to keep his distance from others, so I began to get a glimmer of why Bill frequently insisted that I was just being nice to people because I wanted them to like me. It made me think that maybe that was what *he* was doing!

I periodically brought up the subject of seeing a doctor to have his hearing and sense of balance checked, but he adamantly refused to do so. He didn't want my help with anything so I kept asking God to show me what I could do for *me*. How was *I* going to stay healthy? I remembered the suggestion and even urging of my friends, that I get a job to give me some space away from Bill, so I told God I'd be open to finding a job if he would lead me to one.

Back into the Workforce

After one last phone conversation with Dr. Birkeland, who told me that he thought Bill was so eccentric he was near the edge of insanity, I started looking at possibilities for my future. One of those was serving on the Caribbean Mercy. I had read that the ship was docked at South Haven for a month or so and I had taken Anne-Marie's sons to visit it. When I learned that it was one of a fleet of Mercy ships that take Christian medical personnel to serve in poor countries, treating patients via the medical facilities on the ship, I was interested in signing up for a tour of duty on the ship and asked God to show me if this was what he would like me to do. I read all I could get my hands on about the ministry and completed an application to go on the next trip to the Carribean in November as auxiliary help.

But the day before I received an acceptance letter from the organization, I went for a job interview in Lansing and was hired the same day. One of my long-time Lansing friends, Jean Tubbs, was the Executive Assistant to the head of Capitol Area Community Services in Lansing. They had just received a grant from the state for a new program to hire two Medicaid Ombudsmen to educate Medicaid clients who were being forced into new Health Maintenance Organizations for their medical coverage. She thought I'd be perfect for the job and I was delighted with the opportunity.

My friends, the Shavers, had an extra bedroom and invited me to stay with them, so in August of 1995 I attempted to begin another new life. After a training period, my co-worker and I were outfitted with laptop computers, cell phones, and lots of educational materials, as we went to the homes of Medicaid clients to teach them how to choose an appropriate HMO and then how to correctly use that health coverage.

We quickly began to find cases where people were not receiving adequate health care or were getting into all sorts of trouble with it, so the bulk of the work developed into being advocates for people as much as educators. Vying with health care providers and upper echelon members of state bureaucracy, we spent most of our time going to bat for clients when it appeared they had been treated unjustly.

I absolutely loved the work and living with Dick, Gerry and their daughter, Margaret. Gerry had been my mentor and friend since 1967 so it was wonderful to be in daily contact with her again. What a difference it was to come home every night to an environment where I felt welcomed and appreciated! I can't describe adequately how deeply good that was for my spirit. As anticipated, I was able to cope much better on the weekends in Grand Rapids in spite of Bill's frustration with me.

He had told me before I took the Lansing job, that if I did, he would no longer be my husband. Later that summer, I was sitting out in the yard one sunny, weekend afternoon, watching the antics of my grandkids playing in a wading pool in the driveway, when he came up to me and announced, "I want a annulment!" "Honey, you can't have an annulment until you first get a divorce," I replied. "Then I want a divorce!" he said. "Then go get one, Bill," I replied quietly.

I didn't hear any more talk about that for a while but he kept sending me letters at Shavers, rambling on about many things but mostly talking about what a bad person I was. Since it was impossible to reason with him, I decided not to respond to the letters or refer to them. When I came home each weekend, he usually asked me if I'd read his latest letter and I always gave him a brief "yes" or "no." I did finally ask him to stop sending them the letters, telling him I would not read them anymore. He finally quit doing that when Father Antekeier, our pastor and his confessor, told him not to write to me anymore.

That winter, Bill's behavior became problematic for everyone. A few times he walked several miles to downtown Grand Rapids and took a bus to East Lansing without telling anyone. Nobody knew where he was until he finally showed up at Amy's house or my office. When we discovered him missing one bitter cold, Sunday morning, and then realized he'd left the house around 4:30, we finally called the police for help. It was David who found him that time, around 9:30, way east of where he meant to be. In spite of Matt telling him, very firmly, that he wasn't to leave without telling someone, he did it anyway and got lost again.

Bill had been going to daily Mass and weekly confession with Father Antekeier, so when I went to talk to Father about my struggle, I expected to be told to keep a stiff upper lip and to soldier on with the Lord's grace. So I was shocked when he told me, "Stay completely away from Bill and let your children handle him. You never should have married him. God allowed the marriage to bring seven wonderful children into the world, but some day you may marry again and experience what marriage is supposed to be."

Talking individually with my children regarding my inability to cope with their father's constant emotional abuse anymore, their response ranged from Joe encouraging me to stay away from Bill and "get a life," to the others simply agreeing that we couldn't go on the way we were. They all said I wasn't to worry about their dad. They would take care of him and the problems inherent with that. They're great kids!

Foremost in my mind were the preparations for our Julie's marriage to Darrell in October, and concern about my father's health which was definitely deteriorating. Julie's marriage was a joyous time of celebration in Chicago that fall. During the eight years she had known Darrell, I had grown to love him and appreciate his many attributes. With his deep faith and gentle nature, I couldn't have entrusted her to anyone better. At the other end of the spectrum from the this joy, I was well aware of the sorrow in the pit of my stomach with the significance of the fact that my father was too ill to come to their wedding. Since my mother certainly wouldn't leave his side, the lack of the presence of my parents at Julie's wedding was truly ominous.

Daddy

I had been driving often to Iowa to visit my parents on weekends and keeping in touch by phone. In August of 1994, I had helped them move to an apartment, in anticipation of the time when my father's disease would no longer allow him to drive, and where mother's needs would be met after he died. My parents had sold their home on Hogan Avenue, an avenue named after him, and moved into a 19th-floor apartment downtown in Cedar Rapids, so my mother would have access to her church and hospital activities in spite of the fact that she didn't drive.

It had been obvious to my sisters and me that the closeness of my parents caused a reluctance on the part of our mother to have anyone intruding on their privacy, even their children. But I couldn't stand staying away anymore by late February of 1996. I sensed the anguish in my mother's voice as we talked about her concern for my father and I told her how much I wanted to be with them:

"But you have a job now," exclaimed my mother. "You can't leave your job!" Hesitating to intrude on their privacy, I nevertheless plunged right in. "I'm really upset about not being with you, Mother. I keep picturing you two trying to deal with this illness alone. You don't need to worry about my job because I can get a leave of absence to help you and come back to my job later."

When she understood that I would not lose my job she seemed relieved that I could come. So I made arrangements for a three-month leave of absence, stopped in Grand Rapids to pick up a few things, and by March 13th I had packed up and left for Iowa. Bill looked sad and lost as I went out the door. I felt renewed anguish for him, for what we never had together, for my inability to help him or understand him. My drive to Cedar Rapids was teary, not because of what I was coming to but what I was leaving behind. The burden I was assuming seemed much lighter than the one in Michigan because there was love where I was going.

It was wonderful to hug my father again despite his frailty. Because of the inroads of his Alzheimer's Disease I had wondered if he would know me, but I needn't have worried. As he called out my name and embraced me tightly, his joyful welcome brought me deeply back home. Wasted as he was, glimpses of the old sparkle were still there but the inroads of prostate cancer could no longer be kept at bay.

A visiting nurse came to change his catheter the next day and then he acquiesced when Mother said she thought it would be good for him to accompany us as we ran some errands. I stayed with Daddy in the car while Mother was in a grocery store, and it was obvious that he was in great pain. He used our moment of privacy to tell me how desperately he needed relief. It got to the point where he had me go into the store and get Mother so we could go back home.

While I was still in Lansing, I had tried to talk to Mother about getting Hospice care for Daddy so he could have better pain control, but because that would mean strangers coming into their world, and be admitting that Daddy was dying, she had resisted thus far. And I could see that her determination to keep reorienting him to reality was just causing frustration for both of them.

The next morning Daddy was quite disorientated, asking me if I knew these people we were staying with. I could truthfully tell him I did know them and it was okay for us to be there. When he said he needed to take an automotive part to Vern Michaels in Anamosa, I put him in the car and we rode around for a few minutes. Then, when I asked him if he'd like to go home, he said, "Yes," so we went peacefully home. I was hoping Mother would begin to understand how to ease the frustration of Daddy's disease, but she still seemed locked in her old way of handling his odd behavior.

By the third day with them, I was really disturbed about her attitude toward Daddy, and how impatient she was with him as she kept answering the same questions over and over again. It was a new thing to experience tension between my parents, giving me a taste of what it must be like for people who grow up around parental tension all the time. After they went to bed, I got out my notes from an Alzheimer's Dementia Hospice Training I had attended, and prayed for guidance as to how to approach Mother. For months she had pooh-poohed the doctor's diagnosis, insisting that he only had a touch of dementia.

When Daddy was taking a nap the next day, I said to her, "Mother, there are a lot of things Daddy's just not understanding these days. I can see how exhausted you are and how hard it is to be patient when he asks the same thing over and over again, but things would go smoother if we just answer his questions calmly and go along with whatever he's saying, instead of trying to reorient him to reality. It's not possible to reorient him to reality, so your attempts to do so will only result in frustration for both of you!" I read to her some of my Hospice material and the rest of the day she was really patient with him.

That night when he kept asking over and over if the car was fine and if the horses were watered, Mother let me handle him and watched as I nonchalantly kept assuring him that indeed, the car was fine and the horses had been watered. Daddy's disorientation was sometimes comical. One night he wanted us to change the channel on the big clock that hangs on the livingroom wall!

At other times he was very agitated, coming out of his bedroom in the morning with his clothes donned right over his pajamas, insisting that he must get to work. If he couldn't be dissuaded, I would tell him I'd drive him, and then he'd forget where we were going, so I could just bring him back home.

I was reading *The Road to Daybreak*, by Henri Nouwen, at that time, and had a lot of food for thought when I came across the passage where he had written about how God wants us to recognize the beauty of his presence in our bodies. I had been noticing the beauty of my father's body. As the flesh melted away, his finely chiseled features became more clear, his blue eyes more blue, his skin surprisingly smooth.

My sister, Nancy, the nurse, made a whirlwind visit from California for a few days late in March, mainly to evaluate Daddy's pain. It was a relief to have her there, since Mother respected her medical opinions about what should be done. Before she left, she arranged for Daddy's pain medicine to be upped and backed my recommendation that they initiate Hospice care. I hated to see her go.

I realized that the center of my mother's world was dying and she was desperately trying to keep things going the way she thought she should. But it was a struggle for me to be patient with her controlling ways with both the environment and Daddy. She was torn about me being there because she wanted Daddy all to herself. I knew she couldn't have handled his care now without me, and sometimes we played cards and visited, but she still insisted on forcing Daddy to eat when he didn't want to, and to go for a walk when we practically had to carry him, so I felt torn trying to be an advocate for both of them. She kept acting as if she could keep him up and moving, she wouldn't have to admit that he was dying.

My head was heavy with unshed tears if I didn't keep focused on the tasks around me. Again I was living where I didn't really belong. I regressed to thinking that I didn't have a life of my own and maybe never would. Still I knew my own emotional fragility was minor compared to my mother's. So I just kept praying for God to help me keep everything together.

It was mid-April, after much suffering and many heart-rending days with Daddy, before Mother agreed to Hospice care. When the worker came to initiate my parents into the program, Daddy was in rare good form with his wit, keeping her in stitches as she went through the explanation of what would ensue under their care.

My brother Scott came for a week and was there at a crucial time, when Daddy had gotten up and gone into the bathroom without us realizing it until we heard him fall against the closed door. It took all of Scott's strength to be able to ease the door enough to get his hand in a crack, and then talk Daddy into taking his hand so he could lift him up and away from the door so he could get to him. From then on we made sure one of us was in the same room with him at all times. We moved a card table in the bedroom and played games there beside him.

There were still flashes of humor and wonderful loving interchanges though. I'll always remember, particularly, one time I was kneeling beside his bed, holding his hand in mine, when he reached for me with surprising strength in both arms and pulled me to him, kissing me and telling me how much he loved me.

All of my sisters were with us for the last ten days of his life, and those days were unimaginably precious to all of us. We were all gathered around his bed and I was actually kneeling beside him with my hand on his chest over his heart when it stopped beating, just a week short of his 86th birthday.

After a tumultuous gathering of the Hogan clan for the Irish wake, and a full St. Patrick's Church for the con-celebrated, funeral Mass, a long, long funeral procession led to the little cemetery in the middle of the fields near Fairfax, Iowa, a stone's throw from his boyhood home. It was an incredible time of celebrating his wonderful life, with the stories of his goodness and his fun-loving ways imprinting themselves on the mind and in the spirit of all of his progeny.

None of us could imagine Mother living without Daddy, but she had made firm plans in her mind about how he would want her to behave and continue on afterwards, and she was able to get herself together to the point where I felt I could go back to my life in Lansing and let her get on with hers.

Of Marriage and Divorce

Shortly after I had gone to Cedar Rapids, our David had taken his father on a pilgrimage to Jerusalem with a group of people from our parish, led by Father Antekeier. When they returned, David phoned me with both surprising news and some not so surprising news.

First he said, "Mom, I've met the woman I'm going to marry!" And how my heart did rejoice! Five years previously, David had prayed about becoming a priest, but he felt the Lord tell him that he would marry someday, and that as soon as he met his wife-to-be, he would know she was the one. "Oh, David, I am so thrilled for you! What is she like?" "Well, she's kind of feisty, Mom. She reminds me a little of Aunt Charlotte."

I had to smile at that, picturing my petite, dynamic sister. Then he proceeded to tell me that she had gone with her mother on the same pilgrimage. Although she had been in our parish for a couple of years, they had never met. David said that they still hadn't dated or talked about a relationship, but he was sure in his heart that she was the one he had been waiting for. His second bit of news was regarding Bill.

"Mom, Dad fell down twice over there when there wasn't even anything he could have tripped on. He needs to see a doctor."

"Well, Honey, if you can get him to a doctor that would be great. So far, he's been unwilling to go to one."

A few days later David phoned to say that he couldn't get Bill to agree to go to a doctor, but he told his dad he was making an appointment for him anyway and he was going to take him. However, my sister, Carolyn flew in to Cedar Rapids from Florida for a week, so I was able to drive home and take Bill to the doctor and he went peacefully. Our doctor ordered a bunch of tests and said Bill's problem was most likely Alzheimer's Disease as well as anyone can diagnose it without opening up the brain.

Back at my job in Lansing, all through that summer I rejoiced with David and his Julianne as wedding plans for their October wedding moved forward, and gritted my teeth as I tried to cope with Bill's continued agitation with me. All his medical tests and an evaluation by a psychiatrist who specializes in Alzheimer's

Disease seemed to confirm that diagnosis, so I tried harder to be considerate and patient with him. I couldn't help but notice the difference between him and my father and their way of behaving in spite of this disease. Their basic temperaments hadn't changed.

And it was very hard, grueling. I remember one weekend when I arrived home from Lansing, he was so upset when he saw me, that he couldn't stand still. Jabbing his finger at me with every word, he cried out to me, "*You* are going to hell! And God is holding me responsible for your salvation! You don't do what I tell you to do!" He was on the verge of tears.

I felt practically schizophrenic as I went through the various joyful showers and dinners preceding the wedding, interspersed with the agitated encounters with Bill. But David's wedding day did arrive at the end of October and we celebrated it with great joy. Every one of our children had been able to be present to bask in the happiness of this couple.

Our Tom had come up from Florida, bringing his fourteen-year-old, Katie, with him. Since Bill couldn't drive the bus anymore, we had bequeathed it to Tom, who had hoped that Bill would ride back to Florida with them and stay for a visit, but Bill declined the invitation.

However, a couple of weeks later when I came home for the weekend, I learned that Bill had flown to Florida to stay a month with Tom. He had left a letter on our bed for me, stating that unless I quit my job and came home and learned how to be a good wife, he would no longer be my husband. A few days later, in a phone conversation with my mother, when I told her about Bill again giving me an ultimatum, she asked me:

"What more do you need to put an end to this relationship? What are you waiting for?"

"Well, Mother," I replied. I guess I just wish he would go ahead and start proceedings for the divorce himself."

"You're going to have to do something," she replied.

"Maybe after the holidays," I said to her, changing the conversation then to another topic.

January 1997, arrived with its annual, bitterly cold weather and snow. One weekend as I was about to leave the Shavers' home for Grand Rapids, Dick Shaver said to me, "You do know you have to do something about the situation, don't you?" And I knew I had to. I was more than a bit worn out and it was becoming evident that Bill was agitated more than just when I was home. He couldn't get any peace any more. Then, on the heels of their admonitions, I had an extraordinary dream which was the final impetus for me to start proceedings for a divorce.

In the dream I was wearing my white, terry-cloth bathrobe, lying face-down in a cinder driveway two doors from our house on Sycamore Street. Bill was standing over me (I could see his shoes beside me) ordering me, "You need to get up because I am taking you to some Catholic nuns who will teach you how to behave!"

In the next scene of the dream, I was watching from a distance as he pounded on a bathroom door at my office. I knew I was behind that door as he shouted, "Hurry up and change your clothes so I can take you to the Catholic nuns who will teach you how to behave!"

The last scene took place in our Grand Rapids parish church. I was walking up the right side of the middle aisle in a line of people who were to receive Holy Communion. As usual, there was another line going up the other side of the aisle for the same purpose, as two people at the front distributed Holy Communion. When it came to my turn to receive the Sacred Host, I saw that it was Bill who was holding it up in front of me, but he refused to give it to me. I just stood there.

Father Antekeier was distributing Holy Communion at the head of the other line of people. When he glanced our way and saw what was happening, he motioned for me to come over to him, which I did. And just as Father held up the Host before me, Bill's arm lashed out from the side and knocked it out of Father's hand! I awoke with a start. Once I had calmed down, I realized through that vivid dream, that I was allowing Bill to come between me and my relationship with God and his plan for my life.

As I was leaving Grand Rapids to go back to work I said to him, "I might as well go ahead and file for a divorce since you're not doing anything about it." Without a word, he just looked at me until I left. So I made an appointment with a Lansing attorney to start divorce proceedings and followed through with it.

Since it was uncontested and there were no minor children or property involved, I was told it would be straightforward and simple, and that proved to be true. The lawyer handled the paperwork and I signed the papers, and by the end of May I was legally divorced after almost forty-two years of marriage. I didn't feel emotionally upset with the finality of the divorce. Because of so much strife for so long, what I felt was more like relief. But one spring evening, I was mulling this over, feeling a vague sadness as I went for a long walk after I had gotten home from work.

I had decided to deliver some paperwork to the home of a client, by walking there instead of driving. Because it was such a beautiful evening, it needed to be savored. After I gave my client the papers and started my walk home, feelings of loneliness rose to the surface of my mind as I wished I had someone to share with me the loveliness of the evening.

Then I became aware of a couple of young, African-American children, a boy and a girl, playing on the front porch of a dilapidated house I was approaching. As I came abreast of it, the little girl, who looked to be about five years old, ran down the steps to me with a big smile on her face and threw herself at me, giving me a big hug. Astonished, I exclaimed, "Why! Aren't you a wonderful hugger! I really needed a hug!"

We were beaming at each other, still hugging, when I looked up at the porch where the young boy, who appeared to be nine or ten, was watching us. "Do you want a hug, too?" I called out to him. He broke out into a smile and came running to join us and the three of us hugged and hugged. I thanked them for their loving ways as I left them, walking with a much lighter heart, in wonder at the marvelous ways in which God works. I didn't feel lonely any longer, sensing that God himself had hugged me to cast away my sadness.

A few months later my son, David, said something to me about going ahead and applying for an annulment of my marriage in the Catholic Church. That would provide some closure for me, and Bill would feel he was finally free from the responsibility for a recalcitrant wife. So I did apply for an annulment which was granted nine months later. And that did result in a more peaceful state of mind for my husband, in addition to the relief I felt. What a blessed, blessed relief!

California Joy

That summer of 1997, I rented my own apartment in Lansing and went to live by myself for the first time ever. It was incredibly peaceful to go home each night to my own place, where nobody met me at the door wanting something from me. I was happy there and especially grateful for it after I was talked into accepting the position of Administrative Director of Dimensions of Life, a Substance Abuse Facility for Women. The far too many hours I spent there and the stress of dealing with all the problems inherent with that type of position, caused me to sigh in relief when I was able to go home at the end of each day.

This 27-bed facility was an interesting challenge begun a few years previously and funded by a wealthy Christian man who had hoped it would eventually pay its own way. I was dismayed by a number of things I encountered while working there, in the way of inappropriate staffing and physical problems with an old building, but I grew to love the staff I developed around me, the work itself, and the women we served.

The first of October of 1998, my son, Joe and I were attending a family wedding in Dallas, when we started talking with my sister, Nancy about the possibility of me moving to live with Nancy in California. She was leaving her husband and thought it would be good to have me live with her in her new place. Joe kept urging me to do it, "You need to get a life, Mom," he said.

At that time, the owner of the ministry was running out of money to support us, and I became stressed out with the responsibilities of trying to run a facility without adequate funds to do so. The last straw for me occurred when the state put health care for mentally ill clients and substance abuse clients together into a separate HMO, and then stopped paying us for the care of the Medicaid clients they had placed with us. So I decided to throw in the towel and move to live with my sister, Nancy, in South Pasadena, California.

My family was a bit shocked to think that I would move so far away from all of them. Indeed, even *I* felt guilty at the thought, but not enough to keep me from trying something really different. While my kids were respectful about my decision, my son, Joe, was the one who really encouraged me, saying he would take a week's vacation to drive me and my moving truck across the country. He really understood how stressed I was in my present job.

So that Thanksgiving Day, all of my Michigan and Chicago family members came to the community room in my apartment complex for a lovely meal and good fellowship, and the next day, my sons helped to load the moving truck I had rented. We drove to Grand Rapids for one last hug at Anne-Marie's house where Bill was still living, and with a lump in my throat I climbed back into the truck with my car being towed behind. The lump in my throat was part physical as well as emotional since both Joe and I had colds and laryngitis. We drank tons of Ruby Red Grapefruit Juice and sucked on cough drops throughout the trip. And although we weren't able to talk as much as we normally would have, we both still enjoyed driving the southern route to Los Angeles.

I truly felt like I had been transported to a magical place. Everything around me seemed so fresh and different from what I had known. The house Nancy rented for us was one of those which was built into a cliff overhanging an arroyo, so we entered it either through our front door or through our two-car garage at the top level. Down a flight of stairs to the second level was our kitchen, living/dining room and a bathroom. Two big sliding glass doors led to a generous concrete deck the length of the house, surrounded by a sturdy railing. On down at the third level were our three bedrooms and two baths. Two of the bedrooms also had sliding glass doors to access a porch overlooking the arroyo. I went to sleep at night to the atonal music made by coyotes yipping in the canyon.

The house was located at the southernmost edge of South Pasadena where we looked from our porches, right across the arroyo to a street in the city of Los Angeles. But with the small town ambiance of South Pasadena's shopping area and the rural winding road up to our house, I had no sense of being in a big city environment. The beauty of the surrounding mountains and the sea took my breath away so I thoroughly loved my new life and new surroundings. Nancy and I had so much in common that our daily life together was very enjoyable. The balmy, sunny weather made me feel like I'd died and gone to heaven. We both loved playing tennis, going to the beach, taking long walks, and sitting out on our porch to have a glass of wine in the evening as we lazily watched a long line of planes coming into LAX over the ocean. And I began compiling in my mind, stories about all the funny, quirky things I saw and experienced in La La Land.

I was really happy living with Nancy but I had to make a living too, so after resting up for a couple of weeks, I began to look for a low-stress job that would enable me to meet my financial needs. I hadn't really thought about being a nanny but just before Christmas I met Albert and Pearl Lee and agreed to care for their son at least for a year. As soon as I met three-year old, Ryan, he grabbed my heart. They only lived a few minutes away from me so my life was still grounded in the peaceful enclave of South Pas. Eventually I became comfortable driving on the freeways, taking Ryan to Santa Monica Beach and to visit his mother at Disney headquarters where she worked.

To become acquainted with people in our new environment Nancy and I joined Holy Family Church and I also began meeting some of the members of the Foothill Cycling Club at Cal Tech's campus to ride with them most weekends. We'd leave early in the morning and ride for a few hours through many areas of the Los Angeles basin, having breakfast along the way. They were a very nice bunch of people in my age bracket for the most part and the bicycling was good exercise for me.

The other activity I built into my life was weekly Spanish lessons at a nearby high school. Certainly, in Southern California there were tons of opportunities to use what little Spanish I remembered from my Costa Rican days and I wanted to improve my facility with the language. I also enjoyed the social interaction with the other students.

Then, early in 1999, I came across a book at the library that did more to help me understand my husband than all the forty-some years I lived with him. "*A Beautiful Mind*," the biography of John Nash by Sylvia Nasar, was a gold mine for me. Her account of this genius who won the Pulitzer Prize for Economics in 1994, after suffering from schizophrenia for many years, portrayed many of the man's behaviors that were similar to Bill's.

Although I don't mean to say that I thought Bill was schizophrenic, I do think his genius mind was a terrible handicap when it came to relating to people. So many things fell into place for me. How I wished I had known then what I knew now! But the fact remained, I had not had the insight to understand Bill's torment in such a way as to adjust myself to living with it more gracefully. Eventually, I gave up regretting the struggles of my past, knowing that every bit of that past has been a building block to the person I am now.

With the birth of a the Lees' second child, Connor, in May, my nanny duties doubled, but I knew it would still be a piece of cake. Connor was a darling baby with a happy disposition. When I took Ryan back and fourth to pre-school each day, I carried Connor around in a sling with his back against my chest so he could see where we were going. People responded with big smiles when they noted his merry face peaking out from the sling.

However, Connor grew bigger and heavier; a lot heavier, and I began to experience pain in my wrists, exacerbated when I handled Connor. While the discomfort was minor at first and I scarcely paid any attention to it, as Connor got heavier the pain became more shocking and I could no longer ignore it. I consulted my physician to find some relief and he said, "You need to let your wrists rest for at least a month or so. If you don't, you may get to a point where there won't be anything we can do to make them better." Dismayed by the recommendation, I told the Lees about my dilemma and they arranged to have the boys' grandmother come regularly to manage the care of Connor. However, when it became obvious that my problem wasn't really getting any better, I knew I had to quit and they found someone else to care for their boys by January 15th of 2000.

"Lord, what kind of work can I possibly do that won't make my physical problem worse? You know I want to stay out here, but help me to see what you want me to do and I'll do it. Even if I have to go back to Michigan." I had been flying home to visit about every three months, so I knew some of my kids would take me in if I wanted to return, but I didn't feel ready to do that yet. I kept hoping that I would find work through the classified ads and by networking, but a most surprising thing happened when I was talking to my brother-in-law, Don, one day early in January.

He and my sister, Charlotte, had moved to Pasadena in June of 1999, and since Don had helped me in Dallas in 1993, it was natural for me to brainstorm with him about my present dilemma. At one point he inquired,

"If you could do anything you wanted, what would you like to do?"

After thinking for a while I came up with a thought,

"I'd love to be able to write. I still would like to finish my book, and there are other things I want to write about."

"Well, how much money do you need to keep living out here?"

"Around $1,200 per month."

"Well, don't you know twelve people who love you enough to give you $100 per month for one year?"

What a crazy thought! I was astounded! And then bewildered.

"Well, I don't know if I know enough people who could afford to give me $100 per month but maybe I know twenty-four people who might be willing to give me $50."

"Hell, I'd be willing to support you for a year, and you must know tons of people who would do be happy to do the same. You've spent years taking care of so many people, surely it's not too much to let them know what's going on in your life right now and give them an opportunity to be part of your writing endeavor."

So, with Don egging me on, I composed a letter which basically covered my present situation and Don's suggestion. I wrote asking for their prayers for my writing project and told them I would appreciate anything they felt led to send me. With much trepidation I mailed out the letters to my family members and some close friends.

The first response to my letters came on January 13th in the form of an e-mail from my friends Walter and Ann Kron, who said they would offer up their Jewish prayers as well as pledge $1200 to my writing project. On the 14th my sister Carolyn pledged prayers and financial support. And on the 15th I flew off to Chicago to visit Julie for my regular quarterly visit with her before driving on up into Michigan to visit family there. Elated as I gazed out at the blue sky above the clouds, I was amazed at what was happening to me.

In Search of the Writer in Me

While I was at Julie's home, Joan and Joe O'Halloran came for a visit. Julie is their goddaughter and they live in the Chicago area, so we try to get together whenever I am there. They gave me a check for $1000 to help me with my writing project and Joe had obviously researched the ins and outs of being a professional writer, because he was full of advice. The reality of their gift was incredible to me. What had been only a possibility was now being confirmed by something tangible.

What followed during the coming months was an outpouring of such generosity and love that I positively glowed, I must have. Can you imagine how healing it was for me to keep receiving encouragement and financial support from such a wonderful group of people! And one of the greatest miracles of all was the response of my brother, Steve, who immediately responded with a letter and a check for $1,200. We had not been close to each other since I got married when he was only eight years old. Although I was the godmother of his only child, I had only seen him a couple of times since 1965. And he not only encouraged me, but offered to help me by editing the book for me. What a wonderful gift to have this brother in my life again!

When I got back to California I felt I needed to find a writers group that would function as a support group for me while I took up this new endeavor, so I began checking with the local library and book stores. My search didn't turn up any writers group possibilities but I did find a writers conference to be held on March 4th at Pasadena City College, so I attended the conference and it provided me with more information than I could readily absorb.

One particular workshop I attended was an eye-opener, bringing me up to date with the growing impact the Internet has had on the publishing business, changing drastically the way it was being conducted. The workshop presenter told us that he had bought back his rights to books he had written and published the traditional way. He now had complete control over his work and he also found it more lucrative for him to publish his books himself.

At the conference I came across someone who was a member of a local group of women writers who met weekly so I accepted her invitation to join them a few days later. However, they were simply sharing their work; they were not into critiquing any of their writing so I decided to keep looking for a group that could give me feedback on my output.

Amid my fledgling attempt at writing, I had another huge change to accommodate. While I was in Chicago in February, Nancy and Charlotte had found a house which they decided to buy for us all to live in instead of wasting money renting two homes. So, at the end of March we moved into our new home in Glendale, with the plan being for me to have my own bedroom and pay them rent as I had while living with Nancy.

I remember one Sunday before the move, when Nancy and I were on our way to Mass, we prayed that God would use us to bring Christ into our home with Charlotte and Don. Since they didn't go to church and Charlotte was really angry with God, we knew God's presence within us had the potential to bring greater peace in the house. But I should have paid attention to Charlotte when she called for a household meeting at their condo the next evening and said she was thinking about how hard it was for people to live with her that maybe I should not try to live with them. I had lived with her and Don in Dallas for four months so I knew something about what she was alluding to, but I hadn't come all the way out to Los Angeles to live by myself. So as we talked it over, I just spoke positively about how we could make living together work and she didn't mention anything more about it.

It may have sounded doable, but complicating the move was the fact that several workmen were still completing construction projects inside the house during our first couple of weeks there, and my sisters were in the throes of starting a new business together. While Don, was his usual laid-back self and Nancy and I were coping okay, Charlotte was frantically stressed out with everything. She is a very tense person, needing lots of privacy, so she felt like she was in the middle of a nightmare and her unhappiness cast me back into the struggle I had experienced living with the fury of my husband's ill-concealed anger. When our sister, Carolyn, came in April from Florida to see our new digs, she was appalled by the tension in the house.

Nancy and I attended Holy Family Church in Glendale for the first time on Easter Sunday recognizing the genuine holiness of the pastor, Fr. Joe Shea, as he celebrated the Resurrection of Christ. Caucasians were a minority among the mostly Filipino and Hispanic people there. Both Nancy and I appreciated the enriching environment of other cultures so we looked forward to worshiping there. I had not gotten involved with the parish in South Pasadena but knew that

I would want to serve in some way at our new church. And in early May I attended my first meeting of the Women's Fellowship Bible Study there.

My daily routine was to attend Mass first thing in the morning and then write for a few hours. I still babysat for the Lee family sometimes and in June I began my work as a volunteer at Huntington Memorial Hospital. I absolutely loved being a Patient Advocate there, working one four-hour stint per week assisting the triage nurses in the Emergency Department, focusing on the well-being of the patients and their family members who had accompanied them to the hospital.

June also blessed me with the answer to my prayer for a writers group. The Glendale library put me in touch with a bookshop owner in Montrose, a community just north of us. When I explained to him what I was looking for, he said to me: Oh, you'll be wanting Gen's poetry group that meets in Sunland. Give her a call."

"Bút I don't write poetry."

"Oh that won't matter to Gen. Just give her a call. Here's her number."

"So I phoned Gen and received a most gracious invitation to join them that very night.

Following her instructions, I drove up through the mountains north of our house, noting the beautiful scenery but anxious in my heart. "Oh Lord please let this be okay. After all, this is Los Angeles. Here I am writing about my relationship with God and what if these people are all atheists? What will they think? Will they make fun of me? What am I getting myself into?"

After following narrow, curving, rural-like streets, I found the house, tucked into the side of a mountain and surrounded by huge trees. I had discovered a treasure! I had met the Chuparosas! These were writers who had been meeting to share their work with each other and critique it, since 1985 One of them, Marlene Hitt, was at that time, the official poet laureate of the Sunland/Tujunga area. Most of the half-dozen or so people there were around my age or older, so they had much experience I could learn from and they were most generous in their welcome of me and my writing project.

From then on, every Wednesday night I drove eagerly up the mountain to delicious fellowship and encouragement, and every week I drove back home down the mountain, loving the vista of the lights spread before me showing off the glorious panorama of Los Angeles County. Gen became a very dear friend who shared many times of spiritual fellowship with me, in addition to the Chuparosa meetings. Although a bout with polio limited her ability to get around physically, she traveled the world through her book-selling business operated out of her home, and I can never repay her for the joyful times I had with her, and the comfort her friendship provided when I was distressed. She was a blessing as I headed into a new storm.

Beauty for Ashes

Following June's joyful new beginnings, after dinner one night near the end of the month, Charlotte said she wanted us to sit down together for a household meeting. Then she expressed at great length, the frustration she was having because of living with so many people. She felt that it was too hard for her, so either she was going to move out or someone else had to move.

Of course, we all knew then that I was the one who'd have to move, since the rest of them owned the house. It had been hard living with Charlotte's rampages but I had really tried to be at peace in her presence. Nancy was very distressed at this turn of events but her hands were tied. "You can take as much time as you need," Charlotte said to me, "so you can find something you really like."

I went up to my bedroom and bawled like a baby. All the past rejections came flooding in. Such bitter devastation again engulfed me. What was I going to do? Did this mean I was supposed to go back to Michigan? How could I afford a decent apartment on my own? All I knew to do was to trust the Lord to show me his way for me now.

The next day I prayerfully considered what I would like to have in an apartment and started looking in the paper for possibilities. And although I had not yet met him, I phoned the pastor of my new church to see if I there was anyone at the church I could meet with for some counsel. To my amazement, this man who is responsible for the spiritual care of 5,000 families, answered the phone himself and invited me to come right over. He restored my confidence in myself a bit and offered to let me know if he heard of any apartments nearby.

I asked God to find me an apartment with the amenities I really wanted if he wanted me to stay in California. I wanted my home to be near the church, with light and airy rooms, lots of storage space, my own washer and dryer, a private balcony, and a garage for my car, all for $700.00 or less. The apartments that I saw on Wednesday were disappointing, so when I went to my Thursday bible study group I asked the women to pray for me to find an apartment. Then, one of them, Cathy, waved her hand excitedly. "I have it!" she said. "I've been cleaning out an apartment right next door to church, where the tenant had died. It's a terrible mess but it will be perfect once it's refurbished!

So after our bible study Cathy showed me the place, crawling with roaches and dirt accumulated over the 23 years the elderly man had lived there. But I saw that it could be wonderful once it was restored. I met with the landlord who agreed to rent to me for $650 per month once he had the whole place painted, the wood floors sanded and varnished, the window sashes repaired, and the whole building bombed to get rid of the roaches. It was almost a month before I got into this old Spanish style apartment but it was worth waiting for. And everything I had asked for was there. I rued the fact that when I made my list I had forgotten to tell God that I wanted air conditioning, but I was able to buy a room air conditioner which was all I needed when it was really hot outside.

I could practically roll out of bed and into a pew each morning so my daily routine became even easier. Besides being next to the church I was very near the Glendale Mall and many theaters and shops which were bustling with activity well up to midnight each day. So with my computer classes at the Pasadena Senior Center, my volunteer work at the hospital, my writers group and my bible study group, I was very contented once again, no longer struggling with the tension in the house of my sisters.

Nancy and I continued to play tennis and cards, and enjoy social activities together, so she was in and out of my place all the time. We attended church together and I became more deeply involved in the parish work, helping to facilitate the women's bible study, working with a team of people to form small faith groups within the parish and sharing my faith whenever I was asked to do so. But missing the companionship of living with her, sometimes I felt blue.

Now, I am usually pretty meticulous about my personal appearance, putting my face and clothes tastefully together before I venture out into the world each day. But one morning I overslept and barely had time to throw myself out the door in order to be on time for my monthly haircut appointment, and as I trotted down the block I hoped I wouldn't run into anyone who knew me.

Irritated with the way I looked, I started complaining to You Know Who. "Just look at me, God. Instead of wearing a pretty pair of sandals, I have my big, heavy, walking shoes on because my feet hurt, and I didn't take time to put my contact lenses in, so I'm wearing my ugly glasses, and of course, I didn't fix my hair nicely since I'm getting it cut momentarily. And to think that sometimes I have enough nerve to daydream about meeting a nice man someday who would find me attractive enough to want to marry me—how pathetic can I get?"

With glum thoughts carrying me down the street, I looked up and noticed a man about my age walking briskly toward me with a big smile on his face. As he drew abreast of me, he held out his hand and plunged toward me, saying, "Hello!

I'm Ed from New York!" Stopped in my tracks, I shook his hand and said hesitantly, "Do I know you, Ed from New York?"

"Oh I see you walking in the neighborhood," he replied, "and I wondered if you'd go walking with me."

A bit taken aback, I started scooting along again, saying over my shoulder, "I'm sorry, Ed from New York, but I'm going to be late for an appointment if I don't hurry. It was nice meeting you!" And then, on down the street a ways, I started cracking up!

"You are very funny, Lord. Trying to make some kind of point here?" I really did believe and still do believe that there are few good men left in my age group so I was unlikely to meet a suitable person to date or to marry. So I rarely think about that possibility. But I had another encounter a few weeks later that had me thinking God was working overtime trying to get something across to me.

I was coming out of Penny's one afternoon, joining the crowd hurrying along the sidewalk, when a man's voice beside me said, "Don't you go to Holy Family Church? I see you at Mass there."

I turned to see a young Hispanic man walking beside me. "Yes, I go to Holy Family. Is that your church too?"

"*Si, es mi iglesia.* Do you mind if I walk along with you for a minute?"

He was speaking some English and some Spanish, which gave me a chance to practice my Spanish and I always pick up on chance conversations like this, thinking God possibly set it up as an opportunity to share my faith, so I said, "*Si, es* okay."

With that encouragement, as we crossed Central Avenue, he continued. "I've been wanting to talk to you but I am rather timid," he said.

"You don't seem to be timid"

"Oh but I am because I want to talk to you for a long time but I am afraid."

"What do you want to talk to me about?

"Do you have a husband?"

"No."

"Would you like to have a husband."

"Sometimes I think I would and sometimes I think I wouldn't."

"Well, I have been watching you at church for a long time. I like your smile and the way you look. I have fallen in love with you and I want to marry you."

Well, I wasn't expecting that but I scarcely skipped a beat. "*Que es su nombre, senor*?

"Juan Sanchez"

"Are you an illegal alien, Juan?" Yes, but I wouldn't marry any woman just for that, I would have to love her."

"Juan, you couldn't possibly love me because you don't even know me, and besides that, I am old enough to be your mother! I am 66 years old! You need to find a woman your own age."

"You are not ninety," he replied, grinning. "You are the one I love."

Taking another tactic I ventured, "Look, Juan, let me ask you this. Do you know the Lord?"

"Si, Yo soy Catolica."

"I don't mean that. What does being a Catholic mean to you?"

"I am a good person. I don't steal and I don't lie and I send money every month to my mother in Mexico."

Realizing that he needed to learn a lot more about being a Christian than he had indicated, I told him about the Spanish speaking Charismatic prayer meeting held on Tuesday nights at the church and told him I would pray for him to go there and meet some nice girl his age. Clearly, I was not the one to be talking to him about God. He kept trying to put off my leave-taking as I let myself into my apartment but I finally got my door closed and leaned against it, thinking, "What on earth was that all about?"

I had plenty of time to think about it, since Juan kept showing up at my door off and on for months until I told him I'd call the police if he came again. If God was trying to get me to see that I am not unattractive to men, as sort of a healing for me surely he could have gone about it in a less bizarre fashion. But I had far more pressing things to deal with than Juan.

Leave-Taking

Bill had related politely to me once the divorce and annulment were finalized, and each time I was in Grand Rapids I spent some time with him. He had begun going to the Veterans Administration for his health care and received a new diagnosis for his illness, that of Progressive Supernuclear Palsy. The last time I was able to visit with him at Anne-Marie's home, in February of 2001, we looked through a photo album he had put together when he was in the army, and as I asked him questions about some of the pictures, he made a random comment occasionally, but he didn't initiate any conversation.

He insisted on moving into the Veterans Home in Grand Rapids in March, when it became apparent that his increasing physical weakness needed a higher level of care than could be provided for him in a home setting. He died in July of 2001, from anaplastic thyroid cancer, less than a month after a malignant mass was discovered in his neck. Surgery revealed a tumor so extensive it was not possible to remove it, so Bill was put on a ventilator in order to keep him alive long enough for his family to come to say goodbye to him.

I was in California when our son, David, first told me about the mass in Bill's neck, so I booked a seat on a plane to Grand Rapids, thinking that I might be needed to help with his care in some way after the surgery. Then, when David called me with the surgery result, I was shocked! It all happened so fast! We had expected Bill to live at least another year or two with the Progressive Supernuclear Palsy disease. It was hard to believe that he was dying.

Most distressing to me was seeing this very private man's obvious discomfort, surrounded by monitoring machines. In spite of my Hospice and Emergency Room work, my usual hospital setting demeanor went out the window as I left his room in tears after first seeing him so debilitated. Communication with Bill was then limited to our asking him questions which he answered by nodding his head, or he wrote almost illegibly on a pad of paper when he wanted something. There was still time enough for me and each of our children to say goodbye to him and to share with him and each other, the rich memories of all the interesting things he had introduced into our lives.

I had my private time with him and we both cried as I told him I forgave him for all the times he had hurt me and asked for his forgiveness for the times I had hurt him. All of our children were with me at his bedside in the Intensive Care Unit during the last four days of his life. It was beautiful to see them so tenderly attentive to his every need. And there was beauty for ashes when our four-part singing of favorite music filled his room with sweet memories for us all.

When the physician in charge of his care told us it was time to remove the ventilator we had a hard time agreeing to that, in spite of his Medical Power of Attorney document asserting that he wanted no extraordinary means used to keep him alive. Our son, Paul, needed to talk to a priest about the whole scenario, before he could come to terms with that decision. Then after the ventilator was removed, and with an oxygen mask to help him breath, we took turns being at his bedside for the next 23 hours before he died. I was with him when he died, just a few minutes after Fr. Charles Antekeier prayed over him.

The coming together of his siblings and so many of our extended family members and friends during his wake and funeral Mass in Grand Rapids was a lovely, poignant experience. And, true to Bill's typical non-conforming behavior, he showed up forty-five minutes late for his burial at Ft. Custer National Cemetery, throwing the planned, precision honor guard ceremony out the window. The driver of the hearse had gotten lost during the hour-long trip from Grand Rapids to near Battle Creek, where the cemetery is located, so we laid Bill to rest with a simple rite which he surely would have been happier with in the first place.

During the rest of 2001, I continued with the work on this book, looking forward each week to my Wednesday night meeting with the Chuparosa writers group. The activities with my church were a rock that kept me steady and I continued to love working in the Emergency Department at Huntington Hospital in Pasadena.

Just before Christmas, we learned that Don, my sister Charlotte's husband, had terminal lung cancer so the season was somber with the realization that his time with us was limited. With many of his children and grandchildren visiting during the holidays, we celebrated his life by forming a rag-tag softball team long enough to play against his regular senior softball team. Even the toddler grandkids wore our team's blue T-shirts reading "Don's Delights," and we gave it our best, with Don as our referee.

Then, with the advent of the year 2002, I began a year of increasing stress when I agreed to work part time for Albert Lee in his law office in Pasadena. He had approached me a time or two about doing that since I had left his employment as a nanny, but I had always begged off, stating my need to stay focused on the book. However, I also knew I didn't want to go back into that type of work because of the stress I had endured keeping a lot of details straight in my last office job.

But with the book about finished I agreed to work part-time at his office and also to pick up his son, Ryan, from school one day a week in order to help him practice his tennis and his math. I enjoyed being with Ryan, putting in an hour on the tennis court and then retiring with him to the nearby Starbucks where we sipped juice as he did his math. He's such a special little boy, it was a pleasure to have regular time with him again.

But instead of simply working as a receptionist and re-organizing Albert's filing system as proposed, I kept being asked by some of his staff, to do all sorts of work more suited to a paralegal and it freaked me out. I felt like I didn't know what I was doing. Each time I tried to quit, Albert persuaded me to stay, but it was clear to me that I no longer had the sharp skills that had been mine in the past. I didn't feel like I was doing a good job.

And as I worked through those first few months, determined to get the book done by June, I was also coming to the decision that I needed to move back to the Midwest. My pension from Bill would end in July, leaving me with just Social Security to live on unless I got a serious job. With my hands and wrists giving me so much trouble still, I felt my employment possibilities were limited.

My daughter, Julie had been proposing for months that I make my home in Chicago with her family. Her husband was a dear man and I had been with her for extended visits at the birth of each of her children, so I could easily picture myself enjoying her four little ones and their antics. They had a bedroom with a sunroom on the first floor of their house that could be mine, so I agreed to move to Chicago in July, in spite of not wanting to leave my apartment, my writers group, my church activities, my sisters, and the beautiful, wacky ambiance which was the Los Angeles area that was familiar to me. Sometimes you just have to go forward into the unknown.

But I did look forward to living with Julie's family and being nearer to the rest of my family, and I needed to go. So I resolutely packed up 17 boxes of my books and personal items and I sold or gave away everything else. And after a drive up the coast with Nancy to spend a weekend in San Francisco, I climbed into my car and drove to Chicago. The vistas along the northern route were awesome and I spent a few days visiting with my Denver brothers and my mother in Iowa along the way, all the while oblivious to the fact that I would soon be facing the worst year of my life.

Relinquishment

Reaching Julie's house late in July, I had barely started arranging my new bedroom when we got word on August 8th that Charlotte's husband, Don, had died. We had thought that he still had months to live so I greatly regretted the fact that I had not stayed there a bit longer. In addition to his California funeral, there was a service in Cedar Rapids, where he had taught for years, so my sister, Carolyn, flew into Chicago from Orlando to drive to Cedar Rapids with me for the service there. He had been very instrumental in changing my life. I would miss him, and miss knowing he was still around.

No sooner had I returned to Julie and Darrell's, when they learned that his father, Ernest Streeter, was terminally ill. Since he would remain at home with the help of Hospice workers, Julie was needed to be part of his daily care team during the daytime when Darrell and his siblings were working. I stayed home with the children and helped with the housework until he died on September 18th.

During the next three months my intent had been to get my computer up and running and connected to the Internet so that I could get the final editing done on my book. But I kept running into problems getting my computer connected to the house DSL line. Since Darrell was still in the throes of the circumstances surrounding his fathers illness and death, I certainly didn't want to bother him with my minor glitch. Looking for something else I could do, I tried to put down some roots in the community, looking for a church and new friends, and I also traveled to visit friends and relatives in several parts of the Midwest. And then, devastation became my companion for months as my life changed forever.

We were at the dinner table on Friday, December 20th when the phone rang. Letting the answering machine do its thing, we were only half listening to it until we heard the voice of my son, Michael's ex-wife, Debbie, saying that he was in the hospital with a brain tumor. Julie and I each dashed for a phone.

Michael was a brilliant man, a computer programmer of things mathematical and Russian, working in those disciplines with people from other parts of the world. He was a devout Catholic, pouring his efforts into a number of religious organizations and projects. He was also a very hands-on father to his three daughters, who were ten, twelve and fourteen.

He had been home from work for three days because of an intense headache. That morning, when he discovered that he couldn't make sense of the newspaper, his landlady took him to an emergency room where an MRI revealed a large tumor in the left frontal part of his brain. We immediately phoned family and friends for prayers and I booked an early morning flight to Providence, Rhode Island.

My son Joe, from Boston, had arrived at the hospital by the time I got there, and then my other children put aside their normal lives to help take care of Michael each step of our journey during the next few weeks, taking turns flying across the country as needed. It was a beautiful thing, for me to see the generosity of their families relinquishing them for weeks at a time as they struggled to help their brother.

The following ten weeks were a blur of numbness, terror, and anguish over the realization that we were losing him in spite of surgery to remove the Glioblastoma tumor and follow-up participation in a FDA approved new chemotherapy in Houston. There, a catheter was implanted in his chest and antineoplastins were administered through a small pump that he carried with him everywhere. That made it grueling and exhausting for him and for Julie, who had been designated to prepare and change the bags of antineoplastins every eight hours. The problem with my hands relegated me to monitoring his medications and reverting to caring for his other needs as any mother would do. After almost three weeks in Houston, Julie and I brought him to our home in Chicago to care for him there until he died three weeks later, on March 8, 2003.

I am still grieving too much to write about all that happened during those ten weeks before he died, except to say that the sense of God's presence in the middle of it all was so very tangible. A most extraordinary thing for me was the response of Michael's 140-plus co-workers at the American Mathematical Society in Providence.

While Michael was undergoing surgery, Joe phoned his workplace, and his very distressed supervisor, Janet Simineau, came rushing over to the hospital with papers for me to sign for disability coverage for him, saying, "The whole place has shut down! Nobody can do any work!" Judging from the bewildered looks on our faces, she continued, "You don't understand! Michael is an icon at the place! Everybody loves him!

That was the beginning of a huge outpouring of love from people who knew him or worked with him in the numerous organizations he served. The Fourniers, who had rented him an apartment in their house, the mechanic who worked on his car, the kids in the religion class he taught, all told us how special he was to them. He was such a quiet man that I had often worried about him being so far away where (I thought) nobody knew him well enough to love him. So it comforted me to hear from so many people whom Michael's spirit had touched.

After Michael's Michigan funeral Mass, we buried him in a country cemetery much like his Grandfather Hogan's resting place. Three days later, in Rhode Island, we mourned his death at a con-celebrated Memorial Mass in a church full of his colleagues from the Math Society and then celebrated his life at a reception which followed. Shortly before I left to fly home from there, I met with Michael's CEO at his office. As I was leaving, he said to me, "Michael was the most extraordinary man I have ever met. It wasn't just the brilliance of his mind but the sweetness of his spirit that touched me."

And that spirit of his was evident as he lived within a brain that was crashing under the pressure of the tumor. As I watched him spend hour after hour in patient silence, never complaining, rarely showing any agitation, I was watching the same man who considered every detail of his work and his life to be worth examining and acting upon, whether it meant getting down on his hands and knees to dig up the weeds he had noticed growing on the steps to his parish church, or using his intellect to the best of his ability right up to the last minute.

Just before aphasia set in and Michael's attempt at language became garbled, the last time that he was able to communicate with words, I saw a sentence from a barely legible letter he wrote in response to one he had received from his cousin, Bill Rehg. How like Michael to write, "Oddly enough, my brain tumor has not been about anxieties, but seeing plenty of large and small graces for me, and *more important*, thinking how many *other* people can do *great* things for God if they only realize how much is possible."

After the Memorial Mass for Michael, I remained at his apartment for a week, with my sister, Carolyn, helping me go through his personal effects and his vast library. I was still in a place of numbness and exhaustion when I arrived back home in Chicago, so I went to bed and stayed there for what seemed like days. The exhaustion was accompanied by eyes that constantly leaked tears, especially whenever I tried to pray, even though I wasn't consciously thinking about anything.

I finally started to function again, doing some of the household tasks but I carried an interior heaviness around with me and my eyes still kept leaking. I tried to reason with myself:

"Michael and I used to have long telephone conversations about once a month but he wasn't essential to my day to day living so, logically, it doesn't seem like the impact of his death should trash my life like it has."

When a Hospice Chaplin, Donna Schultz, a made a visit to our home a month after Michael died, she asked us how we were doing. I could only respond that I was sad, exhausted, my eyes kept leaking, and I wasn't thinking very clearly.

"You've got to work through your grief," she said.

"I know the statement but I don't understand it! I know how to work! But what do you mean by '*working* through grief?' What work does one actually *do*?"

"You're doing it right now as you let yourself cry and talk about it."

I was getting a bit frustrated. "But I don't *have* a problem with not crying. I have a problem crying too much.

I took courses in death and dying thirty years ago! I've been a Hospice worker and I was present at the death of my father and my husband without having this continual exhaustion and sorrow. Why is this hitting me so hard? What is going on?"

"There's nothing as hard as losing a child," she replied. "You've been connected to your child since he existed. It's different than losing a parent or a spouse."

Well, she was right about that because it sure is different. To believe that I am so intertwined with my son that I'm experiencing such strong emotions in spite of the logic of it all, still doesn't make sense to me, so somehow, I guess I just need to accept that this is my life right now."

And I've never been one to think that nothing bad should ever happen to me. Why not me? So, when Donna also mentioned that we needed to talk about anger, I was sure I harbored no anger to talk about. However, one morning as I was praying and of course, crying, after Mass, I heard a wrenching cry from my heart come right out of my mouth. "Oh God! How *could* you!" And stunned by my outburst, I began to realize that there's probably a lack of awareness of a lot of what's going on deep inside of me. I just have to keep trusting that the Lord knows exactly where I am and how much I can handle. He's taught me a lot of things by going through hard times with me.

It seemed like I would never feel like getting out of bed again, I just made myself go through the motions of living, but the last week in April I decided I had to do *something*, so I got busy and painted the kitchen. Then my mother phoned, sounding so very confused that I drove to Cedar Rapids to see what was happening to her. The day after I arrived, she fell and injured her left side so it was obvious that she couldn't keep living alone there. After many phone conferences with my sisters, Mother agreed to move to California to live in an apartment near Nancy and Charlotte.

So after ten days with her, I came home and discovered that Darrel and Julie had caught the painting bug and they began painting the other rooms of the house, a process that took up most of the summer. I made a trip back to Cedar Rapids the end of May to supervise the packing of Mother's belongings as my brother, Steve, flew in from Denver in order to accompany her to California.

Michael's two youngest daughters came for a visit in mid-July and I flew back to California with my grandson, David, at the end of the month to visit my mother while he attended a seminar at Thomas Aquinas College, north of Santa Barbara. I made another trip to California in October to speak at a fund-raiser and also made several trips to Michigan during the fall.

My mind is beginning to come out of its numbness so I can think more clearly again and I don't cry nearly as much as I did, so I must be working *through* my grief, although I still don't know how to *do* it. Michael died a year ago, but Julie is expecting a new baby in July, and she and Darrell received another five-year-old boy into our home for the next nine months, so the insistence of life's energy is putting me back on the road to outward productivity again.

Once we learned of the viciousness of Michael's tumor, I remember saying to God: "Oh Lord, is it too much to ask that you would work another miracle for our family like you did with David? Am I being too greedy if I ask? Yet, how can I not ask you to heal him?"

Now I look back and see how many lives Michael has touched and how powerfully each of his funeral services affected the people who attended. God is using him still *because* of his death, as people he knew are moved to try to imitate the holiness that he exemplified.

I have prayed and sung for many years, an ancient prayer that has to do with emptying ourselves so that God can fill us with himself. It has even deeper meaning for me now.

Take, Lord, receive, all my liberty, my memory, understanding, my entire will.
Give me only your love and your grace. That's enough for me.
Your love and your grace are enough for me.
Take, Lord, receive, all I have and possess. You have given all to me. Now I return it.
Give me only your love and your grace. That's enough for me.
Your love and your grace are enough for me.

Take, Lord, receive, all is yours now. Dispose of it wholly according to your will.
Give me only your love and your grace. That's enough for me.
Your love and your grace are enough for me.

Receptive to God's love and grace, we experience the confident assurance that we can do great things for him and with him. With God's love and grace, the tiniest kindness we offer becomes powerful enough to heal whomever it touches. We might want to ponder the last thought Michael left with us. We can do great things for God if we only realize how much is possible. And then offer our potential to God so that we might make a difference in someone else's life.